The Bond of Marriage

THE

AN ECUMENICAL ·

BOND

AND

OF

INTERDISCIPLINARY STUDY

MARRIAGE

*Sponsored by the Canon Law Society
of America*

Edited with Notes and an Introduction by
WILLIAM W. BASSETT

THE UNIVERSITY OF NOTRE DAME PRESS—1968
Notre Dame   London

BX
2250
.B6

Nihil Obstat: *Joseph Hoffman, C.S.C.*
                Censor Deputatus

Imprimatur: *Leo A. Pursley, D.D., LL.D.*
                Bishop of Fort Wayne-South Bend
                June, 1968

Contents

ABBREVIATIONS

CIC — *Codex Iuris Canonici* (Rome, 1917)

C.J. — *Codex Justinianus* in *Corpus Iuris Civilis*, ed. Paul Krueger (Berlin, 1892)

CTh—Theodosiani Libri XVI, ed. T. Mommsen-P. M. Meyer (Berlin, 1905)

D.—Digesta in *Corpus Iuris Civilis*, ed. T. Mommsen (Berlin, 1893)

Denz.—Enchiridion Symbolorum, ed. H. Denzinger; 33rd edition A. Schönmetzer (New York, 1965)

Fontes CIC—Codicis Iuris Canonici Fontes, cura E.mi P. (Card) Gasparri et J. (Card) Seredi, 9 vols. (Rome, 1923-1939)

Mos.Coll—Mosaicarum et Romanarum Legum Collatio, ed. M. Hyamson (Berlin, 1913)

N.—Novellae of Justinian in *Corpus Iuris Civilis*, ed. R. Schoell-W. Kroll (Berlin, 1954).

NTh—Novellae of Theodosius II in *Theodosiani Libri XVI*, ed. T. Mommsen-P. M. Meyer (Berlin, 1905)

NVal—Novellae of Valentinian III in *Theodosiani Libri XVI*, ed. T. Mommsen-P. M. Meyer (Berlin, 1905)

PG—Patrologia Graeca, ed. J. P. Migne

PL—Patrologia Latina, ed. J. P. Migne

AAS—Acta Apostolicae Sedis

ACJI—Acta Congressus Iuridica Internationalis

Ang—Angelicum

AusCRec—The Australasian Catholic Record

Bib—Biblica

CBQ—The Catholic Biblical Quarterly

ClR—The Clergy Review

ConcTM—The Concordia Theological Monthly
DThom—Divus Thomas
Greg—Gregorianum
HarvTR—The Harvard Theological Review
HeythJ—The Heythrop Journal
HomPastR—The Homiletic and Pastoral Review
IrTQ—The Irish Theological Quarterly
JBR—The Journal of Bible and Religion
JTS—The Journal of Theological Studies
NT—Novum Testamentum
NTS—New Testament Studies
OrSyr—Orient Syrien
RB—Revue Biblique
RBibIt—Revista Biblica Italiana
RCuBib—Revista de Cultura Biblica
RechSR—Recherches de Science Religieuse
RDNamur—Revue Diocesaine de Namur
RHPhilRel—Revue d'Histoire et de Philosophie Religieuse
RTPhil—Revue de Théologie et de Philosophie
Script—Scripture
ThQ—Theologische Quartalschrift
TLond—Theology (London)
TS—Theological Studies
TZBas—Theologische Zeitschrift (Basel)
VD—Verbum Domini
VerVid—Verdad y Vida
ZKT—Zeitschrift für Katholische Theologie

Introduction

The bond of marriage is privileged in law because it is sacred for life. It confines and protects the family as the primary community of love. The inherent durability of the marital union is necessary for the realization of the basic values of civilized society, and so it has been sustained in all nations by the rule of law. Within the context of Christian faith the stability of marriage is more than a desirable virtue of the ordered life; it is a demand upon the conscience of individuals that reflects an evangelical ideal of fidelity to man's most holy covenant. This book shall not contest the value or the ideal of the permanency of the bond of marriage. It shall consider the significance of this bond from various points of view, however, in order to evaluate the canonical discipline surrounding it in the Catholic Church.

The love of man and woman, their intimate response to each other and the community of life they form in marriage comprise a rich human experience spread over a broad spectrum of real and symbolic meaning. Marriage is both a deeply personal relationship and a social institution. In many ways it carries the burden of man's most fundamental needs and yet still may soar to meet his grandest dream. Thus within marriage there are many elements of meaning related to its fusion of personal and societal terms. Husband and wife are part of marriage, but so are children and family. Because of the relation of two persons to each other, the life of a third may take its beginning. Marriage is so closely interwoven into the strands of human life that it assumes with the changes of history and culture different modes of form and fulfillment. Yet within these stylistic changes there endures a constancy of ideal. However differently marriage may be patterned by law or custom, its universal goal is that of a special personal devotion found in the sharing of life. Little is more real than this. The quality of this devotion in turn has become the symbol in every language of the deepest longing of mind and heart for unity and acceptance beyond life itself. Because marriage is the incarnate expression of the transcendent meaning of life, in it the symbol is real and its reality is symbolic. The committed love of marriage tells something of the value of life and gives further insight into what is real in being a person.

Marriage is born of the enticement of love and grows in a recurrent challenge to that love. It is a school of perfection and maturation, ever demanding that patience necessary to secure the risk of emptying oneself to be filled again in giving. Manuals of moral theology and canon law for too long a time have spoken only of states of life, of offices, debts and obligations. They have restricted analysis to static categories and confined the framework of evaluation to the lines of contract. But marriage is so much more than a goad and a contract. It is a dynamic, evolving, lived relationship of persons. In the mysterious process of its constantly becoming, as two individuals grope for the ultimate finality of personal commitment, lies its richest symbolism and, perhaps, its deepest reality. For therein marriage bespeaks a sign of God's redeeming love.

There is no single answer to the question of what marriage really means. For society and its legal apparatus it means one thing. For the Church it means another; for husband and wife yet a third. Social order is an institutional meaning, while the values of love and security have a more personal significance. Every marriage for some one husband and wife is "our" marriage. Singly and in concert the human experience of each age contributes the data of description. For Christians the revealing word of God in Sacred Scripture illuminates this reflection in the light of life's eternal dimension.

The polarity of male and female marks the clearest division among us. Yet our sexuality is at once the source of complementarity and reconciliation. Marriage secures the dialectic process of a constant self-giving that makes the discovery of genuine manhood and womanhood possible. Thus marriage enables sexuality to become a catalyst of human personality. It is the normal and natural ambit of self-realization. If, as it has been said, concupiscence can be understood as arising from the radical loneliness of man and his longing for God, then for this, marriage is a remedy. Marriage means integration and a surcease to loneliness, however temporary and partial it may be.

In Christian faith the exemplarity of God's love for man is symbolized in marriage. Marriage is an image, an icon of the kingdom of God. Thus it is holy. It is a sacrament. Even as actions speak more loudly than words, so also do the fidelity, the love, the self-sacrifice and devotion of husband and wife to each other and their children speak more clearly than words the notes of Christ's love for the Church.

Thus in final analysis, human experience and Christian faith see in marriage a lasting bond tied in the oneness of the flesh. When man and woman are given to each other, they must not revoke the gift. They must not break the bond of trust or turn back upon the vow. The Church has always believed this. What God has joined together no man should rend apart. This should not be changed.

To speak with conviction about the permanence of the bond of marriage, however, does not exhaust its meaning nor preclude the possibility of a relaxation of ecclesiastical law surrounding it. Church law and discipline, though ultimately founded upon assumptions of faith, are largely a human response to a human need. Attitudes derived from cultural and historical circumstances are also built into the law. Thus canon law is derivative and dependent. It is a practical instrument for the good of persons and the community of the Church, a prudential measure that takes its sanctity from the purpose it serves and the fidelity to truth it reflects.

Canon law, like any other system of law, approximates a reality it can never perfectly mirror. Within its scope are reflected principles accepted by and acceptable to the society it serves. As that society evolves and develops, these principles must be examined again and again for their consistency with life. Evaluation is important, not because the principles are old, but because their expression is necessarily incomplete and in successive generations loses its cogency of appeal. This age is a time for such thoughtful reevaluation. It may also be the time to lay the foundations in law for a courageous transition to meet the pastoral needs of the future.

The present canon law of marriage rests heavily upon the foundations of a post-tridentine theology that was concerned with organization, institutionalization and codification in terms of Aristotelian science. It is marked by the certainty, necessity and universality of that worldview that is so little shared by men today. Many in the Church are now sincerely convinced the old wineskins of this kind of canon law are too brittle and sour to hold the new wine of marriage in the modern world. They speak of an imperative to renew the pastoral ministry by building a new law on a more dynamic vision of life. Thus they would reject efforts to merely tidy up the old law.

The evolution of social institutions and the progress of the developmental sciences have enriched and liberated our understanding. The growth of knowledge has brought not only a quantitative, but a qualitative change of vision. Men know more than has ever been known before. More than this, however, they judge reality differently. There is not only a larger vision, but a new vision. Freed from the preoccupations of the past, men may now reach for a resolution of the problems of life in terms of a different point of view or mediation of meaning. Specifically, the modern quest for meaning in the area of contingent intersubjectivity makes possible a new approach toward reconciling human freedom and responsibility upon a new level where they may be seen afresh.

Great numbers, perhaps as many as a million adults a year in the United States, cease to share the Holy Eucharist in communion with the Catholic Church because they cannot or will not sustain a permanent marriage. In many countries of Europe as many as seventy percent of mixed marriages are performed outside the Church. In large areas of the world, exploding population growth is forcing a change in the hierarchy of values invested in marriage. Marriages fail with increasing frequency, but the Church is able to help but a few of the millions of those who fail with them. To those who suffer in isolated loneliness, to those who are abandoned or who live in snakepits of hostility, it is not enough to appeal to the consistency of tribunal procedure or even, anymore, to the authority of the Church's law. This law and its authority can no longer help preserve the holiness of marriage for the vast majority of mankind. If sacrificial demands are to be made in God's name, their intrinsic reasonableness must be clearly shown. Service to man in our day demands that the Church reexamine as soberly and as honestly as possible the way it intends to care for those who suffer as victims of the breakdown of marriage.

Historically the response of the Church to the meaning and experience of marriage has passed through stages of varied emphasis. From a natural union blessed in the liturgy, to a procreative bond, to a legally-buttressed social institution the vision has turned in our day to what may be called authentic interpersonal relationship. More so than in the past, the Church now shows the greatest sensitivity to the dignity and responsibility of the individual. The state and shape of the sacraments depend in a real way upon the condition of the Church. Marriage is no exception. The right to marry is more important today than the rights of marriage. New models and new categories have been read into the law in the past. How will the stress upon personal dignity and responsibility so evidently incorporated into the documents of the Vatican Council alter the discipline of the Church governing marriage in future years? What do these terms mean when applied to marriage within the ambit of Christian pastoral concern? What can and should the Church do to be faithful to that which is authentic in the Christian ideal of marriage and still focus its discipline upon the best instincts and needs of modern man who must view the meaning of his life in the lens of contemporary culture? Respect for what is old is a mark of wisdom; blindly clinging to what is antiquated leads only to the abdication of reason. Clearly, because the Church is living and serves the living, adaptation is a part of its saving mission until the Lord shall come.

Can the Church change its basic canon law of marriage so that the evangelical injunction concerning the permanence of marriage can be observed as an ideal rather than as a legal absolute? Should this be done? The freedom of the Church is derived from its submission to Christ. How is submissive obedience to the Lord to be translated into ecclesiastical law today? If a change appears imperative,

what may be predicted as a result? These questions must
be asked. The very importance of marriage for men and
the tragedy of its failure demand an unflagging pursuit of
the best principles of pastoral care for the greatest good.
This pastoral care must be developed and structured upon
a theory supported by faith and reason.

On January 25, 1959, Pope John XXIII called for a
council to renew the Church and announced the formation
of a commission to reform its canon law. Temporarily
suspended during the deliberations of the Vatican Council,
the commission has now resumed the work of legal reform.
To this commission Pope Paul VI has entrusted the challenge of translating into reality the dream of the Council
fathers. In many ways the Council made such departures
from the past that there are no clear legal precedents to
follow. A time of experimentation is necessary. During this
period the commission has requested worldwide consulta-
tion of bishops, universities and laity. The book we are presenting here is a response to this request; it represents the
deliberations of a small group of scholars in various fields
offered for the consideration of the commission and the
faithful. In view of the urgent needs of the present hour,
it is concerned with studying once more the marriage of
Christians "in the light of the Gospel and of human experience."[1]

Because marriage has so many different meanings, it
would be a mistake to entrust the task of reforming the

---

[1] *The Pastoral Constitution on the Church in the Modern World*,
art. 46.

discipline of the sacrament to a single group of specialists. For this reason the Canon Law Society of America was encouraged by the Commission for Canon Law of the National Conference of Catholic Bishops to sponsor a symposium of experts in theology, scriptural studies, sociology, history, psychology, canon and civil law to reexamine all that is implied in the fundamental issue in the renewal of the marriage law, the question of indissolubility. Because Christian marriage is also a matter of ecumenical concern, seven non-Catholic scholars were invited to be among the forty participants. This interdisciplinary and interdenominational Symposium took place at the Center for Continuing Education at the University of Notre Dame, October 15-18, 1967.

Taking the word of an ancient glossator upon the *Decretals*, that water runs purer at the spring than in the river, the Symposium begins with the New Testament and discusses first the meaning of the permanence of marriage in that primal source. What does modern scriptural scholarship say about the permanence of marriage in the sources of Christian revelation? Following this essay is a historical essay presenting evidence in the primitive Church of a discipline that may offer testimony of belief. The first few centuries yield very little that is conclusive. The legislation of the Christian emperors is, however, a major monument of history still largely unexplored. The Symposium weighs this testimony before passing to a study of the ancient theological and canonical traditions of the East.

A statement of the contemporary contractual orientation of canon law and the fundamental principles of the tribunal system in handling marriage cases is necessary. Illustrative of a critique of this position are reflections upon the nature of the judicial decision involved in these cases and the meaning of validity in terms of recent developments in sacramental theology.

To draw the implications of a shift of emphasis in the philosophy of law from stress upon institutional exigencies to greater respect for personal rights, the Symposium next gives thought to the meaning of an appeal to the common good as a source of value in lawmaking. In 1234, Pope Gregory IX justified the promulgation of his *Decretals* in the famous preamble "Rex Pacificus" with the theory that the rights of society uniquely prevail over those of individuals: "lex proditur ut appetitus noxius sub iuris regula limitetur." Today the notion of the common good is identified with the good of persons, not above or beyond them. For Church and society, as Pope Paul VI said in his first encyclical letter *Ecclesiam Suam*, this is "thinking of man in a new way, and in a new way also of man's life in common." What does this understanding of the common good now indicate for canonical reform? Equally important, but perhaps more radically decisive in particular cases, is the psychological nature of the interaction of husband and wife and the complexity of their reciprocal relationship in marriage. The study of personality, specifically its functional needs and disorders, will have great significance in shaping a pastoral discipline to implement the Church's concern in assuaging the hardships caused by marital discord and failure.

Finally to set in proper perspective a real, but scarcely articulated, fear that marriage may not be intrinsically indissoluble after all and that any change in Church law would set off a chaotic chain reaction of divorces, sociology offers for consideration a view of the state of marriage and the family in America today. The investment people place in a stable married life is antecedent to the law and, perhaps, ultimately largely uninfluenced by it. Canonical reform necessary to protect the innocent few need not be prejudicial to the attitudes of the majority.

The participants of the Symposium were given the eight papers for study and deliberation prior to the meeting. During the meetings the authors presented only the salient features of their own research and then directed the discussion and debate that followed. The value of these discussions was such that the integral transmission of the Symposium to the public strongly suggested their preservation. Following each of the papers, therefore, a transaction of the discussion has been prepared that tries to reproduce as faithfully as possible the spoken word. Through these recorded discussions, various ideas appear and are repeated with increasing emphasis. A continuity of thought can be seen gradually developing and emerging in a statement of consensus.

The Symposium was an initial effort to confront the issue of the permanence of Christian marriage from as many points of view as possible. It was intended to be exploratory and questioning in scope. By means of an intensive three-day session of deliberation and debate, the participants hoped to clarify issues and point to further areas of research. Thus the statement of consensus that follows the papers is very modest; some may even find it jejune. It is confined to a statement of issues, reflecting the conviction that the Symposium should speak for itself without running the risk of exceeding premises laid down. Differences of opinion remain. Further research is required. The Symposium is offered as a contribution toward a cooperative effort among Christians to decide upon the equitable and humane response of the Church to marriage and its failure in our day.

There are some for whom discussion of a problem is an exercise in stating an objection to which the answer is already known. They are impatient and distrustful when no clear solution, no satisfying answer, is forthcoming. Yet because marriage is so close to the mystery of life, it offers many questions that elude a comprehensive reply. Surely the problems with which this book grapples have no clear solution. No Catholic will wish to depart from the defined teaching of the Church. Yet neither compilations of dogma nor the standard manuals of moral theology and canon law contain the last word. To gain further insight gives purpose to an honest question, even though no easy answer is at hand. For even a genuine question not answered, as Karl Rahner has said, is better than that dull incomprehension in which everything is always quite sure.

Thus without pretense at having a ready answer we offer this Symposium to the Church and its people for their consideration. The renewal of canon law must ultimately have the consent of the faithful to be accepted with confidence. The people, therefore, should share with their leaders in the deliberations and debate that will one day lead to its enactment.

Through the good graces of Dr. George N. Shuster, Assistant to the President of the University of Notre Dame, a financial grant was obtained to support the Symposium and the facilities of the university were made available to its participants. We are happy to accord him a special word of gratitude. Thanks are also due to the Reverend Peter J. Kearney for suggestions generously given after reading the manuscript and to Anne Kozak for her painstaking editorial services.

William W. Bassett

The Catholic University of America
March 1, 1968

Divorce and Remarriage in the New Testament

DOMINIC CROSSAN, O.S.M.[*]

This paper was requested as a study of the understanding that the New Testament gives of the indissolubility of marriage. "From the study of the New Testament alone, is it certain that Christian marriage is indissoluble?" The study restricts itself accordingly to a discussion of the bond of matrimony in New Testament teaching and ignores other sections, for example, Eph 5, 22-33, which may be of great importance for the ideal of Christian marriage in other contexts. The work has four parts: I. The common teaching of the Synoptics. II. The exception added by Matthew. III. The exception added by Paul. IV. The teaching of the New Testament.

I. THE COMMON TEACHING OF THE SYNOPTICS

There are four texts to be examined: Mk 10,2-12; Mt 5, 31-32 and 19,3-12; and Lk 16,18. Before any comparisons

[*] Professor of Sacred Scripture, St. Mary of the Lake Seminary, Mundelein, Illinois. Father Crossan is the author of *Scanning the Sunday Gospel* (1966), and *The Gospel of Eternal Life* (1967).

are made, each will be first studied in its own proper redactional context.

A. *Text and Context of Mk 10,2-12*

The general context of the pericope is Mk 8,27-10,52
which is composed of a balance of two units of teaching
in 8,27-9,13 and 9,30-10,45 and two healings in 9,14-29
and 10,46-52.[1] The more proximate context is 9,30-10,45
which, like its preceding counterpart in 8,27-9,13, concerns itself with the link between Jesus' destiny of suffering and glory and the same fate which awaits the
Twelve and all other followers of his way. Jesus' destiny
of suffering (8,27-33) and glory (9,2-13) frames the extension of that process to all his followers (8,34-9,1) in
the former teaching complex. The structure and content
of the second unit are similar but more involved. The construction consists of (a) 9,30-32 and 9,33-50 where the
prediction of Jesus' death and resurrection is linked to
the apostolic vocation of service to others. This finds its
parallel in (a') 10,32-34 and 10,35-45 with a similar con-
junction of Jesus' suffering and their call to service.
Within these frames are the three units of (b) 10,1-12;
(c) 10,13-16; (b') 10,17-31. Mark wishes to counterpoint
10,1-12 with 10,17-31 around the centrally located 10,13-
16. In the ideal of the Old Law (10,1-12) a man left one
family (father and mother) to form another family

---

[1] C. E. Faw, "The Heart of the Gospel of Mark," *JBR*, 24 (1956),
77-82 closes this major unit at 10,45.

(wife). But in the ideal of the New Law (10,17-31) a man is called to leave everything for the Kingdom of God. In both pericopes Jesus interprets the law of Moses, but in 10,1-12 it is effected by judging Dt 24,1 in the light of Gn 2,24, while in 10,17-31 Jesus explains requirements far beyond those of Ex 20,12-16 = Dt 5,11-20 on his own authority alone. Mark's purpose in using 10,1-12 in the overall construction of 9,30-10,45 and 8,27-10,52 exists primarily in this heightening of the demands of Jesus from 10,1-12 (leave family for wife) into 10,17-31 (leave all for the Kingdom).[2]

The text of 10,2-12 is comprised of a double dialogue between the questioner and Jesus in 10,2.3.4.5-9. After the teaching is stated generally in 10,2-9, it is spelled out more explicitly for the special disciples alone in 10,10-12.[3]

[2] This linkage of 10,1-12 and 10,17-31 shows up again in the similar construction of both units. Each has a double dialogue between Jesus and questioner(s) in 10,2.3.4.5-9 and 10,17.18-19.20.21-22 beginning with the *epērōtōn* of 10,2 and the *eperōta* of 10,17. Each has Jesus turn from questioner(s) to his own disciples in 10,10-12 and 10,23-27: *'oi mathētai* in 10,10 and *tois mathētais* in 10,23.

[3] Mark structures Jesus' discourses through four rubrics: (a) controversies with the inimical authorities, (b) public teaching of the crowds, (c) private interpretation for the Twelve, (d) special instruction for the inner Three. This artificial construction marks off the deepening layers of revelation, as Mark sees it. Cf. 2,16-28 (a); 3,21-4,34 (abc); 7,1-13.14-16.17-23 (abc); 8,27-9,13;9,30-10,45 (bcd); and 11,27-12,34; 12,35-37; 12,38-44; 13,1-37 (abcd). In the light of this rhythm of exposition the *proselthontes Pharisaioi* of 10,2 should be omitted, with D a b k r sy[s], as an import from the parallel Mt 19,3. The transition from Mk 10,2-9 to 10,10-12 is an artificial Mkan device to denote a deepening level of statement.

B. *Text and Context of Mt 5,31-32*

The general context of Mt 5,31-32 is the long inaugural discourse of 5,1-7,29. The more immediate location is in a series of antitheses introduced by the polemical statement of 5,20. In the examples which follow it in 5,21-26. 27-30.31-32.33-37.38-42.43-48, Jesus opposes his own understanding of the law of God to that advocated by the Pharisees. The sixfold *errethē* of 5,21.27.31.33.38.43 is replaced by the sixfold *egō de legō 'ymin* of 5,22.28.32.34. 39.44, and this exemplifies how the *dikaiosynē* of Jesus' followers must abound above that of the Pharisees (5,20).

The third antithesis in 5,31-32 stands out from this list for three reasons. The openings of the other five examples are in standard form: *ēkoysate 'oti errethē* in 5,21.27. 33.38.42 with the appended *tois archaiois* of the initial 5,21 presumed in all. But 5,31-32 has only the brief *errethē de*, and the next antithesis in 5,33-37 begins with *palin* as if after an interruption. Finally, the content of 5,31-32 is closely linked to that of the preceding 5,27-30: *moicheyseis* (27), *emoicheysen* (28), *moicheythēnai* (32a), *moichatai* (32b). The unit of 5,31-32 seems to have been added into an already constituted list of five antitheses in an already established pattern (*ekoysate 'oti errethē . . . egō de legō 'ymin*).[4] This is confirmed by the fact that Matthew has another version of 5,31-32 in a context parallel to Mark's in Mt 19,3-9. In 5,31-32 the text

[4] J. Dupont, *Les Béatitudes* (Louvain, 1958), pp. 145-147: "cette troisième antithèse est un élément adventrice dans le discours" (p. 147).

is composed of Dt 24,1 (=5,31) and Jesus' own apodictic
statement against it (=5,32).

C. The Text and Context of Mt 19,3-12

The general context of Mt 19,3-12 is similar to that of
Mk 10,2-12. The three pericopes of Mk 10,1-12.13-16.17-
31 find their parallels in Mt 19,1-12.13-15.16-30. But the
balance of Mk 10,2-12 and 17-31 is spoiled in Matthew
because he has a double dialogue in 19,3.4-6.7.8-9 (like
Mark) but a triple interchange in 19,16.17.18a.18b.20.21
(unlike Mark). Matthew has also the distinction of questioners[5] and disciples ('oi mathētai in 19,10). But what
Mk 10,10-12 addresses to the disciples alone in the house,
as an artificial indication of the development of 10,10-12
over 10,2-9, Mt 19,9 addresses to the original questioners.
The added section to the disciples in Mt 19,10-12 is proper
to Matthew alone.

D. Text and Context of Lk 16,18

The general context is the literary unity of Lk 16.[6] Two
parables serve as major frames for various terse logia

---

[5] Presumably the ('oi) Pharisaioi of Mt 19,3 passed over scribally
into Mk 10,2. It could not have been allowed there by Mark because of his fourfold structuring of Jesus' discourses. This was not
the place for a clash with the hostile authorities for Mark's own
sequence. Cf. C. H. Turner, "Western Readings in the Second Half
of St. Mark's Gospel," JTS, 29 (1928), 1-18.

[6] J. D. M. Derrett, "Fresh Light on St. Luke xvi. I. The Parable
of the Unjust Steward; II. Dives and Lazarus and the Preceding
Sayings," NTS, 7 (1961), 198-219, 364-380.

whose association is often verbal and mnemonic. The opening parable of 16,1-8[7] and the closing one in 16,19-31 alike begin with *anthrōpos* (*de*) *tis ēn ploysios* (16,1 = 19). Within these frames the theme of possession continues through the logia of 16,9 (*mamōna tēs adikias*), 16,10 (*adikos*), 16,11-12 (*adikō mamona*), 16, 13 (*mamōna*) and 16,14-15 (*philargyroi*). The three isolated statements of 16,16.17.18 break into this common theme.[8] It would seem that they are placed here as totally isolated logia which could find no other place for retention, and they are simply appended to the logia on possession in 16,9-15 between the parables on possession in 16,1-8. 19-31.[9] Lk 16,18 has very little connection with the immediate context in which it now stands.

E. *The Literary Relations of the Texts*

Before considering the theological problem of these texts, it will be useful to study their literary relationship. In general it is already clear that we have a dialogue

[7] A. Descamps, "La composition littéraire de Luc XVI, 9-13," *NT*, 1 (1956), 49-53; J. A. Fitzmyer, "The Story of the Dishonest Manager (Lk 16,1-13)," *TS*, 25 (1964), 23-42. The former writer begins the appended logia with 16,9, the latter at 16,8b.

[8] E. Bammel, "Is Luke 16,16-18 of Baptist's Provenience?" 51, *HarvTR* (1958), 101-106 suggests that they came from the Baptist and are transposed to the mouth of Jesus by Lk.

[9] There is a mnemonic connection between the *theoy* of 16,16 and the *theos* of 16,14-15 and between the *nomoy* of 16,17 and the *nomos* of 16,16. If 16,18 had originally some such mnemonic verbal connection in the Aramaic substratum, it is no longer evident in the present Greek of Luke, but cf. J. Dupont, *Mariage et divorce dans l'Evangile* (Brussels, 1959), pp. 47-48.

situation in Mk 10,2-12; Mt 19,3-12 and a logion in Mt 5,31-32 and Lk 16,18.

1. The Debate in Mark and Matthew

Two questions arise. Did the aphorism of Mk 10,11-12 = Mt 19,9 ever exist as a separate unit which was then appended to Mk 10,2-9 = Mt 19,3-8? Does Mk 10,2-9 or Mt 19,3-8 represent the earlier level of the tradition? It has been shown that there existed a standard pedagogic device in rabbinical circles of the first and second post-Christian centuries whereby (1) an inimical or tricky question (2) received an enigmatic, interrogatory or *ad hominem* response, but (3) the disciples in private later ask and (4) receive the full proper answer to the problem. Secondly, it was been argued that Mk 10,2.3-9.10.11-12 fits into this four-point pattern, and does so better than Matthew. Mark is therefore a literary unity and earlier than Matthew according to this theory.[10] But it is not at all clear that Mk 10,3-9 can be considered as such as enigmatic response, and it is equally unclear that Mk 10,11-12 is the type of development over Mk 10,9 which this literary device usually demands. The shift from questioners to disciples in 10,10 has already been noted as part of a much wider redactional activity on the part of Mark.[11] More positively, Mk 10,9 makes a better climactic aphorism in the historical situation than does 10,11-12. Whether Mk 10,2 or Mt 19,3 better represents the original ques-

---

[10] D. Daube, *The New Testament and Rabbinic Judaism* (London, 1956), pp. 141-150; cf. discussion by Dupont, *Mariage et divorce . . .* , pp. 39-43.

[11] Cf. notes 3 and 5 above.

tion, the purpose of the debate must have been to bog Jesus down in rabbinical disputation over the sufficient reasons for divorce.[12] The answer of Jesus does not merely strike at divorce and divorced people but at the questioning Pharisees who argue on the reason for which *they* can grant a divorce. The concluding aphorism of Mk 10,9 compares *'o theos*, who created marriage, and *anthrōpos*, the Pharisees who discuss reasons for their dissolving it, and the power of each over marriage. Once again the Pharisees are against God, just as in Mt 15,1-9 where the Pharisees replace the *logon toy theoy* (15,6) with their own *entalmata anthrōpōn* (15,9). As stated in Mk 10,2-9 the trick question has been turned on those who posed it. Jesus will not side with any rabbinical reasons for granting divorce but denies them power over it under any circumstances. He will not debate Dt 24,1 but simply cite Gn 2,24. The addition of the section in Mk 10,10-12 would merely take the pressure off the Pharisees and transport it to those seeking divorce and planning remarriage. Mk 10,2-9 and 10-12 represent originally distinct units[13] and Mark has combined them as part of his overall structuring of Jesus' teaching.

[12] Dupont, *Mariage et divorce . . .* , p. 16 argues that Matthew is more original, but that Mark found questions of sufficient motive useless for a Gentile audience. E. G. Selwyn, "Christ's Teaching on Marriage and Divorce. A Reply to Dr. Charles," *TLond*, 15 (1927), 88-101 preferred Mark as more original since his text better hid the trap imbedded in an innocent question.

[13] F. Vogt, *Das Ehegesetz Jesu. Eine exegetisch-kanonistische Untersuchung von Mt 19,3-12; 5,27-32; Mc 10,1-12 und Lk 16,18* (Fribourg-i-B., 1936), pp. 163-176.

When Mk 10,2-9 is compared with the parallel Mt 19, 3-8, the former appears as the earlier level of transmission. In Mk 10,2-9 there is a harmonious balance of (1) question "by the Pharisees" (10,2), (2) counter question by Jesus (10,3), (3) answer by the questioners from Dt 24,1 (10,4) and (4) counter answer by Jesus from Gn 2,24 (10,5-9). The concluding dictum by Jesus is simply an obvious corollary from Gn itself. But Matthew has literary and theological intentions over and above those of Mark. He does not want the disciples to appear as recipients of Jesus' special teaching until they receive something really so intended, his own proper unit in 19,11-12. He wishes to have the isolated aphorism appended (= Mk 10,10-12) as climactic statement to the debate with the Pharisees, so that the solemn *legō de 'ymin* of Jesus ends the discussion, and not the quotation from Gn 2,24. For this reason he must reconstruct Mark's sequence into (1) question by the Pharisees (19,3), (2) answer by Jesus from Gn 2,24 (19,4-6), (3) counter question by the Pharisees from Dt 24,1 (19,7) and (4) counter answer by Jesus' own apodictic statement (19,8-9). But a suture shows up in his work. He has to repeat the *ap' archēs* of Mt 19,4 (=Mk 10,6) in 19,8. The debate consists of Mk 10,2-9 at the earliest level of the transmission and of Mt 19,3-9 as a later reworked version of it.

2. The Logion in Mark, Matthew and Luke

It has been argued that Mk 10,11-12 is an isolated saying of Jesus appended to 10,3-9 through the standard redactional device of 10,10 and that in Mt 19,3-9 it has

been more fully integrated into a parallel context as Mt
19,9. The logion appears four times: appended in Mk 10,
11-12, integrated in Mt 19,9, relocated in Mt 5,32 and
isolated in Lk 16,18. It is no longer possible to find its
original location in time and space. It is an isolated saying
of Jesus, striking in its apodictic novelty and aphoristic
brevity.

Within these four instances, which at first glance seem
so similar, three levels of development are visible. In Mt
5,31-32 there is no explicit question of monogamy. Among
the Jews adultery was an act against the right of the husband only. Since a man could have more than one wife,
adultery only occurred when a married woman was unfaithful to her husband or when a man was associated
with such a woman. It could not take place between a
married man and a single woman.[14] In itself Mt 5,31-32
says nothing against polygamy. It states that the husband
who divorces his wife is responsible for the adultery which
takes place if and when she remarries (*poiei aytēn moicheythēnai*) and in which the new husband partakes
(*moichatai*). In other words the case is exactly as if she
had received no divorce, but the divorcing husband
stands guilty in Mt 5,31-32. The text is against divorce
and remarriage on the part of the woman. It says nothing
of the former husband, and even less is said about polygamy without divorce. To obtain this in Matthew, one
would have to go not only to 19,9 but to 19,3-6. This means
that Mt 5,32 is the earliest and most primitive form of

[14] J. Bonsirven, *Le divorce dans le Nouveau Testament* (Paris,
1948), pp. 7-24; W. Kornfeld, "L'Adultère dans l'Orient antique,"
RB, 57 (1950), 92-109.

the logion. It looks only to what the husband should not do to his wife.

The second level of development appears in Lk 16, 18 = Mt 19,9. In these two versions of the dictum the point of view is still primarily that of the husband, but monogamy is also presumed. Adultery is committed when the husband divorces the wife and *he* marries another, and the second husband of the repudiated wife is also in adultery. But what is new is that the former husband commits adultery in remarrying and so it is committed *against* the rights of his former wife. When this isolated logion in Lk 16,18 is attached and imbedded into Mt 19,3-9, it is clear that monogamy is being presumed at the same time that divorce and remarriage for either party is being prohibited.

The third stage of the phrase appears in Mk 10,11-12. Here attention is equally divided and structurally paralleled between husband and wife. The viewpoint is no longer exclusively male as in Mt 5,31-32, or even primarily male as in Lk 16,18 = Mt 19,9, but completely balanced between both; if husband divorces wife and remarries, he commits adultery (10,11); and if wife divorces husband and remarries, she commits adultery (10, 12). The new consorts of such people are not even mentioned. No doubt this speaks much more of a Graeco-Roman situation than a Hebraic one.[15] But it also brings

---

[15] Daube, *op. cit.*, p. 367; V. Taylor, *The Gospel According to St. Mark* (London, 1952), p. 420. Because of the unusual articulation of Mk 10,11-12 as compared with Mt 19,9; 5,32 or Lk 16,18 copyists attempted harmonizations which resulted in the textual variants noted in the critical editions.

to logical conclusion and impartial statement the mutuality inherent in Mt 19,19 = Lk 16,18 and even in Mt 5,31-32 as part of a writing later to contain Mt 19, 3-9.

The literary history of the four texts thus consists of two events. The development of an isolated saying whose time and place setting is completely lost, and its integration into the development of another pericope, that of a debate with the authorities. There are five steps in the process. Mt 5,31-32 represents the earliest statement of the logion, although in a later redactional setting. Lk 16,18 is a second stage in the development of the aphorism, and Mk 10,11-12 is the third stage of the process. This third stage is closely linked to the fourth, the appendage of Mk 10,11-12 to Mk 10,2-9. The last stage is the transition of Mk 10,2-9 into Mt 19,3-8 and the complete integration of the saying as found in its stage two (= Lk 16,18) into that newly phrased debate.

F. *The Consensus of the Synoptics*

For the moment we ignore the special clauses in Mt 5,32 and 19,9 and look only at what is the common teaching in the texts just studied. In the debate texts of Mark and Matthew both agree that Gn 2,24 forbids a man from divorcing and repudiating his wife. In itself nothing is said of remarriage or of monogamy. This arises from the nature of the incident. The answer of Jesus is not directed primarily on the level of the personal and the moral, as against the person contracting divorce and remarriage. It is intended for the Pharisees who discuss motives whereby they can permit divorce, and Jesus' answer is that they have no such power over marriage at all. It is on the level of the public and the juridical. No doubt remarriage after divorce and even polygamy itself can logically be precluded as deductions from the "two in one flesh" principle, but the debate texts do not draw this conclusion explicitly.

The logion texts go farther along the road of explicit statement. The teaching of Mt 5,32 and 19,9 can be considered as the full expression of Matthew's mind. In itself 5,32 says nothing against the husband's remarriage. It only denies the validity of the wife's remarriage. But Mt 19,9, Lk 16,18 and especially Mk 10,11-12 make it quite clear that (1) divorce is invalid, (2) the divorced husband cannot remarry, (3) the divorced wife cannot remarry. Leaving aside for the moment the enigmatic exceptions of Mt 5,32 = 19,9, the Synoptics agree in placing on Jesus' lips the refusal to accept valid divorce, a refusal without qualification or exception in Mark and Luke.

II. THE EXCEPTION ADDED BY MATTHEW

The two phrases *parektos logoy porneias* in Mt 5,32 and *mē epi porneią* in Mt 19,9 represent some sort of qualification of the statement recorded of Jesus in Mk 10,11-12 and Lk 16,18. The question arises whether Matthew has added them to the common tradition or whether he records this faithfully and Mark and Luke made the omissions. If the common tradition behind Mark-Matthew-Luke is taken as being ultimately the teaching of Jesus, we are then asking whether Matthew records Jesus' words with their original qualification while Mark-Luke omitted this qualification, or whether Mark-Luke record basically the unqualified absolutes of Jesus' teaching and Matthew has himself appended the qualifying clauses.

A. *The Insertion of the Clauses in Matthew*

From the convergence of two reasons these clauses are accepted as Matthew's additions and not the omissions of Mark-Luke. If these latter writers omitted the clauses, they did so separately, and no reasons for such omissions are easily available.[16] It was already seen that Lk 18,16 and Mk 10,11-12 represent two different stages in the saying's transmission. They are neither both dependent for it on some single common source, nor as yet immediately dependent on one another. Secondly, the edition of qualifying remarks which make the statements of Jesus more precise for Matthew's own audience is a well-known phenomenon of that writer. Among the Beatitudes, for example, compare the *tǭ pneymati* of Mt 5,3 with its absence in the corresponding Lk 6,20 or the *tēn dikaiosynēn* of Mt 5,6 and the absence of it in Lk 6,21.[17] The most

---

[16] As will be seen later (cf. pp. 24-25) Paul would have to represent a third omission of the clause.

[17] Many examples of such are given in Dupont, *Les Béatitudes*, pp. 209-243 and *Mariage et divorce dans l'Evangile*, pp. 87-92. He concludes that such arguments for Matthew's addition of the clauses

likely supposition is that Matthew has added the special
clauses found in the logion in 5,32 and 19,9.[18]

B. The Meaning of the Clauses in Matthew

The clauses in question do not need any extensive textual criticism. The *parektos logoy porneias* of Mt 5,32 is
supported by the manuscript tradition. The only problem
is with the *mē epi porneią* of 19,9. In certain manuscripts
this appears in the 5,32 form, but this is quite easily
explained as textual influence from that preceding statement.[19] The opinion that the clauses are very ancient interpolations can hardly be taken as a valid scientific possibility,[20] for the claim of interpolation without manuscript
evidence is at best most doubtful exegesis.

in 5,32 and 19,9, "ne constituent pas une preuve positive établissant
que l'évangelists a réellement ajouté les clausules; elles suffisent
cependant à créer une présumption, invitant ainsi l'exégète à
expliquer ces clausules en fonction de l'intérêt que l'évangéliste
porte aux besoins immédiats de la vie de l'Eglise" (p. 92). Cf. also
the extensive bibliography on p. 92 of authors who support this
interpretation of the clauses.

[18] A. Descamps, "Essai d'interprétation de Mt. 5,17-48. 'Form-
geschichte' ou 'Redaktionsgeschichte'?" *Studia Evangelica* ("Texte
und Untersuchungen," 73; Berlin, 1959), 156-173.

[19] For example, in B D φ 1 al.

[20] Both clauses are interpolations for G. Bonaccorsi, *Primi saggi
di filologia neotestamentica. Letture scelte dal Nuovo Testamento
greco con introduzione e commento* (Turin, 1933), I, 37. Others
have denied the authenticity of 19,9 alone, cf. J.-M. Vosté in *RB*, 15
(1918), 576-578; A. Allgeier, "Die crux interpretum im neutesta-
mentlichen Ehescheidungsverbot. Eine philologische Untersuchung," *Ang*, 20 (1943), 128-142; S. Larranga, "San Mateo (5,32;

1. Synopsis of Critical Discussion

A useful summary of opinions on the meaning of the two clauses has been presented by B. Vawter.[21] He gives six main explanations. (1) Adultery is allowed as sufficient reason but only for separation, not for divorce and remarriage.[22] (2) Adultery is allowed as the exceptional reason for divorce, and eventual remarriage is legitimate only in this case.[23] (3) The meaning is "not even in the-

19,9) y la indisolubilidad del matrimonio cristiano," *VerVid*, 7 (1949), 53-74; F. C. Millington "A Spoilt Masterpiece," *Studia Evangelica* ("Texte und Untersuchungen," 73; Berlin, 1959), 506-509.

[21] "The Divorce Clauses in Mt 5,32 and 19,9," *CBQ*, 16 (1954), 155-167. Cf. also U. Holzmeister, "Die Streitfrage über die Ehescheidungstexte bei Matthäus 5,32, 19,9," *Bib*, 26 (1945), 133-146 which summarizes opinion for the preceding decade.

[22] This opinion is still quite alive, cf. T. Fahy, "St. Mt 19,9– Divorce or Separation?" *IrTQ*, 24 (1957), 173-174; J. Dupont, *Mariage et divorce* . . . , p. 157, but cf. reviews by M.-E. Boismard in *RB*, 67 (1960), 463-464 and T. Worden in *Script*, 12 (1960), 57-59.

[23] This might be termed the classical Protestant position, just as the preceding one is the traditional Catholic one, cf., for example, W. C. Allen, *A Critical and Exegetical Commentary on the Gospel according to S. Matthew* ("International Critical Commentary"; New York, 1907). A. M. Dubarle, "Mariage et divorce dans l'Evangile," *OrSyr*, 9 (1964), 61-73 notes how Eastern discipline has accepted the Mtan phrases as denoting the legitimacy of divorce for serious and reiterated adultery. This article is disputed by J. Dauvillier, "L'indissolubilité du mariage dans la nouvelle Loi," *ibid.*, 265-289. Cf. also J. J. Rabinowitz, "The Sermon on the Mount and the School of Shammai," *HarvTR*, 49 (1956), 79.

case of uncleanness" (as in Dt 24,1), an explanation requiring linguistic gymnastics of a high order.[24] (4) The phrases are intended to decide in favor of the Shammai school (divorce only for adultery) rather than the Hillel school (divorce for many other reasons), as exegesis of Dt 24,1 while actually revoking Dt 24,1 at the same time.[25] (5) The sentences denote Jesus' intention of by-passing the whole problem of *porneia* while excluding all other alleged reasons.[26] This preterition makes much more sense as explained by Vawter himself. He sees in it a direct contradiction of Dt 24,1 so that Jesus states his absolute refusal of divorce and remarriage "Dt 24,1 not withstanding," where the *'erwat dābār* of Dt 24,1 is the *porneia* of Mt 5,32 and 19,9. Hence the clauses summarize the contradiction already established by Mk 10,6-9 = Mt 19,4-6 against Dt 24,1 quoted in Mk 10,3-5 = Mt 19,7-8. However, it is questionable if the language (*parektos* or *mē epi*) can bear this transition from neutral preterition ("setting aside the matter of *porneia*") to direct contradiction ("Dt 24,1 not withstanding"). (6) The theory which has become known as the rabbinic interpretation

[24] M. Brunec, "Tertio de clausulis divortii," *VD*, 27 (1949), 3-16 translates with "etiam non praeter" (10).

[25] A. Tafi, " 'Excepta fornicationis causa' (Mt 5,32); 'Nisi ob fornicationem' (19,9)," *VD*, 26 (1948), 18-26. This is opposed by T. Schwegler, "De clausulis divortii (Mt 5,32 et 19,9)," *ibid.*, 214-217, but more negatively than positively.

[26] Recently defended by T. V. Fleming, "Christ and Divorce," *TS*, 24 (1963), 106-120. Reason for the preterition is the hardness of the Pharisaic hearts.

holds that *porneia* in the two clauses is neither adultery (*moicheia*) nor the *'erwat dābār* of Dt 24,1,[27] but translates the technical rabbinical term *z^enut* which denotes illegitimate marriages.[28]

It is not the intention here to repeat the excellent arguments adduced by B. Vawter against the first four opinions. Neither do we wish to argue against his own interpretation. This has already been done elsewhere.[29] But in his review of the rabbinic interpretation of the clauses, he constantly argued from the point of view of Jesus' speaking the phrases: "why should Christ be imagined," "to what purpose, moreover, would Our Lord" and "there was no logion of Christ" (p. 163). Rather our purpose is to take another look at the clauses in the rabbinic interpretation, but to consider these clauses as insertions of Matthew rather than as statements of Jesus.

2. *Porneia* and Invalid Marriage

The finest presentation of the rabbinic interpretation of the clauses in Matthew is undoubtedly that of J. Bon-

[27] T. Considine, "'Except it be for the fornication.' A Suggested Interpretation," *AusCRec*, 33 (1956), 214-223 thinks *porneia* is adultery in the OT sense of infidelity to God, and in this case divorce and remarriage is possible. A. Mahoney, "A New Look at the Divorce Clauses in Mt 5,32, and 19,9" *CBQ*, 30 (1968), 29-38, translates them by: "Not because of *porneia* (i.e., something unseemly in the eyes of God)" and "except for *porneia* (i.e., something unseemly in the eyes of God)."

[28] This meaning for *porneia* has been noted since the middle of the last century in authors cited by Bonsirven, *op. cit.*, p. 46.

[29] A. Vaccari, "De matrimonio et divortio apud Matthaeum," *Bib*, 36 (1955), 149-151 denies that *logos porneias* in Mt 5,32 translates and intends the *'erwat dābār* of Dt 24,1.

sirven,[30] whose arguments have been accepted by many
other scholars.[31] The core of the theory is the meaning
given to *porneia*, the only word which is common to both
qualifying clauses. The term does not mean adultery
which has its own quite specific word, *moicheia*. Neither
does it refer to the general *'erwat dābār* ("shameful matter") of Dt 24,1, which is cited as sufficient reason for
divorce. It translates the technical term *zᵉnut* used for
irregular and illegitimate marriage by the rabbinical commentators. Bonsirven has argued from rabbinical examples that this term (literally "prostitution") took on a
more and more precise technical meaning in postbiblical
Hebrew, and designated a marriage in some way illicit,
illegitimate, null and void. Secondly, the Greek word
porneia which could also have a wider connotation of any
sort of illegitimate union was often used to translate *zᵉnut*
in its precise technical meaning. An example can be cited
from 1 Cor 5,1 where *porneia* is used for the incestuous

[30] *Le Divorce dans le Nouveau Testament;* cf. also his "'Nisi ob
fornicationem,' exégèse primitive," *Mélanges Cavallera* (Toulouse,
1948), 47-63; "'Excepta fornicationis causa.' Comment résoudre
cette 'crux interpretum,'" *RechSR*, 35 (1948), 442-464. This thesis
had been argued earlier by R. Dyson and B. Leeming, "'Except it be
for fornication.' A Note on Mt 19,3-12," *ClR*, 20 (1941), 283-294
and reiterated again in B. Leeming and R. A. Dyson, "'Except it be
for fornication'?" *Script*, 8 (1956), 75-82. Cf. also note 28 above.

[31] Vaccari, 149-151; "La clausula sul divorzio in Mt 5,32; 19,9,"
RBiblt 3 (1955), 97-119; "A cláusula sobre o divórcio en Mt
5,32 e 19,9," *RCuBib*, 1 (1956), 1-16; A. Alberti, "Il divorzio nel
Vangelo di Matteo," *DThom*, 60 (1957), 398-410; M. Zerwick,
"De matrimonio et divortio in Evangelio," *VD*, 38 (1960), 193-212;
J. B. Bauer, "De coniugali foedere quid edixerit Matthaeus? (Mt
5, 31s; 19, 3-9)," *VD*, 44 (1966), 74-78.

union of a man with the wife of his own father. Another
and even more significant example will be studied later
in Acts 15,20.29; 21,25.

But when *porneia* is taken in Mt 5,32 and 19,9 as denoting invalid marriage is not Jesus forced to state a rather
trite tautology: "if a man divorce his wife, unless they
were never really married . . ."? The proponents of this
theory already mentioned all speak of Jesus' having inserted the qualifications himself and thus lay their entire
argument open to a serious objection. They are much
more secure than others on the historical and grammati-
cal levels but can be easily attacked by "objections . . . of
the logical order."[32] However, if the clauses are taken as
Matthew's own proper insertion, this objection falls as
long as it can be shown that Matthew is not himself
trapped in the same tautology.[33]

3. The Historical Situation of Matthew

The explanation offered here is not a new one. It com-
bines two points already noted: the theory of Bonsirven

[32] So Vawter, cf. 163. The answer of Vaccari, "De matrimonio
et divortio apud Mt," is not very convincing. He claims that the
Sermon on the Mount is given, "ad instar codicis legum . . . ut nil
restet ambigui" (151). Nor is one too ready to accept Leeming
and Dyson "'Except it be for fornication'?" (*Script*) who refer it
to the case of Antipas and Herodias (81).

[33] After this paper was delivered and completed for publica-
tion a more recent analysis by B. Vawter changed his earlier position to one closer to that argued here; cf. "The Biblical Theology
of Divorce" in *The Proceedings of the Twenty-Second Annual Con-
vention: The American Catholic Theological Society* (New York,
1968).

and others on the meaning of the clauses with the arguments of Dupont and others for their Matthew origin. This combination has already been made by other scholars.[34] The interpretation seeks to give an historical setting to Matthew's insertion of these exceptive phrases into the common teaching of the Synoptic tradition.

a. Porneia *in Acts* In three texts of Acts, the four requirements of the Mosaic Law still to be observed by Gentile converts are enumerated: to refrain from the flesh of animals slain for pagan sacrifices, from consuming the blood of animals, and therefore from eating strangled meat, and from *porneia*. The sequence of the prohibitions is very important. In 15,20 it is: idol-offerings (*tōn alisgēmatōn tōn eidōlōn*), *kai tēs porneias*, strangled food (*kai pniktoy*) and blood (*kai toy 'aimatos*).[35] Immediately following this text the order is changed in 15,29: idol-offerings (*eidōlothytōn*), blood (*kai 'aimatos*), strangled meat (*kai pniktōn*) and *porneia*. The same sequence appears in 21,25, and once again idol-offerings are

[34] H. J. Richards, "Christ and Divorce," *Script*, 11 (1959), 22-32; H. Baltensweiler, "Die Ehebruchsklauseln bei Mt (5,32; 19,9)," *TZBas*, 15 (1959), 340-346. Cf. also the review by J. A. Fitzmyer in *TS*, 27 (1966), 451-454 of A. Isaksson, *Marriage and Ministry in the New Temple. A Study with special reference to Mt. 19.3-12 and i. Cor. 11.3-16*, tr. N. Tomkinson ("Acta Seminarii Neotestamentici Upsaliensis," XXIV; Lund, 1956).

[35] T. Boman, "Das Textkritische Problem des sogennanten Aposteldekrets," *NT*, 7 (1964), 26-36 discusses why the Western text omits *kai pniktōn* (*pniktoy*) in Acts 15,20.29; 21,25 and substitutes Mt 7,12 instead. It is a case of irrelevance noted and redressed as the NT text moved deeper into completely Gentile areas.

eidōlothytōn as in 15,29 and not the earlier term *tōn alis-gēmatōn tōn eidōlōn* as in 15,20.

The problem of analyzing the sources of Acts is very difficult. No doubt Luke used prior sources but he so integrated his materials and dominated them from a literary point of view that precise division and separation is almost impossible.[36] This general difficulty has shown up specifically in the attempt to analyze the sources of Acts 15. While some scholars maintain it can be broken down into its separate sources,[37] others argue that it is a purely Lucan composition.[38] It is also debated whether the speech of James in 15,14-18 is a composition of Luke's[39] or stems from some such prior source.[40] It is not possible here to go more fully into this disputed area; but if this speech of James is a composition of Luke's, the change in sequence between the four conditions in 15,20 and 15,29 would be quite understandable. The sequence in 15,29 would be from whatever tradition, oral or written, which Luke had for the decree itself. But in placing the decree on the lips of James, Luke reversed the sequence as a nicety of literary style. The last three conditions imposed

[36] J. Dupont, *Les sources du Livre des Actes. État de la question,* (Brussels, 1960).

[37] R. Bultmann, "Zur Frage nach den Quellen de Apostelgeschichte," *New Testament Essays* ("Studies in memory of T. W. Manson"; Manchester, 1959), pp. 68-80.

[38] E. Haenchen, "Quellenanalyse und Kompositionsanalyse in Act 15," *Judentum, Urchristentum, Kirche* (1960), 153-164.

[39] J. Dupont, *"Laos ex ethnōn,"* NTS, 3 (1956), 47-50.

[40] N. A. Dahl, "'A People for His Name' (Acts xv.14)," *NTS,* 4 (1958), 319-327.

on the Gentiles in the catalogue of 15,29 are actually reversed in 15,20. When the list comes up again in 21,25, the traditional sequence given in the decree is again used. If the speech of James in 21,18-25 was given in Luke's traditions, this may be the actual source for that now written in 15,13-21. In other words, the sequence of the four conditions in 15,29 is most likely older than Luke's own composition of Acts 15.

This exact sequence is important because it is the same sequence of conditions imposed on the proselytes who lived among the Israelites in Lv 17-18. The legal requirements demanded of such people are four in number: (1) avoidance of idol-offerings in Lv 17,1-9, (2) the prohibition against blood in 17,10-12, (3) the prohibition against meat with blood in it in 17,13-16 and (4) the catalogue of forbidden marriages in 18,1-18. It is clear that the same four requirements for proselytes living in Israel in Lv 17, 8.10.13.15; 18,26 are found in Acts 15,29 = 21,25 and in precisely the same order—*if* the *porneia* of Acts 15 is accepted as synonymous with the forbidden marriages of Lv 18.

b. Acts and Matthew · The historical events which lie behind the present smooth literary unity of Acts 15 are not at all clear. Many scholars are convinced that two events are combined into one incident by Luke.[41] As the

---

[41] For a discussion cf. S. Giet, "L'assemblée apostolique et le décret de Jérusalem. Qui était Siméon?" *RechSR*, 39 (1951), 203-220 (=Mélanges J. Lebreton, I); J. H. Crehan, "Peter at the Council of Jerusalem," *Script*, 6 (1954), 175-180; M. Miguens, "Pietro nel concilio apostolico," *RBiblIt*, 10 (1962), 240-251; T.

narrative now stands the theological problem seems one
of universal import (15,1.5) and yet the decree goes out
only to Antioch, Syria and Cilicia (15,23, but cf. 22 and
30). Neither does Paul use its decisions when confronted
with similar problems in the church of Corinth, cf. 1 Cor
5,1-5 (*porneia*) or 8,1-13 (*peri de tōn eidōlothytōn*). But
whether Acts 15,29 represents the universal decree of a
council or the private interpretation of James on the minimal requirements for peaceful coexistence between Jew
and Gentile Christians will not effect this interpretation
of Matthew. Were it universal Matthew would know of
it and if it were directed exclusively to Antioch and its
provincial surroundings (Syria and Cilicia), it would
have been centered in the area most closely associated
with the situation in which and for which Matthew was
written.[42]

Matthew is writing his gospel within the historical situation which gave rise to the decree of Acts 15,20.29; 21,25.
He has in his traditions the common Synoptic statement
of Jesus' categorical condemnation of divorce. But he records it with the added exceptive clauses to indicate that
it would not apply to pagans married within the forbid-

Fahy, "A Phenomenon of Literary Style in Acts of Apostles," *IrTQ*,
29 (1962), 314-318; "The Council of Jerusalem," 30 (1963), 232-
261; P. Gaechter, "Geschichtliches zum Apostelkonzil," *ZKT*, 85
(1963), 339-354.

[42] F. V. Filson, *A Commentary on the Gospel according to St.
Matthew* ("Black's NT Commentaries"; London, 1960) notes that,
rather than Jerusalem, "Antioch in Syria might be a better setting
for a Gospel which shows no interest in Levitical regulations" (p.
15).

den kinship of Lv 18. Two such pagans who wished to
become Christians and live at peace with Christians of
Jewish background could (should? must?) divorce and
were then free to remarry if they so wished.[43]

The clauses of Matthew have been called an exception.
There is an obvious objection which could be made to
this. Matthew has Jesus say, it would seem: "Divorce and
remarriage is adultery, unless they were not really married in the first place." Therefore, it is argued, we do not
have a real exception but only the verbal appearance of
one. Yet this objection is not quite accurate. Matthew
does not say, "if they were not really married in the first
place," but, "if they were not really married because married within Lv 18,1-8," as *porneia* has been interpreted in
this paper. This leaves the Christian reader with a di-
lemma. If the special clauses in Matthew are not really
added exceptions but qualifications implicitly contained
in Jesus' apodictic condemnation, then Lv 18,1-18 and
those marriages judged *porneia* in the historical perspective of Acts and Matthew are normative also for us.[44] For

---

[43] Ed. Massaux, "Les relations entre la Loi Ancienne et la Loi
Nouvelle selon Mt., 5,17-48," *RDNamur*, 12 (1958), 265-283
speaks of ecclesial discipline rather too rigidly: "Cette incise n'est
donc pas l'idée de Jesus, mais la répercussion d'une discipline
particulière à certaine communauté chrétienne palestinienne qui,
sur ce point, s'éloignait de l'idée de Jésus et qui, par le fait même,
s'oppose à la doctrine ecclésiastique actuelle" (277). If one exception is recorded, others may be presumed to have existed unre-
corded.

[44] This was exactly the argument used by Henry VIII of England
when demanding a declaration of nullity for his marriage to

example, a nephew and aunt who were already married could not become Christians and remain married (cf. Lv 18,12). Exceptive clauses and unqalified absolute would be on the same level for us. But if these are admitted as real exceptions from Matthew's historical circumstances, as qualifications of Jesus' absolute condemnation because of special difficulties of time and place and common life between converted Jews and converted pagans, we have in Matthew both (1) the common tradition of Jesus' unspecified condemnation and (2) the first exception which the community found itself forced to make because of the exigencies of historical situations.

III. THE EXCEPTION ADDED BY PAUL

The section in 1 Cor 7 is headed by Paul *peri de 'ōn egrapsate* "concerning the matters about which you wrote." The subject in general is the relationship between men and women, and the problems of marriage and celibacy.[45] The general context which concerns us here is 7,8-16. This has three subsections. The first one deals with

Katherine, his brother's widow. "From the beginning of the divorce proceedings he was convinced that his marriage with Katherine was contrary to the law of God and therefore beyond the jurisdiction of the Pope" as T. Maynard, *Henry the Eighth* (Milwaukee, 1949), p. 123 states.

[45] For Paul's general teaching on these subjects cf. P. H. Menoud, "Mariage et célibat selon S. Paul," *RTPhil*, 1 (1951), 21-34; X. Léon-Dufour, "Mariage et continence selon S. Paul," *A la rencontre de Dieu* ("Mémorial A. Gelin" Le Puy, 1961) 319-329; "Mariage et virginité selon S. Paul," *Christus*, 11 (1964), 179-194.

the unmarried and widows and begins *legō de tois aga-mois* in 7,8-9. The second part talks to married people and starts *tois de gegamēkosin* in 7,10-11. The third section speaks of the special case of the believer married to the unbeliever, where one party to a marriage has become a Christian while the other remained a pagan. This is addressed *tois de loipois* in 7,12-16. The last two divisions mentioned above are carefully qualified. The words to married people in 7,10-11 stem not from Paul but from Jesus, *oyk egō alla 'o kyrios* (7,10), while the advice in 7,12-16 is from Paul and not from Jesus, *egō oych 'o kyrios*. The argument here is that in 1 Cor 7, 10-16 we have a recall of Jesus' categorical imperative against divorce in 7,10-11 and a special Pauline exception or qualification added to this in 7,12-16.

The prohibition of 7,10-11 is that already seen in Mk 10,2-12; Mt 19,3-12; 5,31-32; Lk 16,18. The *chōristhēnai* of 7,10 and *chōristhē* of 7,11 recall the *mē chorizetō* of Mk 10,9 = Mt 19,6. Paul cites this as coming from Jesus himself. Separation is prohibited but more especially is divorce and marriage forbidden. And Paul alone has the sequence of wife mentioned first and then husband. No doubt this represents the final stage of the logion's development from Mt 5,32 through Mt 19,9 = Lk 16,18 and into Mk 10,11-12. Paul finds it expedient to address himself to wives first and husbands second. The special exception to the general rule is then appended in 7,12-16. Two cases are given and a reason added for each. First case: if the husband has an unbelieving wife who wishes to stay with him, it should be so (7,12) and so also for the believing wife with an unbelieving husband (7,13a). The reason is that the entire small community of the family is sanctified through the one who believes (7,13b-14). Second case: if peaceful life is impossible, they can separate (7,15a). The reason added is that God's call should beget peace not strife and there is no guarantee that life in strife will save the unbelieving party in any case (7,15b-16).

Is it correct to consider 7,12-16 as a real exception to Jesus' apodictic prohibition of divorce and remarriage?[46] It has been argued that the clause added on Paul's own authority is not a real exception since Paul would not dare to make such an addition. It must merely be permission to separate without remarriage, and not divorce with the possibility of a later new marriage.[47] The argumentation

[46] The traditional discipline of the Roman church has accepted it as such naming it, somewhat unhappily, the "pauline privilege." It has been extended even beyond the immediate case originally intended by Paul. Cf. A. C. Jemolo, *Il Privilegio Paolino (1 Cor. 7,12-15) dal principio del sec. XI agli albori del XV* (Sassari, 1922); G. Arendt, "La tradizione cattolica in favore de Privilegio Paolino nel coniuge infedele battezzato in una setta acattolica (1 Cor 7,15)," *Greg*, 4 (1923), 241-270, 329-354; S. Woywood, "Marriage Laws of the Church: The Pauline Privilege," *HomPastR*, 25 (1924-25), 272-282; L. Chaussegros de Lery, *Le Privilège de la Foi* (Montreal, 1938); J. J. O'Rourke, "The Scriptural Background of Canon 1120," *The Jurist*, 15 (1955), 132-137.

[47] T. P. Considine, "The Pauline Privilege," *AusCRec*, 40 (1963), 107-119 argues that the text does not intend "the permission to divorce a pagan spouse in certain circumstances but rather the counsel, or even command, to retain her" (108). In this he is even more negative than P. Dulau, "The Pauline Privilege. Is it promulgated in the first epistle to the Corinthians?" *CBQ*, 13 (1951), 146-152.

is scarcely convincing. The institution of separation without real divorce was not known in Greek or Roman Law and can hardly be presumed for 1 Cor 7,15.[48] Besides this general fact, the *chōrizatai, chōrizesthō* of 7,15 should be taken in the same sense as the *chōristhēnai, chōristhē* of 7,10-12. The context is divorce and remarriage in each case. More importantly, Paul presents the exception as based in its own way on Christ. The principle given for his exception is: "God has called you (us) to peace" (7,15b). The word of Christ forbids divorce but the call of Christ begets peace. The Pauline exception in 7,12-16 is how the Apostle reconciles the two imperatives.

IV. THE TEACHING OF THE NEW TESTAMENT

The teaching of the New Testament on divorce and remarriage must include two facets: (1) the apodictic and unqualified condemnation of divorce and remarriage which is the common teaching of the Synoptics and of Paul and which all cite as stemming from Jesus' own teaching; (2) the different exceptions added by Matthew and by Paul.[49] The community represented by Matthew found itself faced with the historical problem of pagans married against the laws of Lv 18 and wishing to be baptized and live with the Christian Jews. They allowed or

[48] O'Rourke, *op. cit.*, 132-137.

[49] These two exceptions have already been studied together by J. J. O'Rourke, "A Note on an Exception: Mt 5,32 (19,9) and 1 Cor 7,12 Compared," *HeythJ*, 5 (1964), 299-302. But the presence of an exception in 1 Cor does not prove that the one in Mt stemmed from Jesus himself.

indeed demanded divorce and remarriage. Paul found a different historical problem—pagans who could no longer live in peace and harmony after the baptism of one party. He also allowed divorce and remarriage. If there were already two exceptions born of divergent historical problems admitted within the New Testament itself, how did the early community consider the apodictic condemnation of divorce and remarriage made by Jesus? This is obviously of primary importance for the Christian reaction to divorce and remarriage today. Modern Christian communities will likewise have to face historical problems in which they must reconcile the unqualified condemnation of Jesus with the call of God which is to a life of peace.

The best way to understand this categorical imperative of Jesus is to replace it in the redactional setting which Mt 5,31-32 has given it. In the Sermon on the Mount of Mt 5-7, Jesus is depicted as bringing the Mosaic Covenant to its divinely intended perfection, as opposing himself not to Moses but to the interpretations of the Pharisees.[50] It has always been recognized that the passage from the magnificent ethical ideals of this anthology to the practical policies and prudential programs of daily life is no easy transition.[51] These ideals represent where a man must go but do not tell him what to do while he

---

[50] E. P. Blair, *Jesus in the Gospel of Matthew* (New York, 1960); W. D. Davies, *The Setting of the Sermon on the Mount* (Cambridge, Eng., 1964).

[51] J. Knox, *The Ethic of Jesus in the Teaching of the Church: Its Authority and Relevance* (New York, 1961).

struggles toward that goal trapped as he is in his own and society's weaknesses and limitations. In dealing, for example, with the six antitheses of Mt 5,21-26.27-30.31 32.33-37.38-42.43-48 commentators have been quite ready to distinguish ideal and program, perfection and development. Examples would be the categorical prohibition against swearing and the necessity of restraining untruth in serious situations (5,33-37),[52] or the unqualified injunction to nonresistance and the necessity of containing aggressive violence (5,38-48).[53] But there has always been a far greater reluctance to apply similar norms of interpretation to Jesus' prohibition of divorce and remarriage. Commentators were much more ready to sanction the possibility of self-defense and war, despite Jesus, than to permit divorce and remarriage, despite that same Jesus.[54] Both divorce and war are tragic human fail-

[52] T. R. Milford, "Is all this swearing necessary?" *TLond*, 68 (1965), 410-417.

[53] H. Clavier, *The Duty and Right of Resistance according to the Bible and the Church* (Leiden, 1956); "Mt 5,39 et la non-resistance," *RHPhilRel*, 37 (1957), 44-57; J. Rausch, "The Principle of Nonresistance and Love of Enemy in Mt 5,38-48," *CBQ*, 28 (1966), 31-41.

[54] This is especially true in the Roman tradition. But cf. the recent works of V. J. Pospishil, "The Eastern Churches and the Question of Remarriage of Divorced Catholics," *Diakonia*, 1 (1966), 302-314; *Divorce and Remarriage. A New Approach Towards a New Catholic Teaching* (New York, 1967). Most significant is the recent study by B. Häring, "The Normative Value of the Sermon on the Mount," *CBQ*, 29 (1967), 375-385 (="Studies in Honor of L. F. Hartman," 69-79). After studying the type of imperatives in the Mtan anthology he notes: "Examined and evaluated against the

ure, but once they have irrevocably happened no apodictic condemnation of their possibility tells us how to handle their actuality. Two human beings who enter into ongoing personal community should develop together and develop each other mutually so that no reason for divorce would ever arise.[55] Jesus insists on the utter reality of this ideal since it alone will bring lasting happiness to man.[56] But this still leaves us today as it left Matthew and Paul then with problems of how to go on with life among weak human beings. For them it was how to preserve peace between converted Jewish and Gentile couples. We have different problems, cases, hypotheses today. We have different reasons why the Christian community in love and forgiveness understands divorce and remarriage among its human members. The categorical imperative of Jesus can never be used as a casuistic absolute but only

background of this context, the saying 'whoever marries a divorced woman commits adultery' just by itself is not sufficient to prove that under the new law of the covenant the remarriage of an innocently divorced woman excludes such a person under all circumstances from the kingdom of God" (383 or 77).

[55] B. Wambacq, "De libello repudii," *VD*, 33 (1955), 331-335 is quite correct in noting that the OT never really favored divorce. At best it received reluctant toleration and legislation. On the relations between divorce in OT and NT, cf. A. Allgeier, "Alttestamentliche beiträge zum neutestamentliche Ehescheidungsverbot." *ThQ*, 126 (1946), 290-292; A. Alberti *Matrimonio e divorzio nella Bibbia* (Milan, 1962); F. Vattioni, "Il divorzio nella Bibbia," *Studi Sociali*, 3 (1962), 235-260.

[56] H. G. Coiner, "Divorce and Remarriage. Toward Pastoral Practice," *ConcTM*, 34 (1963), 541-554: "Where husband and wife are united in a living Christian faith, the ideal of indissolubility of marriage will be realized" (553).

as a catechetical ideal. The New Testament itself recorded two exceptions as its experience of life progressed.
There will be unfortunately many more exceptions, many
more cases where divorce and remarriage must be sorrowfully accepted as part of our human weakness and
our failure to form community, before Christ is all in all.

COMMENT

AND

DISCUSSION

The biblical basis of our common Christian conviction of the permanence of marriage is firm and authoritative. Traditionally the evangelical precept has been looked upon from two different points of view. The Protestant ethic tends to locate the injunction against divorce and remarriage among the imperative ideals of the Kingdom of God, while Catholic belief has seen it as an absolute legal norm, admitting only such exceptions as have been given under the same inspiration as the norm itself.

An ideal is indivisible and unexceptionable, yet there are degrees of both success and failure in its attainment. It is a goal set in concert with other equally important ideals, demanding continual, responsible choice in life-situations of conflict and human weakness. The ideals of the Gospel are unceasing in their demand, and in this sense they are absolute. However, rather than pointing to an order of life in detail, they stand as primary criteria for value judgments in the choice of constantly occurring alternative ways to their fulfillment. A legal norm, on the other hand, embodies not merely a goal, but also a clear and definitive way of attainment. It derives its absoluteness from the unicity of precise positive prescription and can achieve flexibility only from dispensation. When lost, an ideal can be regained. But a legal norm is lost in the breaking.

Since the New Testament remains the fundamental source of Christian morality, it is crucial to derive the meaning of the permanence of marriage from the biblical context in which it is enunciated. Thus we ask if the prohibition of divorce and remarriage may be considered as an ideal or must fidelity to the Lord's imperative be determined in ecclesiastical discipline by the enforcement of a legal norm? The immediate context does not contain the answer. Rather a solution to this question must be found not only in a supportable exegesis of the meaning of words and phrases, but also, and perhaps more basically, in the vision of New Testament morality as a whole.

Biblical hermeneutics discloses various levels of meaning and importance in moral precepts. There are those of a general nature binding in all circumstances, such as the love of neighbor or respect for human life. These precepts are normative for our moral judgments, yet contain within them no specific action-pattern, no clear specification of agency or circumstance. Other precepts, however, go beyond the mere statement of principle to the determination of definitely expected action, such as the command to reiterate the Eucharistic banquet in remembrance of the Lord or, in this case, not to put away one's wife. Absoluteness in this latter case embraces not only principle, but also the specific action-pattern attached to it. It is not a teaching such as turn the other cheek, as an imaginative instance of loving nonresistance, that may sometimes allow not turning the cheek in self-defense. Rather it is a teaching that is very firm and unfolds as a principle in a definitely expected action.

The context of the injunction against divorce and remarriage seems to mix both types of precept. The principle itself is univocal, but the exceptions present alternatives. We must ask why were both the principle and the exceptions given in the same context. Perhaps the reasoning underlying both principle and exceptions will lead to a more adequate statement of the norm itself. Would this same basic understanding then permit other exceptions for the same reasons as those mentioned? If so, the theological rationale of the injunction against divorce and remarriage would also explain exceptions. This line of reasoning would offer a consistent interpretation and broaden the base of exception beyond these specific cases. Theological support could be found both for the precept and actions in exception to it.

The words of Jesus were cast in historical circumstances and were levelled against an evil attacking men and women in that day. He acted to curtail man's right and inhibit man's malice. Thus Jesus enabled marriage to serve a more authentic human good. In this sense the Lord restored a godly ideal of creation and made it workable. Today there is a responsibility to give adequate weight to that historical circumstance and clothe the ideal in a workable flesh and blood expression to serve the authentic good for man in our world. If the exceptions in Matthew and Paul are exemplary of the ways Christians may strive for the ideal of life and marriage, then it is not enough for the Church merely to repeat them. The Church must ask how right they are for people today. It must translate their deepest meaning for the direction of contemporary man. Human lives, met with adversities unknown in the ancient world, articulate needs that cannot be served by a fundamentalism that merely repeats the words of the past without distinguishing the conditioning factors of history.

In the cases of exception contained in Matthew and Paul, the Christian community expressed the conviction that it was not right to enforce the injunction against divorce and forbid remarriage. Are there not cases today of a different nature that make it equally destructive of the Christian life to press this norm as a legal absolute? Scripture itself provides criteria for assessing the rightfulness of particular norms in the ordinary events of life. To ask the reason why Jesus gave a particular precept would entail understanding it in relationship to other norms. New forms of the rule might then develop and be authenticated in concert.

Paul apparently saw no contradiction to Christ's prohibition of divorce and remarriage in the exception he allowed. He gave as the overriding reason for the exception the necessity of two persons living in peace with each other. If this same reasoning were seen as necessary to a more adequate expression of the primary norm of indissolubility, it would allow even further extension of exceptions. In Paul peace supercedes the absoluteness of the marriage bond itself. Living at peace in a common faith with one another for Paul and at peace with the community of Christian Jews for Matthew was a fundamental Christian principle that made exceptions to indissolubility possible. Within the New Testament itself there is apparent then a principle of evolution and adaptation. The indissolubility of marriage itself may be seen in the service of Christian peace and, indeed, conditioned by it.

If a marriage simply ceases to be, for example, because of incurable insanity or abandonment, may the innocent party remarry? It is not clear that Christ intended to forbid this. In his carefully written study of the normative value of the Sermon on the Mount, Bernard Häring says the text of Matthew does not lend itself to this type of casuistry. Christian moralists generally accept ethical principles from the New Testament that allow adaptation in other areas of conflict. We wage war and yet strive to be peacemakers. In the face of the strong injunction against taking oaths, the Church carefully fortifies her judicial processes with a proliferation of oaths.

Why must adaptation stop at the door of sex and marriage? It is difficult to establish an inherent reason for the special treatment of the isolated prohibition of divorce and remarriage.

This line of reasoning still leaves debatable many particulars of premise and logical derivation. In this vein there remain questions of exegesis that need further clarification.

The logion of Matthew, "what God has joined together, let no man put asunder," taken in itself, may not be used to prove that divine law forbids only consensual divorce. Christ clashed with public authority in contradicting the Pharisees. This logion and that which follows, "if a man divorces his wife and marries another, he commits adultery," must be taken together with the debate context in which they were spoken. Basing his answer upon Genesis, Christ enunciates the creative purpose of God in marriage. God made man and woman in such a way that in marriage they should be one. It is not directly relevant to distinguish between human authorities, private or public, to retain an acceptable source of the power to grant divorce. Once man and wife are joined in marriage, they should not separate or be separated.

Later in Matthew (19,10), Christ speaks of the difficulty men will have in accepting this precept. Clement of Alexandria interprets this to mean that the very nature of marriage precludes divorce. Those intending to marry should accept it as a permanent union, or not marry at all. This would seem to indicate that Clement did not understand *porneia* in the sense of an exception. A verifiable tradition in the Fathers leans also to this interpretation. This should be taken into account as an objection against interpreting *porneia* in the light of Leviticus as a statement of exception.

J. Massingberd Ford, in an article in *New Testament Studies*, 10 (1964), 361-365, supports the opinion that in I Cor 7,12-16

Paul did not intend another exception, but the same as that found in Matthew. Paul did not grant a concession of divorce, but a concession to those who have married contrary to the prescriptions of Leviticus. He enabled them to live at peace with the community. The children of such marriages should not be considered tainted, as in Jewish law, but holy and good. Ford claims that the Pauline Privilege, understood as it is today, is found first in the writings of Ambrosiaster (370-384). Did a more primitive tradition hold I Cor 7, 12-16 as an exception to indissolubility or not?

Acts 15 coincides with and follows the same sequence as the prescriptions against incestuous marriage in Leviticus 17-18. Thus follows the use of the word *porneia*. This would indicate that these prescriptions had a particular importance for Luke. Why then did he not include the exception of *porneia* in his Gospel (16,18), as did Matthew? This is simply not known. The reason may have been, however, that the specific concern in the situation of the Jewish converts was more pressing upon Matthew than Luke. Thus Matthew would have found it more necessary to clarify the prohibition by recalling Leviticus. Another reason may be that Luke intended to separate the period of Christ in his Gospel from the period of the Church in Acts. Also Luke presents the teachings of Christ in a radical, unconditioned form, as in his special emphasis upon absolute poverty. He seems to be reluctant to add any qualifications.

Should it make any difference for Christians today whether the logion was actually ever spoken by Jesus or was an addition of Matthew? Edward Schillebeeckx, O.P., in his *Marriage, Human Reality and Saving Mystery* (New York, 1966) develops a lengthy theological argument from this distinction. The authority of the New Testament for Christians, however, rests upon its inspiration as the word of God. It does not basically depend on exact phrasing of Jesus' words. Nor does a distinction between Jesus' words and the interpretation of the evangelists alter the value of scriptural principles.

Within the New Testament itself it seems clear that there was a development of thought regarding the indissolubility of marriage. The fact of this evolutionary development coinciding with a deeper understanding of the Christian life is a significant factor in the interpretation of Scripture. It would clearly point to the impossibility of merely repeating the statements of Scripture as an adequate compendium of Christian ethics. It would further indicate the possibility of development today in the positive direction of a richer theological understanding of marriage and its permanence.

Scripture contains archetypal models of human behavior and above all the model of a dialectic constantly transcending itself. Continuing this dialectic, human life responds to Scripture and transcends it. Theological reflection upon this fact gives reason to both freedom from the words of Scripture and fidelity to its principle. Within the balance of these, the Lord's prohibition of divorce and remarriage and the reasons for it can be interpreted to answer more effectively the needs of twentieth-century man.

2

Novel 22

JOHN T. NOONAN, JR.[*]

The customary perspective from which the Roman law
on divorce in Christian times has been viewed is from a
supposed Christian position on divorce, which the Roman
law is seen as reflecting, rejecting or accommodating.[1]
The perspective of this paper is different. It asks: What
do we know of the Christian teaching on divorce from
the laws of the Christian emperors? I shall set out what
was the law on divorce, the reason given for it and the

[*] Professor of Law, The University of California School of Law,
Boalt Hall, Berkeley. Professor Noonan is the author of *The Scho-
lastic Analysis of Usury* (1957), and *Contraception: A History of
Its Treatment by Catholic Theologians and Canonists* (1965).

[1] Thus A. H. M. Jones declares that "on one point all Christians
were agreed, that marriage was indissoluble except for adultery,"
and Roman divorce legislation as late as Justinian and Justin
"shows how impotent was the Church to change accepted moral
standards on which it felt so strongly as the sanctity of marriage,"
The Later Roman Empire (Norman, Okla., 1964), ıı, 974, 975.
Herbert Hunger sees a contradiction between "Christian principles"
on marriage and *raison d'ètat* in the Byzantine legislation before
the eighth century, Herbert Hunger, "Christliches und Nichtchrist-
liches im byzantischen Eherecht," *Österreichisches Archiv für
Kirchenrecht*, 18 (1967), 30. J. B. Bury, speaking of the divorce
law, says "here ecclesiastical influence was active and the Emperors from Constantine to Justinian fluctuated between the

explanations one might find; I shall then assess the value of this limited, but substantial, evidence in determining the belief of the Christian faithful.

I. THE ROMAN LAW OF DIVORCE IN CHRISTIAN TIMES

In 331, about twenty years after his conversion and the events of the Milvian bridge, Constantine established three grounds on which a libel of divorce (*repudium*) could lawfully be given by a wife to a husband: a man could be divorced if he was a homicide or a medicine man or a destroyer of tombs. A husband could divorce his wife if she were an adulteress, a medicine woman or a procuress (*C.Th.* 3.16.1). The lawgiver also felt obliged to specify three grounds which did not give a woman cause: that her husband was a drunkard, a gambler or a womanizer. Further it was necessary to state that a husband might not dismiss a wife on "every sort of pretext" and that one of the effective grounds must be provable in

wishes of the Church on one side, and on the other common sense and Roman tradition," *The History of the Later Roman Empire* (London, 1923), ii, 406. Yet Bury himself notes that "the ecclesiastics themselves had not yet arrived at a clear and definite doctrine" —an admission which makes suspect his sweeping "the wishes of the Church." Somewhat similarly Biondi, *Il diritto Romano Cristiano* (Milan, 1954), iii, 169 attributes the fluctuations of Roman divorce law to a conflict between "a divine conception" of marriage as a sacrament and a "human conception according to which marriage is a bilateral act, free and voluntary and hence soluble." Yet Biondi also states, "I do not believe that at bottom the civil rule was different from that of the Church of the time, or at least from a current in it."

court on subsequent investigation. The penalty for a wife's divorcing without grounds was loss of her property down to her hairpins and deportation to an island; the penalty for a husband was loss of his wife's dowry and a prohibition to remarry.

Relevant points may be underlined in this legislation. The grounds given the husband seem to be a reminiscence of the grounds on which Romulus is said to have permitted divorce—a possibly conscious invocation of the morals of the founding father.[2] There was no symmetry between the husband's grounds and the wife's. The wife was explicitly denied the right of divorce for adultery.

Children were neglected by the legislation. Only a spouse who did not want to be divorced was protected by its thrust. At the same time, the law projected the view that divorce against the will of one party was a bad thing, to be restrained and not encouraged. Treating man and woman unequally was probably of more help to a woman than a man, simply because without any law a woman could have been more easily cast off.

There seems to have been no connection between this law and any special religious view of remarriage. Remar-

---

[2] The legendary account of the legislation of Romulus is provided by Plutarch, *Romulus* 22 in his *Parallel Lives*. Divorce was permitted for adultery, for "counterfeiting of the keys" and for "medicine" toward children. In this context medicine indicated drugs preventing conception or provoking abortion, see my *Contraception: A History of Its Treatment by the Catholic Theologians and Canonists*, p. 25. Biondi, III, 163 ridicules the idea that Romulus was being copied, which was advanced by C. Dupont, *La Réglementation Économique dans les constitutions de Constantin* (Lisle, 1963), p. 113, but he gives no reason for his ridicule.

riage, indeed, was assumed to be the regular sequel to divorce, as deprivation of the right to remarry was a principal part of the sanction aimed at a lawbreaking husband; even for him a second marriage was not void but subject to property claims of his first wife. Moreover, if a wife wrongly sought a divorce, her action had the paradoxical effect of freeing her husband: her punishment of deportation itself dissolved the marriage;[3] nothing prevented her husband from taking advantage of this turn if he chose. After a divorce for cause, remarriage was entirely within the spirit and policy of the law.

The law did symbolize in a limited way that divorce was a matter of social concern, but the concern was limited to the upper classes who would marry with dowries and possibly be influenced by considerations of property. Did the concern extend to divorces by mutual consent? The old principle, enunciated by Diocletian, was: "No one can be compelled to contract marriage to start with or to recompose a broken marriage. Hence understand that it is not right that the free faculty of contracting and of dissolving marriages be transferred to the realm of the obligatory" (*C.J.* 5.4.14). It was not entirely clear if the law of Constantine trenched upon this liberty of contract; at least the man by contract with his wife seemed able to avoid any sanctions provided by law against his divorcing without grounds.[4]

---

[3] So *D.*24.1.43 holding a gift made by one spouse to another, *causa exilii* valid, for the marriage was dissolved.

[4] Biondi, iii, 173 simply asserts that divorce by mutual consent continued to exist but cites no evidence.

But was this law Christian legislation? I will postpone
this question until I have set out the principal steps
taken by Constantine's Christian successors.[5] Almost a
century later, in 421, the Emperor Honorius issued at
Ravenna a new schema for involuntary divorce. A trial
after a *repudium* had been given might show (1) no
ground at all, (2) moral flaws and average faults or (3)
crimes. A wife divorcing on no grounds was deported and
lost all her property, together with the opportunity of
recovering it if she ever was allowed to return. She was
also denied the right to remarry. If she proved moral
fault, she still lost her dowry and marriage gifts and the
right to remarry, and her husband could charge her with
adultery if she did remarry. If she proved crimes, she
kept both dowry and marriage gifts, and five years after
the divorce she "received the power to remarry." A husband without grounds lost dowry and gifts and the right

[5] The one ex-Christian in the interval, Julian, issued a law which
enlarged the possibility of divorce for women, according to Pseudo-
Augustine, *Questiones de utroque testamento*, c.115.12, *PL* 35.
2348-49. The text of the law has not survived, and the casual
reference here makes it hard to reconstruct its terms. No mention
of divorce is made in the anonymous fourth-century comparison of
Roman and Mosaic law, *Mos. coll.* This work, sometimes attributed
to Christian authorship including that of St. Ambrose, is probably
that of a Jew, see Jean Gaudemet, *La Formation du droit séculier
et du droit de l'église aux 4e et 5e siècles* (Paris, 1957), p. 90. The
Jewish and Mosaic law on the killing of an adulteress is compared
(*Mos. coll.* 4). The silence on divorce may indicate a sense that
the Roman law is now committed to a Christian position which
will not support the author's thesis of a strong similarity between
Mosaic and Roman legislation.

to remarry; proving moral fault, he kept the gifts, lost the dowry and could remarry in two years; if he established a crime, he got dowry and gifts and the immediate right to remarry (*C. Th.* 3.16.2).

This legislation, like Constantine's, used the property right and the remarriage right together as the chief sanction against the male. The dissolubility of marriage was thus part of the structure of the law. Not only did the law assume that divorce was for the purpose of remarriage; it was expressly provided that where the husband failed to prove any grounds, the wife could remarry after a year. The penalty of celibacy for the husband in this case was not because his marriage survived, but because he was to be punished for his "insolence" or lack of moderation.

There was no suggestion of religious reasons for the law. Indeed the only reason that appeared on the face of it was the thought that a woman who convicted her husband of crimes showed that she acted from loathing of her husband rather than from a desire for a new husband —a dubious enough assumption, which, at least, suggested a legislative antipathy to adultery. The provisions aimed at husbands' dismissing their wives for slight or no grounds meant that the Constantinian edict was probably not very well enforced, and the *Interpretation* of the law noted that it was common for husbands to be displeased with their wives' characters without being able to prove crimes. The law slightly strengthened the woman's position by regulating dismissal for moral fault and giving her equal grounds on which to seek an unpenalized divorce.

As adultery was a crime with a married woman,[6] she could now at least divorce her husband for adultery if he committed it with a married woman. Divorce by consent was not mentioned explicitly by the law.

The composition and experience of the imperial family in the West may have had some impact on the law, although their personal participation in its drafting cannot be proven. Honorius himself had been married twice. The first time was in 398, when he was fourteen, to Maria, the daughter of Stilicho, the regent of the Empire. On her death about 408, Stilicho married off a second daughter Aemilia to him, but in the same year Stilicho fell from power and was executed, and Honorius returned Aemilia to her family, the marriage unconsummated and she still a virgin. Neither of the wives seem to have been as important to him as his half-sister Galla Placidia. Taken captive by the Visigoths in 410, Galla Placidia was married in 414 at the age of twenty-six to the barbarian king Athaulf. After his assassination she was enslaved by his successor, but soon freed and traded back to the Romans and, more or less unwillingly, married to the consul Constantius in 417. On February 8, 421, Constantius was crowned Augustus, and then he and Honorius together crowned Galla Placidia as Augusta. She was again widowed in September, 421, and Honorius proceeded to embarrass his court by public displays of affection to her. She

[6] Theodore Mommsen, *Le droit penal romain* (French trans. by J. Duquesne, Paris, 1907), II, 420-421.

later fell out with Honorius and fled to her nephew Theodore in Constantinople. On Honorius' death in 423, she became regent of the empire in the West and ruled until 435. Galla Placidia, in short, was a remarkable woman who survived captivity, enslavement and widowhood to become a Roman empress.[7] The divorce legislation was enacted in 421 when she was coming into her own as a powerful force at court. It may not be unreasonable to speculate that she is the first of several Roman empresses to have taken an interest in the law of divorce and to see the stronger provisions in favor of women as a reflection of her experience.

In the East another woman may have had a part in the most violent change in the divorce law to occur under a Christian emperor. The East was ruled by Theodosius II, the nephew of Honorius and Galla Placidia. He had been educated by his older sister, Pulcheria, a devout and dedicated Christian virgin. When he was twenty, his sister had picked his wife for him—a bright, energetic and well-educated pagan girl, Atheneis, who had come to court to plead her inheritance rights in a quarrel with her brothers. Atheneis became a Christian with the baptismal name of Eudocia. Her intellectual and legal interests are presumed to have continued, and her sympathy with some pagan thought may well have remained.[8]

It is difficult to attribute to other than pagan influence what took place. In 439, the time-hallowed provisions of

[7] On this history, see Bury, I, 125, 184, 194, 197, 203, 204, 209-210.

[8] Bury, I, 214-215, 220-221, 231-232.

Constantine were repealed. Saying that "it is harsh to exceed the regulations of the ancient laws," the emperor abrogated "the constitutions" which bound husband or wife by the gravest penalties when a marriage "was dissolved" and decreed that blame and coercion should be governed by the ancient laws and responses of the jurisconsults (N. Th. 12). Only a year before, the Code which bears Theodosius' name had been issued containing both the laws of Constantine and of Honorius on divorce; the plural, "constitutions," was used in the abrogating act, so that both laws were meant. The law was returned to a pre-Christian state. Probably the reform had been contemplated for some time but not undertaken before the Code was issued so as not to jeopardize the concurrence of the Emperor of the West in the Code.

The repealing act did enunciate the general principle that out of "favor for the children" divorce ought "to be more difficult" than marriages, and in the interest of this principle the law decreed that divorce must be by a libel of repudiation, viewed as a more formal act than the consent constituting marriage. This provision seemed to assert that even divorce by mutual consent fell within the sphere of social control, a social control exercised on behalf of the children. Nothing explicit was said about consensual divorces, so presumably they were accepted. The rejection of Honorius as "harsh" indicated a belief that divorce against the will of one spouse was often an acceptable solution.

The divorce law continued to concern the lawmakers of Constantinople. Again in the regime of Theodosius II,

in 449, but now without the help of Eudocia, a new law
was enacted on a mixture of the Constantinian and
Honorian models. It took the substantial step of clearly
eliminating consensual divorce. The dissolution of marriages "without just cause" was prohibited. Agreements
to the contrary were "null as contrary to law." Yet the
legislator declared himself desirous of giving the necessary help to "him or her oppressed by adverse and unhappy necessity" (*C.J.* 5.17.8). An expanded list of just
causes was therefore provided. For both husband and
wife adultery was placed at the head of the list. This
provision was not to accord completely equal treatment,
as adultery for the man had to be an act committed
with another married woman, but near equality was
achieved by providing that a wife could divorce her husband if he actually brought lewd women home. Homicide
continued to be a ground for either husband or wife, and
a plan to commit homicide was ground when the intended victim was the spouse. The old ground of tomb-
disturbing was probably embraced in a clause on "taking
something from the sacred edifices," with a specific additional reference to women who were destroyers of tombs.
Only male medicine men were specified. With these variations, the old Constantinian crimes—adultery, homicide,
medicine and burial violation—were retained. To them
were added several grounds probably of special concern
to the government: for either husband or wife, plotting
against the empire or kidnapping; for wives, their husbands' cattle rustling, counterfeiting, robbing or receiving

robbers; for husbands, their wives' fostering robbers. To this extent, the grounds were restricted to crimes. But what the schema of Honorius had provided for husband, this law provided for both spouses: divorce on moral grounds. A wife could divorce her husband for beating her with blows unfit for a free woman; a husband could divorce a wife who struck him. Acts which perhaps were thought to raise a presumption of adultery but were not themselves the crime of adultery were also specified: a wife's frequenting the theatre, circus or arena against her husband's prohibition or dining with strange men behind his back. Five years before, Theodosius II had executed Paulinus, his Master of Offices, on similar presumptive evidence of adultery with the Empress Eudocia while she, his wife of twenty-four years, had withdrawn in voluntary exile.[9]

The sanctions relied on to enforce the law were the familiar ones of property and remarriage rights, but the old severe sanction of deportation of the woman was dropped. If a wife was unjustified in her divorce, she lost her dowry and marriage gift and the right to remarry for five years; a man merely lost the dowry and gift. The trend

[9] Bury, I, 230. According to the story told by John Malalas, *Chronicle* 14, p. 356, Theodosius was given a gift of an enormous Phrygian apple. He presented it in turn to Eudocia. She gave it to Paulinus, who, unaware of its origin, presented it to Theodosius. When the Emperor asked the Empress where the apple he gave her was, she said, "I ate it." This statement intensified his suspicions, and he had Paulinus killed.

of legislation to treat women more like men thus continued, with the elimination of the unusual penalty for the
woman. Still not equal, they were a little less unequal.

The use of remarriage rights as sanction again expressly
incorporated a belief that remarriage was permissible
after divorce. The reason given for barring the unjustified
divorcee from marriage for five years was "that it is just
that she lack marriage for a while when she has demon-
strated that she is unworthy of it." There was no suggestion that her unjustified divorce left a valid marriage
in her path. If she succeeded in proving good grounds,
she could marry within a year. The reason given for the
delay was "lest anyone suspect the offspring," that is, lest
there be a doubt whether a new child was her first or
second husband's. The law thus assumed that she would
marry again and procreate at once.

In Rome three years later in 452, Valentinian III issued
a law which took no notice of the efforts of his father-
in-law, Theodosius II, at Constantinople. In the course
of a constitution chiefly directed to judicial procedure,
Valentinian III referred to a "new law which permitted
marriages to be dissolved by a contrary will alone," and
abrogated it (*N.*Val. 35.11 of 452 A.D.). Presumably the
law of 439 was meant. The Roman law now declared that
what had been decreed by Constantine was to be left
inviolate. The reason given was that it was "for the bond
of reverence of marriages, lest they everywhere be rashly
dissolved." This language came close to sacramental
terminology but seemed to object to the rash dissolution
of marriage rather than to all dissolutions. It is not clear

why the more sophisticated scheme of the East was ignored and why Constantine was treated as the acme of ancestral wisdom. A good guess would be that Rome had been outraged at the abolition measure of 439 and wanted only to assert the tried and true wisdom of the Founding Father of the Christian empire. It has been suggested Pope Leo I was behind the law, and no doubt he was a more influential force on marriage legislation than the undistinguished reigning emperor of the West.[10]

Divorce continued to interest the empire in the East. The Emperor Leo I legislated extensively on the question between 457 and 474, and his legislation was largely in force at the beginning of the sixth century (N. 22, pr.). What its provisions consisted in are unknown since they were not preserved by the later codifiers. It became clear at any rate that the issue of consensual divorce had not been decided for the East. The Emperor Anastasius provided in 497 that if a libel of repudiation was given with mutual consent, the wife did not have to wait five years, though no ground sanctioned by the 449 law was alleged: she could pass to a second marriage after a year's wait (C.J. 5.17.9). Presumably the other penal provisions of the law were waived in this case.

It was, in any event, a good question as to whether the prohibitions of divorce from Constantine to Anastasius had any teeth to them. The pecuniary penalties of the law had the self-interest of the parties to assure their enforce-

---

[10] For the suggestion as to the influence of Pope Leo, see Biondi III, 176; on "weak and worthless" Valentinian III, see Bury I, 250.

ment. But if someone cared to pay this price or could work out a settlement with his spouse, was there any public machinery which prevented remarriage? Adultery with a married woman was a crime, but a legally invalid *repudium* was sufficient defense against a charge of adultery for a man who married a woman believing that there had been a legal divorce (*D.* 48.5.44). To enforce the penalties of deportation of the woman or simple denial of remarriage to man or woman would have required the efforts of the state, and there is no evidence that the state carried out these provisions. Of special significance is that the grounds established by law were not proved before the *repudium* was sent and became effective. The *repudium* was sent first. Only later might there be a trial on the grounds alleged—a trial either for adultery or for property rights.[11] Hence, judicial supervision of the divorce was not built into the act of divorce itself, and it may be supposed that the invocation of the judicial machinery to investigate what had already happened was spotty and infrequent.

Divorce then had been a subject much considered, much legislated on, unevenly regulated by 529 when Justinian authorized the work of collecting and codifying the law. But Justinian brought to the subject special insights. None of his predecessors had taken such a deep

---

[11] For an example of a sixth-century *repudium* from Egypt, see A. S. Hunt and C. S. Edgar, *Selected Papyri* I (1932), 29. In this example, the father of the wife is dismissing the husband. The grounds given are rather general—crimes which "should not be mentioned."

personal interest in theology. None of his predecessors
had been so interested in the law as an instrument for
the welfare of the empire and the good of its subjects'
souls. In addition to these theoretical qualifications,
Justinian was joined in marriage to his intellectual equal,
Theodora, whom he, at the age of forty-one, had married
from love. He responded to her abilities by taking counsel
in the making of at least some laws from "our most pious
consort given to us by God" (*N.* 8.1 of 535). He responded
to her person by the confession he put into law itself:
"We know, though we are lovers of chastity, that nothing
is more vehement than the fury of love" (*N.* 74.4 of 538
A.D.).[12] He had special reason to consider the law of
marriage with respect to Theodora, because he had been
enabled to marry the ex-actress and to legitimate their
potential offspring only by persuading his uncle Justin I
to change the marriage law in force in 523 to what
became *C. J.* 5.4.23.[13] It is impossible to show that
Theodora actually advised on the divorce laws or to
establish how great a part Justinian played personally
in their composition. It does seem likely, however, that
in the later legislation after the work of collecting old law
had been done, the personal valuations of Justinian, in-

[12] It has been observed that only the emperor himself would in-
sert such a personal note: David Daube, "The Marriage of Justinian and Theodora," *The Catholic University of America Law Review*, 16 (1967), 397. Another personal note is the pun in which
he acknowledged Theodora's help in Novel 8.1: he took counsel
from his *theou dedomenen* wife.

[13] *Ibid.*, 381-394.

fluenced by Theodora, were reflected and that this emperor, who proclaimed himself a "lover of chastity," struggled to find the right course to take on questions of remarriage.

In the Code, Justinian ignored Emperor Leo I and began with Theodosius II's law of 449 and Anastasius' of 497 (*C.J.* 5.17.9, 5.17.11). To their provisions he added these grounds in 533: a wife's procuring an intentional abortion, bathing in common with men for a lustful purpose or attempting marriage to another man (*C.J.* 5.17.11). The last two grounds were in the Theodosian area of acts proximate to adultery; the first was in the area of medicine making. A special provision specified, for the first time, a sanction against divorce in a marriage contracted without dowry. In this case, the man acting without cause had to pay his divorced wife one-quarter of his substance up to a maximum payment of one hundred pounds; the wife, if it were her fault, was subjected to the standard five-year waiting period (*C.J.* 5.17.11). In addition, a husband was permitted to withdraw from marriage to choose "a solitary life" or a wife to choose "monastic practice" without the usual penalties for dissolution of marriage. If a spouse thus embarked on religious life, the law treated the withdrawal from marriage as equivalent to death. Any agreement the spouses had made in case of the death of one came into play, "as if he who withdraws from living together in marriage appears to be dead, since he is fully useless to his partner" (*C.J.* 1.3.52.15 of 531).

These provisions were just the beginning of Justinian's work. The correct treatment of remarriage continued to

concern him. In the same period in which the greatest
church of Christendom, St. Sophia, was being built, a
new code on divorce was being prepared. It was issued
in 535 as Novel 22.

Marriage, Novel 22 began, gives an "artificial im-
mortality to our nature"; through it, "God, so far as
possible, gives eternal existence to our species." Hence,
"rightly marriage is our study." Unlike other matters
which concern only parts of mankind, "the study of marriage is of importance to the whole of human offspring."
The ancients did not sufficiently consider the question of
second marriages. Theodosius II paid more attention to
them; other emperors issued laws on them; Leo I acted
vigorously to decree much on them; so too have we. But
now we improve our earlier laws. In short, in view of the
prime importance of the matter, Justinian has prepared
with thoughtful care a comprehensive schema on remarriage, repealing all previous legislation.

What constitutes marriage? "Mutual affection makes
marriage." Justinian answered with the classical formula
which he emphasized to indicate that a dowry was not
necessary to bring a marriage into being.[14] Hence, he
said, marriage can be dissolved, with or without penalty,
"for, of those things which occur among men, whatever
is bound is soluble" (N. 22.3). The solubility of marriage
was the basic premise of Novel 22; on this foundation
the juridical edifice was rested.

---

[14] For a study of Justinian's use of marital affection as the key
element in constituting a marriage, see Gianetto Longo, "Affectio
maritalis," *Bollettino di istituto di diritto romano*, 46 (1939), 194.

In the *Timaeus* of Plato the phrase "whatever is bound is soluble" occurs, and Schoell's edition of Novel 22 puts the phrase as used by Justinian in quotation marks as a quotation from Plato. In the *Timaeus*, 41, the words are spoken by the Author of the Universe to the assembled gods before he has made any mortals. As Francis Cornford translates,

> Gods, of gods whereof I am the maker and of works the father, those which are my own handiwork are indissoluble save with my consent. Now, although whatsoever bond has been fastened may be loosened, yet only an evil will could consent to dissolve what has been well-fitted together and in good state; therefore, although you, having come into being are not immortal nor indissoluble altogether, nevertheless you shall not be dissolved nor taste of death, finding my will a bond yet stronger and more sovereign than those wherewith you are bound together when you came to be.

The passage thus dealt with a relative indissolubility of being which was conferred by the divine will. In the allusion to it by Justinian, the context is altered: now solubility is "among things which happen among men." The solubility of human affairs is delicately contrasted with the relative indissolubility enjoyed by the gods.[15]

There are four ways, Novel 22 continued, in which dissolution is effected during the life of the parties to the

---

[15] Biondi III, 185 notes that Justinian could have drawn different consequences from Plato's passage, "transporting the concept into the Christian orbit"; that is, in Biondi's view, asserting the indissolubility of marriage. Surely what is significant is that, instead, the solubility is what the allusion underlines.

contract: (1) by the consent of both, (2) for rational ground which is called "good grace," *bona gratia*, (3) without cause and (4) with rational cause, which is not *bona gratia* (*N. 22.4*). Of the first, nothing was to be said here, for the parties could arrange the matter by agreement as it pleased them. Novel 22 directed itself to the last three classes.

On divorce for rational cause Justinian followed what was already in his own Code: the grounds were those given by Theodosius II plus those added in 533. The sanction of suspension of marriage rights for the woman remained unchanged. An explanation was added as to why the man could remarry at once, whether he had acted on rational grounds or not; it was, symmetrically with the reason given for delaying marriage for the wife, lest there be confusion of offspring (*N. 22.16*); that is, the law assumed an incontinent man who would have intercourse whether married or not and thought it better to provide for immediate marriage. Justinian observed further that marriages were frequently dissolved where there had been no dowry, because here there was no fear of penalty. He reaffirmed his own legislative efforts of 533 to discourage this casual treatment of lower class marriages (*N. 22.10*). In general, however, a new approach was taken to the property of a divorced couple. It was based on concern for the children.

It may be, said Novel 22, that when a marriage is dissolved, the parties will "perdure in their first marriage and perchance not sadden their procreated offspring by a subsequent marriage"; it will be a happy and blessed thing if they do not do this (*N. 22.20*). But if "not content with

marriage," they remarry, the law must regulate their
property. If there were no children of the first marriage,
there are no financial penalties for either man or woman.
But if there are children, any property the wife receives
or has received from the husband is hers only to the extent
of a usufruct; similarly the husband holds property from
his wife only in usufruct (*N.* 22.23). Neither the husband
or wife in such a situation can alienate or pledge the
property subject to usufruct; any such transfer is null
(*N.* 22.24). In this property the children of the first marriage share equally, for all have equally been "dishonored"
by the second marriage (*N.* 22.25). Only if one child
dies, his portion of the property may then be alienated
(*N.* 22.26). Moreover, a remarried husband or wife may
not give his new spouse a gift greater than the portion of
a child in the first marriage, so that an upper limit is introduced on marriage gifts in second marriages, a limit intended to conserve property for children of the first
marriage (*N.* 22.27). In these provisions, dowry and marriage gifts ceased to be used as sanctions which operated
to favor the innocent spouse; regulation of them became
a sanction which operated to benefit the children. It was
explicitly stated that these provisions held whatever the
cause of dissolution of the marriage and whoever's fault
it was (*N.* 22.30). All of this legislation seemed to reflect
a view that divorce was undesirable for its effect on the
property rights of the children, not because of its severing
of a natural or indissoluble bond.

Fault, then, remained important only to determine the
wife's waiting period for remarriage and to assess a penalty

where a man dissolved a dowerless marriage. The reorientation of sanctions made the Theodosian list of causes of far less significance than it had been when supported by its original sanctions. Justinian, moreover, now codified a number of causes for dissolution which were not only rational but had the special appellation "good grace." Here fault was entirely eliminated.

The first and chief of good grace causes was the desire "to pass to a better life and to practice chastity." Only one spouse need have such a desire; the consent of the other was not required. No special formula or vow was specified. It was sufficient that one "put an end to the marriage" and withdrew. The reason for dissolution was a shorter form of that given in *C.J.* 1.3.52.15: "he seems to die as to the marriage" (*N.* 22.5). Presumably this rationale implied that the other spouse was now free to remarry.

The other good grace grounds were involuntary. First there was impotence of the man to copulate. Impotence was not viewed as nullifying the marriage as in later canon law, but as creating a ground for divorce. In 528 Justinian had required that there be a period of two years in which the man's inability was established; only after that could the wife, or her parents, divorce him (*C.J.* 5.17.10). Now he stated that experience had shown that some who were impotent for two years had been able later "to minister to procreation." Instead of concluding from this that impotence might be a psychological problem, the legislator merely extended the period of trial from two years to three (*N.* 22.6). Nothing was said as to the impotence being antecedent, natural, incurable and perpetual. Apparently impotence occuring at any time in marriage could dissolve it. Inability of the woman to have intercourse was not considered.[16]

The other involuntary good grace grounds depended on action taken by others and rested on the juridical effects of slavery. Slaves were juridically incapable of marriage (*C.Th.* 12.1.6). By what seemed an inescapable logical corollary, if a free spouse became a slave, his marriage was dissolved: he no longer had a juridically cognizable will capable of expressing the marital affection which classical pagan jurisprudence made essential to marriage (*D.* 49.15.12.4).[17] By the time of Justinian the continuation of marital affection was no longer necessary for continuation of the marriage.[18] But Justinian found another rationale for the old result: "[slavery] as our predecessors have taught us, is not far from death" (*N.* 22.8). Accordingly, enslavement, like death, dissolved a marriage.

---

[16] Insanity was not mentioned as ground for divorce. In the *Digest* as interpolated, it was held that "if a marriage is established," an insane woman can be dismissed, *D.*24.2.4. The implication is that there may be no marriage at all because of the insanity, but this is not said explicitly, and this apparently obvious ground for nullity or for good grace divorce was not picked up by the later legislation of Justinian.

Sterility as ground for divorce was mentioned in an interpolation in the *Digest*, *D.*24.1.60, but it was also ignored by Justinian.

[17] See Edouardo Volterra, *La conception du mariage d'après les juristes romains* (Padua, 1940), pp. 2 and 61.

[18] See Volterra, pp. 2-37; Giuseppe D'Ercole, "Il consenso degli sposi e la perpetuità del matrimonio nel diritto romano e nei Padri della Chiesa," *Studia et documenta historiae iuris*, 5 (1939), 23.

The Roman captured by the enemy was in the position of a slave. Classical jurisprudence held that his marriage was dissolved; the right of a returning captive to regain his property did not include a right to regain his wife (*D.* 23.2.1; *D.* 49.15.14.1). Two Popes undertook modest modifications of this view. In 410, Innocent I taught that a woman captive, Ursa, returning home was entitled to take back her remarried husband, Fortunius, for the Pope so ruled on the explicit understanding that she had "not been cast out by divorce."[19] Asked to rule on the rights of a returned prisoner, Pope Leo the Great in 458 urged that what was granted as to property should be granted as to the wife: the returning soldier should be entitled to a "reintegration" of the marriage, if he wished. But the Pope did not say that the marriage endured without the reintegration or that the soldier was bound to take back his now remarried wife.[20] In 529, Justinian had taken two more steps to protect the soldier: he gave him the right to accuse his wife of adultery committed while he was a captive (*D.* 48.5.14), and he prohibited the wife from marrying while it was uncertain whether the man was dead or a prisoner (*D.* 24.2.6).[21] The protection was not

[19] Innocent 1, *Letter 36, PL* 20.602.

[20] Leo 1, *Letter 159*, 1-2, *PL* 54.1136. He does cite Mt 19,6, "What God has joined together."

[21] Both provisions are held by many authorities to be interpolations by Justinian's codifiers, see Ernst Levy and Ernst Rabel, *Index interpolationum quae in Justiniani Digestis inesse dicuntur* (Weimar, 1929) I, 88-89 and 530.

absolute: after waiting five years, the wife was free to marry. Apparently after such a time, captivity looked enough like death to dissolve the marriage. The treatment was modeled on the Constantinian law that required a four-year waiting period where a wife had not heard from a soldier husband on an expedition. After she had "borne the yoke such a great length of time" with no word, she was free to marry (*C.J.* 5.11.1). In Novel 22 Justinian explained his thought more fully and applied the rule not only to captured men but to captured women. It was, he said, a "punctilious and subtle reason" which broke the marriage by the mere fact of captivity—the reason that the spouses were no longer of equal condition as one was now a slave. But he himself, he said, had viewed the matter "more humanely" and "therefore determined that the marriage lasted" as long as it was evident that the captive survived; five years' wait dissolved the marriage only if, at the end of it, the existence of the captive was uncertain (*N.* 22.7).

In dissolutions by good grace no penal provisions applied, the wife still had to wait one year to marry (except where she had already waited five), the husband could marry at once, the property rules in favor of the children applied (*N.* 22.30). Good grace divorce was thus distinguished from rational cause divorce only by its express avoidance of moral blame being assigned to either party. The technical term used—*bona gratia* in Latin even in the Greek text—does not seem to imply more than this absence of fault. The grace referred to was certainly not sacramental grace. The divorces given did not require any special dispensation or grace from the emperor, although two of the cases looked like the cases of dissolution by religious profession and for nonconsummation where the Pope later was said to dispense from the bond. The term was used strongly and affirmatively to indicate what was entirely proper. For example, "such is the case of captivity that it is good grace to dissolve the marriage."[22]

Novel 22 was not the last word of Justinian on marriage, but I shall argue in a moment why it may be the most significant Roman legislation on divorce. It is necessary, however, to set out first its sequel. Seven years later, in 542, Justinian undertook further marriage legislation. In part, he aimed to strengthen the status of marriage established by affection alone, without dowry. He reaffirmed the pecuniary penalty for its dissolution and provided further for the property rights of children of such a union (N. 117.5). More comprehensively, he attempted to guard the rights of all children where marriages were "dissolved," so that "in no way may the children be injured by the separation of the marriage"; guidelines were given as to which parent they should stay with, and their support was regulated (N. 117.7).

Following this legislation for the children, the emperor stated bluntly that, reviewing the causes established for

[22] In an interpolated passage of the *Digest* on the marriage of captives, the phrase "good grace" is somewhat differently introduced: "by good grace the first marriage seems dissolved," D.24.2.6.

divorce, he had found several by which dissolution
"easily" occurred and had decided to strike "unworthy"
grounds. "Unworthiness" was not defined, but the rational
causes of divorce were drastically reduced. Eliminated
were most of the grounds where the spouse performed
some criminal act against one other than the spouse—
homicide, sorcery, burial violation, kidnapping, cattle-
rustling, robbery. The only ground of this kind left was
plotting against the empire or failing to reveal such a plot.
Homicide was grounds only where it was attempted
against a husband (*N*. 117.8). Wife-beating was justified
by the same grounds which justified dissolution, was never
itself to be grounds for dissolution and was to be punished
only by an assessment in favor of the injured wife against
the husband's antenuptial gift (*N*. 117.14). The grounds
which created suspicion of adultery were retained and
slightly altered—a wife's dining or bathing with other
men, staying outside her husband's or her parents' home,
frequenting circuses, theatres or arenas. The grounds
which, while not constituting adultery by the husband,
were now made grounds for divorce, were keeping another
woman in the house or, after warning by his wife or her
parents, frequenting another women in the same city. A
wife might also divorce her husband if he accused her of
adultery and did not prove it (*N*. 117.9).

Good grace divorce was also limited. Impotence had to
be from the beginning of a marriage. Divorce for the sake
of chastity had to be with the consent of the other spouse
and then had to be choice of a monastic life. The case of

dissolution by captivity was preserved, but dissolution for any other cause was abolished (N. 117.12). Even the term "good grace" disappeared from the law.

The most striking features of the new law were three: first, there was the elimination of consensual divorce except where the monastic life was elected. No reason for this change was given, although it was laconically observed that, "up to the present," such divorces had been had (N. 117.10). Second, there was a one-sided increase in penalty for unjustified divorce, for it was observed that some women desired to live indecently and hastened to break their marriages. To check them, the law stipulated that if a woman divorced without cause, she lost her dowry to her husband, two-thirds of her other property went to her children and one-third to a monastery, and the bishop of the city of her domicile was to order her put into a monastery for life (N. 117.13). The law was no harsher than the old penalty of deportation for the dismissed wife, but after a century since abolition of this penalty, the new sanction must have appeared sharp and unequal. Moreover, the wife's enclosure in a monastery presumably had the effect of freeing the husband to remarry; hence, there was no need to provide explicitly for him that he could remarry when his wife unjustifiably sought a divorce. Thirdly, Novel 117 set out in detail a process by which a husband could lawfully kill an adulterer. It required not only three written warnings, witnessed by three reliable witnesses, but also the husband's surprising the man with the husband's wife in the husband's home, the wife's house, the adulterer's home or in a tavern or in the suburbs (*N.* 117.15). Significantly, even in this drastic effort to formalize the killing of adulterers, no right was given to the husband to kill his guilty wife; here divorce remained the approved legal outlet for his passion.

Novel 117 breathed a much more restrictive spirit than Novel 22. It did not, however, assert any general principle of indissolubility. Its vigorous reform provisions seemed to aim at helping the children of a first marriage and at discouraging easy divorce. But there was no invalidation of second marriages made by husbands in defiance of the law; and, even more significantly, a saving clause specifically exempted from the law's operation what had already been decided by judicial decree or "friendly agreement" (*N.* 117, Epilogue). What the law objected to was not the principle of consensual divorce, but the spread of divorce that the principle made possible.

The unequal treatment of women was righted in 548, the same year in which Theodora died. In the course of a constitution on various matters, a section on divorce was inserted in which Justinian said that now he changed the law "for the better" and decreed that there be "no difference" between the punishments of men and women divorcing without cause recognized by law. The reason was simply given: "In an equal crime we have judged it just to threaten them with similar punishments" (*N.* 127.4).

In Justinian's final legislation on the subject, Novel 134, issued in 556, divorce was even more closely restricted.

For adultery, hitherto the prime ground for divorce, a new approach was set out. When a woman was convicted of adultery, she was to be beaten and confined in a monastery. Her husband then had two years within which to take her back. If he did not, she had to receive the monastic habit, and presumably the marriage was dissolved. In the case of a man, adultery was punished by the loss of his marriage gifts to his wife (*N.* 134.10). The law did not repeal the old divorce provisions, but apparently was intended to offer an alternative sanction for adultery less drastic than divorce. At the same time it assimilated divorce for adultery by the woman to dissolution by religious profession.

In addition, Novel 134 took notice that "some" studied to evade the existing divorce law. Once more divorce by consent was forbidden. Once more it was repeated that divorce was permitted only on the grounds enumerated by law. But, beyond exhortation, the law enacted new and severe punishments. If a couple dissolved a marriage without legal cause, they were to be confined to a monastery and to lose all their property either to their descendants or ascendants if they had any or, if they had none, to the monastery. The reason given for the law was "lest because of this contempt both the judgment of God be scorned and our law be transgressed." Yet Novel 134 was less punitive than medicinal. If, before being sent to their

---

[23] Nonetheless a divorce obtained in violation of Novel 134 was valid, Theodore of Hermupolis, a legal commentator of the sixth century, cited in Hunger, *op. cit*, p. 308, n.l.

monasteries, the couple decided that they preferred to live together after all, all penalties were cancelled; and if one was willing "to call back the marriage," and the other refused, only the dissenter was subject to the law (*N.* 134.11).

This law, for the first time, had enough teeth in it to discourage consensual divorce.[23] It was abrogated ten years later by the next emperor, Justin II. In the repealing legislation, the Preface stated that "a great many" had petitioned for the change, alleging that there was "warfare and battle" in their homes but that they could not show the causes allowed by law. They alleged that sometimes this domestic battle reached the point where lethal acts were attempted by spouses—acts, of course, which constituted legal grounds but which these petitioners were either unable to prove or asserted by way of rhetorical exaggeration. The emperor observed that, given the multitude of marriages, it was "assuredly impossible that some cruel and irreconcilable enmities not occur." He repeated the old principle of Diocletian in the more current phraseology of marital affection: "If mutual affection makes a marriage, diverse wills by mutual consent rightly dissolve it." He added only that the dissolution must be effected by the legal sending of the libel of repudiation. The law on consensual divorce was to be "as it once had been" (*N.* 140).

With Justin II's repeal of one portion of Justinian's legislation, leaving in force all the rest, a period in divorce reform ended; and at this point it is convenient to assess the view of marriage taken by the emperors from Constantine to Justin II and its significance in manifesting Christian beliefs.[24]

II. THE RELIGIOUS SIGNIFICANCE
OF THE DIVORCE LAW

From Constantine to Justin II there was in Roman divorce law no assertion that marriage was indissoluble or irrevocable by the law of God, nature or man; no assertion that marriage was a mystery or sacrament; no assertion that a valid first marriage was any barrier to a valid second marriage. Divorce was regulated not only as matter of property rights, but the crucial question of remarriage was treated by the law, and where divorce was admitted, remarriage at once or after a period followed as a consequence which the law explicitly allowed. The historians who find inconsistency in the divorce law are insensitive to the kind of changes that would occur in any effort to grapple with a serious social problem.[25] Except for the

[24] On the subsequent use of the marriage and divorce law of Justinian in the Greek Church, see Emil Herman, S.J., "Ius Justinianeum qua ratione conservatum sit in iure ecclesiastico orientali," *ACJI*, 2 (1935), 152-154.

[25] *E.g.* Bury's peevish comment, "The result was confusion, no less absurd to a lawyer's sense of fitness than offensive to the reason of ordinary men" (II, 406). I am afraid that most human law presents a mixed and perplexing picture, not offensive to a lawyer but to a layman who believes that law must look like geometry.

repeal by Theodosius II in 439, the basic pattern is coherent. A structure is provided which favors marriage but for various reasons permits divorce.

Divorce was discouraged by law because easy divorce was against "the bond of reverence" (*N.*Th. 12), because it often reflected a desire to live indecently (*N.* 117.13), because it injured the children of the first marriage (*N.* 117.7). "The bond of reverence" suggested that marriage was a sacred contract, not lightly to be broken; the characterization of indecency in seeking to dissolve the marriage implied the same attitude. But while these terms bespoke a religious view of marriage, they did not amount to assertions of indissolubility. What of Justinian's phrase, "lest the judgment of God be scorned" (*N.* 134.11)? The phrase indicated that there was a divine interest to be protected in marriage; in its context, it implied that this interest could not be ignored by consent of the parties; at the same time, referring to a law which permitted a variety of grounds for dissolution, it was far from being an invocation of "what God has joined together, let no man put asunder."

The phrase "judgment of God," *judicium Dei*, was also used in the Code in 531 or 532 when Justinian revoked an earlier law. Ulpian taught that a marriage between a citizen and a freedwoman was dissolved by the citizen's elevation to the senatorial class. Justinian declared: "We, following the judgment of God, do not permit in one and the same marriage the fortune of the husband to be the misfortune of the wife. . . . Let severity of this kind be absent in our days, and let the marriage remain firm" (*C.J.*

5.4.28). Here there was very much the sense of correcting of what was harsh and inequitable, not of asserting a general teaching that "the judgment of God" was that marriage was indissoluble.[26] The phrase probably meant "the will of God" rather than any such specific teaching. A phrase that refers to the corresponding subjective response is "the fear of God" which Justinian invoked when he corrected the old law imposing financial penalties on those dissolving a marriage to enter a monastery. The correction was made of "what up to now has happened against the fear of God," *timor Dei*, (*C.J.* 1.3.54). Similarly when Justinian told the Senate and people of the magnitude of his lawgiving work, he said, "ancient times did not seem worthy to divine judgment, *judicium divinum*; these have been granted in your times" (*C.J.* 1.17.2.19). The divine judgment here is the general will of God. As in *C.J.* 5.4.28, the will of God is manifested in the new and better laws of Justinian. It seems probable that "judgment of God" in Novel 134 has no more specific sense.

One hypothesis that might be suggested to account for the failure to treat second marriages as invalid is that the Romans either lacked a concept of nullity of contract or hesitated to apply such a concept to a sacred institution

[26] The case had been precisely that of Justinian's aunt Euphemia, the slave girl, who had been married by Justin I while he was a young army officer. Presumably her right to continue as Justin's wife had been assured only by an imperial rescript retroactively declaring her freeborn. Euphemia later had stubbornly opposed Theodora's entering the imperial family as Justinian's wife. On the whole question, see Daube, "The Marriage of Justinian and Theodora," 385.

such as marriage. The old law said very generally, "when a marriage is legally contracted it cannot be invalidated *'ex post facto'*" (*C.J.* 5.6.3; the Emperor Gordian). But, in fact, nullity of marriage was completely familiar to Roman law. Simulated marriage was null (*D.*23.30).[27] The marriage of a Christian and a Jew, according to Valentinian II's law of 388, was the crime of adultery, open to attack by anyone (*C.J.* 1.9.6). The marriage of a freed-woman was treated as null under the following circumstances: a slave's master had freed her to marry her; against his will she had divorced him. Her next marriage was invalid as long as her old master wanted her back (*D.* 24.2.11). Justinian continued this rule in the Code (*C.J.* 5.1), and in Novel 22 he declared that the law judged the second union "not marriage or nuptials, but as fornication and corruption" (*N.* 22.37). What was particularly striking here was that the divorce itself was treated as effective; "marriage is customarily dissolved by civil law" (*D.* 24,2.11). The bar to remarriage in this special case was created by force of the law. This case is the only one where remarriage after a prohibited divorce was declared to be null. The law might conceivably have nullified all second marriages after a prohibited divorce; in this case alone did it say expressly there was "no marriage."

Novel 22 also nullified the marriage of a man who, mistakenly believing she was free, married a slave girl:

[27] Whether this passage has been interpolated by Christians has been argued, Henry Insadowski, "Quid momenti habuerit christianismus ad ius romanum matrimoniale evolvendum," *ACJI*, 2 (1935), 63. Levy and Rabel list no interpolation.

"We do not say the marriage is dissolved, but from its very beginning a marriage never occurred" (*N.* 22.10). The existence of the marriage here depended on the law; if the girl's master had permitted the marriage and not disclosed her servitude, she became free and the marriage stood (*N.* 22.11). These provisions of Novel 22 show the precision and sophistication with which the legislator acted in the making and unmaking of marriage.

A second possible explanation of the Roman divorce legislation is that it took account of the religious pluralism of the Empire and tolerated practices inconsistent with accepted Christian morality. This hypothesis of religious or moral toleration is, however, disproved in two ways. It was inconsistent with the express affirmations of dissolubility of marriage made by the legislator and by the use of the remarriage right as a flexible sanction to discourage some divorces and to permit others. In none of this legislation is there any thought that remarriage in itself is invalid or evil. The statements of the law on marriage are made about an institution which is itself a sacred legal creation. As Diocletian and Maximian had once put it, "the only legal marriages are those permitted by Roman law" (*Mos.Coll* 6). For the law to say a marriage was lawful was not to tolerate an act of significance without legal authorization, but to give status to what otherwise had no being for the law.

Secondly, toleration of this kind was inconsistent with the spirit and intent of the emperors to legislate the Catholic faith. Theodosius II proclaimed that the people of the Empire should follow the Catholic religion (*C.Th.*

16.1.2). The declaration was repeated by Justinian (*C.J.* 1.1.1). Some 150 laws in the Theodosian Code were intended to assume the establishment of the orthodox Catholic faith (*C.Th.* 6.5-11); some 50 laws in Justinian had the same objective (*C.J.* 1.5-11).[28] Marcian in 451 legislated that any of the less formal imperial decrees called pragmatic sanctions which were contrary to the ecclesiastical canons were invalid (*C.J.* 2.12.1). Theodosius II, legislating for the province of Illyria, gave the status of law to ancient Christian practice "and the pristine ecclesiastical canons which have been in force," and this law was repeated in both codes (*C.Th.* 16.2.45, *C.J.* 1.2.6). More generally, Novel 131 of Justinian provided that "the ecclesiastical rules which have been set out by the four holy councils or confirmed by them" obtained as law (*N.* 131.1). More specifically, legislating against the marriage of priests, Justinian said, "We do not want our laws to have less force in regard to them than the sacred canons," and legislating in the same decree against incest, he said, "For what the sacred canons prohibit we also prohibit by our laws" (*C.J.* 1.3.44). The legislator did not hesitate to regulate important questions of ecclesiastical order, as in the detailed provisions of Novel 6 of 535 governing the ordination of bishops and priests. The administration of the sacraments was determined, not only as to sacrodotal ordinations, but in the prohibition of the repetition of baptism (*C.Th.* 16.6.2).

---

[28] In general, on the legislation intended to assure the triumph of the Catholic faith, see Gaudemet, 194-196.

The consciousness of enacting belief into law was especially strong in Justinian, who has been described by a great historian of dogma as "the finest dogmatician of his time and country."[29] "Theology and legislation are inseparably bound in his person."[30] In his statement on "The Conception of the Digest" in 528 Justinian referred "all hope only to the Supreme Province of the Trinity," for "authority of laws which well dispose divine and human affairs and expel all evils." Justinian's statement in 534 "On Composing and Confirming the New Code" referred frequently to God's help given to this work. The Code began "in the name of Our Lord Jesus Christ" and set out Justinian's confession of faith (*C.J.* 1.1.5) and his reference of all things pertaining "to the ecclesiastical state" to the Roman pope (*C.J.* 1.1.7). The religious note was even stronger in later legislation. Novel 119 proclaimed God to be the emperor's sole hope, who gave salvation to soul and empire; "hence it is fitting that our laws depend on him and look to him, and this is the beginning and the middle and the end" (*N.* 119.10).[31]

The religious zeal of the ruler was paternalistic in its care to provide for the belief of the Empire. Justinian gave

[29] Adolf Harnack, *Dogmengeschichte* (4th ed.), II, 422.

[30] Erich-Hans Kaden, "L'église et l'état sous Justinien," in University of Geneva, Faculty of Law, *Mémoires publiés par le faculté de droit*, 9 (1952), p. 113.

[31] See *ibid.*, p. 137 for an enumeration of the numerous testimonies of Justinian to his faith, his service to the Church and his desire to be "the least slave" of God. Approximately one-fifth of Justinian's own extensive legislation was devoted to religious affairs, *ibid.*, p. 113.

what was "useful to our subjects," "so that we may preserve their souls" (*C.J.* 1.5.18). This declaration occurred
in a constitution directed to orthodoxy of belief, but sometimes this paternal religious zeal was expressly moral. In
Novel 77 Justinian stated that his aim and prayer was
that "those entrusted to God live well and find His will."
Accordingly, he exhorted sodomites who "act against
nature to fear God and the future judgment" and ad-
monished men not to blaspheme "lest they lose their souls"
(*N.* 77.1). The emperor Justin II, who repealed Justinian
on consensual divorce, expressly invoked the instructions
of God in legislating on sodomy (*N.* 141).

This religious zeal did not tolerate dissent. The Theodosian Code adjudged those who were not Catholics to be
crazy (*C.Th.* 16.1.2). Justinian's Code said that it was
right to withhold "earthy goods" from those not orthodox
in their worship (*C.J.* 1.5.12.5). Pagans were expressly excluded from the bar in 468 (*C.J.* 1.4.15), and although the
chief composer of the Code, Tribonian, was a pagan, pro-
fessorships of law were closed to pagans (*C.J.* 1.11.10.2).
Justinian conducted several purges of pagans from office.[32]

In the same spirit the religious practice of non-Christians
was subjected to regulation. While Jews were tolerated,

[32] Jones, II, 945; Bury, II, 367-368. Bury observes at II, 261
that Justinian "set before himself the ideal of an empire which
should be populated only by the orthodox Christians." "'One state,
one law and one church'—such was the brief formula of Justinian's
entire political career," A. A. Vasiliev, *History of the Byzantine
Empire* (trans. by S. Ragozin, Madison, 1928), I, 181.

those Jews who did not believe in the resurrection of the body or the last judgment were to be given "the ultimate punishment." The translations of the Bible which the Jews could use in their worship were regulated (N. 146). This provision occurred in a late Novel of 553, but much earlier legislation had shown the same willingness to control the practice of peoples who did not profess Christianity. A law of Diocletian and Maximian in 285 legislated against polygamy despite its acceptance by Jewish theology (C.J. 5.5.2). Marriage to a brother-in-law was punished as incest in 355 without recognition of the Jewish levirate law (C.Th. 3.12.2). The Jews of the East were expressly told not to follow their law in marriages by Theodosius I in 393 (C.J. 1.8.7).

The inhabitants of Syndios and the Jews of Tyre were reported to Justinian as having disobeyed his marriage laws. They petitioned him not to be compelled to send away their wives. For a fine of ten pounds of gold per man, their petition was granted (N. 139.1). They kept their wives, not because they were exempt from the law, but because flexibility in application of the law distinguished the administration of Justinian. In the same way when it was related to him that there were many illicit marriages in Mesopotamia and Osdraesa, he held that they might be excused, if they had been contracted far in the past, especially because the region was exposed to enemy attack and the offenders were from the rural masses (N. 153.37). This kind of tolerance, tolerance in enforcement of law, stemmed from both the shrewdness and inefficiency of Roman administration. But it was not the kind of tolerance that found recognition in the formal statement of the law.

The extent to which the bishops were involved in the operation of the divorce laws has also some bearing on their religious significance. The bishops had courts, perhaps as early as Constantine (*C.Th.* 1.27.1),[33] at least by consent of the parties a fifth-century bishop could acquire civil jurisdiction (*N.Val.* 35.1). It may be more than mere coincidence that the statute so providing, entitled "The Episcopal Court," was also the statute containing Valentinian III's provisions on divorce (*N.Val.* 35.1.11). The account of Pope Leo the Great's judgment for the returned soldier indicates that the bishop of Rome heard divorce cases, and it would seem probable that, once submitted to the bishop, the case was decided as to both religious and civil effects. In the later legislation of Justinian the "defenders of the Church" had the job of confirming the existence of a marriage (*N.* 117.4), and presumably in the exercise of this function could have raised objection to illegal remarriages.[34] Bishops were given the responsibility of consigning to monasteries those who sought to evade the law on divorce for cause (*N.* 134.11). Since this confinement to a monastery could be the first step in dis-

[33] The authenticity of this decree has been much debated.

[34] The defenders of a church, *defensores ecclesiae*, were church-appointed officials, who carried out a number of legal and administrative functions where the property rights or religious interests of the Church were involved (see *C.J.* 1.3.32.2-4; 1.3.54.9).

solving a marriage, the bishops had a key role to play in such dissolution. Moreover, bishops also enjoyed a supervisory function in the overall legal system—either to report negligence in hearing a case to the emperor or to sit with a judge recused for bias (*N.* 86). In these several ways the bishops were tied into the court system. If it functioned to sanction divorce and remarriage, the bishops helped make this system work.

It might, however, be suggested that the true Christian ideal was recognized by law to be indissolubility when the legislation of Justinian forbade priests to marry divorcees (*N.* 123.14). It might be argued that what was thought impossible to ask of the laity was asked of the more sacred body, the clergy. The rule for the clergy would embody the true view. Such an argument would seem to carry too far. The same legislation prohibited candidates for the priesthood from marrying widows or from remarrying. Clearly there was a belief that there was something less than ideal in a second marriage; one cannot infer from this belief that second marriages were considered evil. The penalty for a candidate marrying a once-married woman was not invalidity of his marriage, but ineligibility for ordination. The rule on the twice-married thus affirmed an ascetic ideal but did not condemn remarriage as ungodly (*N.* 123.14). If a priest married anyone at all after ordination, he suffered "loss of the priesthood" (*C.J.* 1.3.44). Children born from this union were illegitimate, and marital intercourse therein was stigmatized as an "absurd embrace" (*ibid.*), so that the marriage was almost regarded as null. The rule on postordination celibacy showed that the rules for priests had a different objective than those for the laity.

It may be asked, however, if Roman legislation on divorce has any more significance as evidence of Christian belief than Roman legislation on prostitution, the theatre or slavery. In each of these areas, institutions were embedded in contemporary society and undisturbed by the Christians who became its rulers. What would Roman law indicate as a basic Christian's attitude to these institutions? A brief comparison of law on these subjects with the divorce law may afford some enlightenment.

On prostitution, the first legislation of a Christian emperor was simply to prevent dedicated Christian women from being sold to brothels (*C.Th.* 15.8.1). Almost a century later legislation protected daughters from being made prostitutes by their fathers or female slaves being made prostitutes by their masters (*C.Th.* 15.8.2). In 439 the state renounced a tax received from procurers and ordered the exile of procurers from Constantinople (*N. Th.* 18). All of these steps were modest enough efforts to repress a practice which St. Paul had denounced with such vigor in the First Epistle to the Corinthians (1 Cor 6,15-18). What is striking, however, in comparison with the divorce legislation is that there is nothing in the legislative enactments which accepts prostitution as a good; in various ways the lawmakers characterize it as evil, although the limitations of each law show that the evil is accepted. Prostitution, at least until 439, was a source of revenue to the state (*D.* 22.5.3.5), but no law declared that the state was permitting a lawful occupation in levying the tax. Only some forms of prostitution were condemned, but unlike the elaborate rules on remarriage rights after divorce, rules on prostitution were not part of a structure designed to discriminate between good prostitution and bad prostitution. The qualitative difference in the approach to the two questions is marked.

In regard to acting, the law took the position that it was a necessary but indecent profession (*C.Th.* 15.7.1-12).[35] From what was legalized one could reach the same conclusion as that inculcated by Christian moralists, that being a person of the stage was incompatible with being a Christian. It was provided that if a person of the stage received the sacraments, he could not be recalled to his stage occupation; to prevent this law from being a way out of an important public service, it was legislated in 367 that the sacraments should be administered to actors only if they were actually in danger of death (*C.Th.* 15.7.1). Legislation of 380 permitted any Christian woman to escape the stage (*C.Th.* 15.7.4), but it was immediately provided in 381 that if a woman thereafter became "involved in indecent embraces" and "remained a woman of the stage in spirit," she should be dragged back to her old occupation and never receive absolution (*C.Th.* 15.7.5).

These provisions reflected the current Christian attitude to penance. Only one chance was given for repentance for major sins. Absolution even at death might be denied

[35] The law made a clear distinction between prostitutes and actresses, however poor the reputation of the latter; see Daube, "The Marriage of Justinian and Theodora," 395.

to the sinner.[36] The legislation translated this attitude into
law. It seemed no more an infringement of Christian liberty to put the fallen actress back into a position where
she was likely to sin again than it did to put the fallen
Christian out of hope of ever receiving the sacrament. The
law on actresses is good evidence of the contemporary
Christian's positions on sin and penance. It is not evidence
that the Christians approved of acting. Unlike remarriage
after divorce, the return to the stage of a Christian girl
who had sinned was not to enter again into an honorable
estate, but to suffer a penalty prescribed by law for her sin.

As for slavery, it was accepted by Christian moralists
and fortified as an institution by law. Hundreds of provisions of the Codes were directed to establishing, protecting and carrying out the difference between free man
and slave. No one would suspect from the massive legislation of the emperors that the mere ownership of one
human being by another might be inconsistent with the
New Law of Christ, "Love one another as I have loved
you" (John 15,12).

The slave laws, in fact, reflected the predominance
among Christians of a view that could be labelled Platonic
or Stoic or other-worldly—the view that what mattered
was the state of a man's soul. Whatever his servile condition, a man's soul could be saved. No fundamental injury
to his soul was done by his enslavement. Hence, the slave
owner by the mere fact of owning another human being
did him no injury. If the slave owner did something more—

[36] So the Council of Elvira (305), canon 53, excommunicating
women who committed abortions to conceal adultery, Mansi,
II, 16.

such as to cause a female slave to become a prostitute—he did something immoral, and here the law did in fact intervene to prevent the injury of "women being made to have coition against their will" (*C.Th.* 15.8.2). If the slave owner interfered with his slave's religious life—such as a Donatist master forcing his slave to be rebaptized—the law again intervened (*C.Th.* 16.6.4). The distinction in legal protection roughly corresponded to the distinctions of Christian thought. To free slaves was better than to make slaves, as Justinian declared (*N.* 22.8). But there was no essential objection to slavery as an institution by Christian moralists often otherwise outraged by pagan practices. The massive support given the slave system from Constantine to Justinian is evidence that Christians thought the institution was basically compatible with Christianity.

The slavery example, of course, suggests that what Christians believed right from 331 A.D. to 566 A.D. is no necessary criterion for Christian doctrine. Moral teaching develops. The criteria of development are the great commandments of love and the experience of the Christian people. In the light of these criteria, slavery by the nineteenth century was recognized as inhuman, unnatural, un-Christian. It would have been absurd to check this development by appealing to Christian belief at the time of the Roman Empire. Analogously, the evidence on Christian beliefs furnished by the Roman law on divorce is by no means decisive in determining whether the later development of indissolubility was right or wrong. All that this historical evidence establishes is that for a substantial period of time marriages were viewed by many Christians as dissoluble.

Another hypothesis to account for the legislation would be that the question of remarriage and divorce had never been fully delated in the Church. Divorce was not a cause embraced by any major religious group within or outside the Church. There was nothing comparable to the issue raised as to rebaptism by the Donatists or the issue raised as to procreation by the Manichees. Without any significant religious agitation pro or con divorce, the Church did not have to make up its mind, and individual Christians accordingly took individual positions without reflecting a corporate judgment.

This line of argument surely has much force. Yet, there were Christians who felt that marriage was indissoluble. If they commanded no party, men like Jerome and Augustine were not unknown in ecclesiastical circles.[37] Their belief that remarriage could never validly occur while a spouse was alive was an opinion that must have been known by many theologians and shared by some. If the Christian emperors took no notice of their thought, it indicated that opinion on the question of indissolubility was not yet crystallized. In 407 the provincial Council of Carthage, in which Augustine played an important role, declared: "We decree that, according to the evangelical and apostolic discipline, neither a man dismissed by his wife nor a woman dismissed by her husband may be mar-

---

[37] The texts of the Fathers on divorce and remarriage are assembled and analyzed in Victor Pospishil, *Divorce and Remarriage* (New York, 1967), pp. 141-165. The most famous single quotation, perhaps, is Jerome's: "One matter are the laws of Caesar, another those of Christ, Papinian commands one thing, our Paul another," Epistle 77.3 *PL* 22.691.

ried at the altar: but let them remain as they are or be reconciled to each other. If they defy this, let them be reduced to penance. In this matter the promulgation of an imperial law should be sought."[38] A strict reading of this canon may confine it to the case of the dismissed party remarrying. It is clear, however, that the emperor would have been apprised that some churchmen disagreed with existing law.

The most important bishop to teach the indissolubility of marriage was Ambrose. He held an influential see and could speak with authority to the emperor. One need only recall his protest to Theodosius I on the massacre at Thessalonica, his letter to Valentinian I on the proposed restoration of the altar of the gods to the Senate House, his rejection of imperial jurisdiction to try a matter of faith,[39] to believe that if Ambrose had thought that any matter of great principle was involved he would probably have urged it on the court. For Ambrose stated explicitly that the Christian law on marriage differed from the imperial law permitting divorce and remarriage.[40] Yet there is no record of his protesting to the emperor on the laws on divorce in force in his day. Christians in good faith could believe that marriage was dissoluble or indissoluble without anyone's calling his opponent a heretic. The calm acceptance of dissolubility by the law shows that at this time, between 331 and 566, no definitive Christian position had been established on remarriage and divorce.

[38] G. D. Mansi ed., *Sacrorum conciliorum nova et amplissima collectio*, IV, 556.

[39] Ambrose, *Letters* 51, 18 and 21 respectively.

[40] Ambrose, *Expositio in Lucam*, 8.5 CSEL 324.

The evidence of Christian belief afforded by the law is, to be sure, of an ideal character. That is, the provisions of the emperors must not be taken as a description of the practices of the people. By the nature of their sanctions, the laws were based to affect generally only what the Romans called the *honestiores*, the upper classes. Even as to them the impact of the laws must be largely a guess. The opportunities for evasion by corruption or legal artifice, noted by the laws themselves, must have been considerable. It cannot be supposed that such laws, so significantly restricting human action, were perfectly applied. Nor can it be shown that the laws represent optimum conduct; the conduct of many Christians may have been stricter than the laws. That divorce was a social concern and that its regulation was found appropriate for the state are of course shown by the laws. Beyond these general and important truths, the laws do testify to what was abstractly believed to be a good system for regulating divorce and remarriage. They show that for the emperors and their administrations no principle existed to prohibit divorce and remarriage.

It may be argued that the laws show more, that the laws disfavored divorce, that the laws reflected a tendency to do away with divorce.[41] Certainly in the work of Justinian

---

[41] This contention is strenuously advanced by Biondi. He argues that Roman law eschewed general principles, but that step by step it advanced eliminating the grounds of divorce and so laying the bases for a theory of indissolubility (III, 186). But the very general principle of dissolubility in Novel 22.3 seems to be counter to this contention.

there was such a tendency. The grounds for divorce were restricted by him to cases which judicial fiction could assimilate to death and to cases, such as plotting against the empire, where death would be the penalty if the grounds were criminally proved.[42] Adultery remained an exception, but in the last legislation of Novel 556, adultery even when proved, did not dissolve the marriage; the monastic profession was made the method of dissolution. There was thus within Justinian's own life considerable change. But if the overall development from Constantine to Justin is considered, the tendency against divorce is much less marked. In 566 as in 331 divorce by consent was allowed, in 566 as in 331 divorce was possible for certain grave crimes; the more sophisticated legislation of Justinian provided causes like monastic profession unknown to the earlier law. If fiction assimilated monastic profession to death, it was consciously done, simply recognizing that the partner who had left was "fully useless" to his spouse (*C.J.* 1.3.52.15). The death contemplated was not the

---

[42] Biondi, III, 173-174 argues that even in the Constantinian law the grounds specified were "crimes for which the death penalty was threatened," and hence the admission of the *repudium* "did not in fact clash too openly with the indissolubility of the marriage, which would equally be dissolved by execution of the penalty." But Biondi seems to have confused crimes punishable with death and "capital crimes." Adultery, medicine and tomb-violations were all capital crimes (Mommsen, III, 407-411), but capital crimes could be punished by loss of citizenship or servitude (*D.*2.11.4 pr; *D.*48.19.2), see Mommsen, *op. cit.* III, 241-242. It is true that such punishments before Justinian also ended the marriage, but not by death itself.

"civil death" to which later scholastic theologians compared religious profession, but a "death" in regard to the marriage. What is much more noticeable than a trend against divorce is a trend to treat man and woman more equally and to provide greater protection for the children. In respect to both these matters, the laws of Justinian marked a great advance on Constantine: in respect to them there had been an evolution.

The trend of Justinian's own thinking on divorce is, of course, good evidence of Christian reflection on what good legislation on the matter should be. But all of Justinian's work took place within a framework in which he accepted the human malleability of the law on remarriage. The dominant principle of his legislation was the essential dissolubility of marriage. Neither Novel 117 nor Novel 134 reflected the guiding thought, but Novel 22: "Of those things which occur among men, whatever is bound is soluble."

COMMENT

AND

DISCUSSION

The admission of divorce with the right to remarry in the legislation of the Christian emperors is a fact beyond controversy. It is also certain that the theological premises contained in the general corpus of these laws reflect a studied purpose to conform with the divine law in moral principle. The significance of these facts as a monument of faith, however, must be carefully weighed against the testimony of other sources of the Church's teaching in this era. There is evidence from several of the Fathers, as well as from the canons of the North African councils, that many in the Church opposed the civil law and strongly affirmed the indissolubility of marriage.

St. Ambrose (340-397) urged the faithful not to be deceived by the law:

Do not be deceived by the laws of men. Every immorality is adultery and what is not licit for a wife is neither licit for the husband. The same chastity is due on the husband's part as on the wife's. . . . You put away your wife as though you had a right to do so and are open to no guilt. You think you are free to do this because the human law does not forbid it. But the divine law does forbid it. You obey human rulers, but you should stand in fear of God. Heed the laws of God, to whom those who make the laws themselves owe obedience. (*Expositio in Lucam*)

In *De Abraham,* Ambrose further states:

> No one is permitted to know any other woman except his
> wife. You have been given the right of marriage so that
> you do not fall into a snare and become involved with any
> other woman. You are bound to your wife. Do not seek to
> be free because you are not allowed to marry another
> woman while your wife is alive. Seek another wife while
> you have your own and you are guilty of the crime of
> adultery, which is all the more grave because you think the
> law covers your sin with its authority.

Before the time of Justinian, Athanagoras (177) protested
to the Roman emperor that Christian morality is higher than
the morality of the Romans. Justin Martyr, in his *Apologia*
(165), says, "he who marries her who has been put away by
another man commits adultery." St. Jerome (340-420) seems
to have interpreted St. Paul in favor of the absolute indissolubility of marriage. How may we understand the belief
that underlies these isolated statements? Were these Fathers
proposing a Christian ideal of marriage or witnessing belief
in indissolubility as an enforceable imperative? Were they
opposing only consensual divorce or all divorce? They were
certainly concerned to teach the holiness of Christian marriage
against the evident moral evils of promiscuity.

Josef Zhishman, the great historian of Oriental canon law,
warns against broad assumptions taken from statements of the
Fathers and the early councils (*Das Eherecht der orien-
talischen Kirche* [Vienna, 1864]). He interprets the canons of
the Council of Carthage as a condemnation of consensual
divorce, not of divorce for cause by judicial decision. Furthermore, he assigns to the Fathers a pedagogic, rather than a
judicial, role in converting the populace to a Christian ideal
of marriage.

A critical examination of these and other patristic and canonical sources is necessary to gain a total picture of what must have been the accepted practice of the Church at this time. The Roman legislation is certainly a valid testimony of the belief of a great part of Christianity. To what extent it prevailed over the whole Church is a matter of speculation.

It is of great significance that Justinian was a well-educated theologian, deeply sensitive to his responsibility of giving spiritual direction to his subjects. He purposely sought the counsel of outstanding contemporary theologians to enact a law of unimpeachable orthodoxy. It is difficult to imagine that he could have misinterpreted the faith of the Church so grossly and not met with strenuous opposition. More than a century after the condemnation of divorce by the Council of Carthage, the promulgation of Justinian's law on divorce and remarriage was received without any official contradiction from the Church.

From the fourth to the sixth centuries there was a very close connection between the Church and the government of the Roman empire. St. Ambrose had access to the imperial court at the time when Theodosius' law was being drafted. From the writings of St. Ambrose it appears that he felt himself responsible for the laws of the emperor. When the emperor Valentinian wanted to move the altar of the gods back to the senate house as a gesture of good will to the pagans of Rome, St. Ambrose excoriated him. He told Valentinian that this would be an outrageous violation of the faith, no matter how much the Romans may have wanted it. Yet he made no direct representation to the emperor against the laws of divorce. Did he consider this issue less important or less surely a matter of the faith?

The Fathers of the Church were a heterogeneous group of people. Many of them were little known and had only a minor influence upon their contemporaries. Who better reflects the living practice of the Church, the Christian emperors or the Fathers? Would Justinian have taken St. Jerome very seriously? Both the emperor and the legislative experts aiding him thought of themselves as knowledgeable Christians. When no important bishop of the Church told them they were wrong, they must have thought their law was a valid representation of Christian belief. The laws of Justinian manifest so clearly the conviction that he was doing the right thing for the salvation of souls that it is inconceivable that he was aware of a deliberate error in faith and morals.

Throughout Justinian's Code there can be found instances of the enactment of the sacred canons of the councils into civil law. Nowhere is there a consciousness of conflict between the civil law and the canons of the Church. The fact that the canons of the councils are found side by side in the Code with the elaborate divorce legislation bears out the conclusion that contradiction was not to be expected.

Another factor to be considered is that the empire at the time of Justinian was still far from being completely Christian. The heart of Rome itself was fully pagan. Is it possible that the laws on divorce and remarriage reflect a toleration of social conditions that could not be changed? Between the pagan and Christian extremes were the floating masses, the more or less converted Christian generation, some of them fully Christian, others on their way to Christianity. Was the law a compromise with prevailing pagan mores?

Toleration of moral evil by local administrators may be admitted. It would be unlikely, however, to find its way into the principles of Roman Law itself. If a compromise with the pagan subjects were necessary, Justinian would not have needed to commit himself so strongly to the principle that anything can be dissolved, as he does in Novel 22. Furthermore, the general law itself shows no evidence of compromise in other matters where Christian principles are at stake. In later legislation Justinian uses incarceration in monasteries as a penalty for the violation of certain laws. This assumes that he was dealing with Christians whom he would banish to the cloister if they disobeyed. A forced monastic profession for the crime of adultery would dissolve a marriage in Justinian's law. Religious sensitivity here hardly corresponds to a compromise with pagan morality.

In the Roman empire of the sixth century, marriage had already achieved deep legal and religious significance. Yet it was an upper-class institution, gradually being extended to the lower classes and still denied to slaves. In many cities of the empire more than half the population would have been numbered among the slaves. They had neither property nor inheritance rights. The legal prerogatives of citizens of the middle and upper classes were simply unknown to them. The laws of Justinian on marriage and divorce did not touch this vast populace. Slaves could be sold away from their consorts. They had no recourse in law against adultery or abandonment. What must Christian slaves have believed about the permanency of marriage if the emperor's law granted their marriages no legal protection or acknowledgment?

Many important questions remain to be investigated beyond the scope of this presentation. These lie principally in the interpretation of the teaching of the Fathers of the Church and the primitive canonical sources. It seems clear that there has been a gradual development of doctrine. A rudimentary awareness of the holiness of marriage slowly evolved to the affirmation of its full sacramentality in the thirteenth century. Was there a parallel development in the concept of indissolubility? Does the doctrine of the indissolubility of marriage with which we are familiar today represent the triumph of a central belief of the faith? Or may we honestly seek a greater latitude in canonical discipline today by harking back to the practices of Christian antiquity?

3

The Indissolubility of Marriage: The Theological Tradition of the East

ALEXANDER SCHMEMANN[*]

I.

I must begin this paper by stating the initial paradox of the Eastern Orthodox approach toward marriage. On the one hand, the Orthodox Church explicitly affirms the indissolubility of marriage;[1] yet, on the other hand, she seems to accept divorce and has in her canonical tradition several regulations concerning it.[2] How can these apparently contradictory positions be reconciled? And, first of all, what does this paradox mean? Is it an uneasy compromise between the maximalism of theory and the minimalism of practice, that famous "economy" which the

[*]Dean of St. Vladimir's Theological Seminary, Tuckahoe, New York. Father Schmemann is the author of *Sacraments and Orthodoxy* (1965), and *The World as Sacrament* (1967).

[1] See F. Gavin, *Some Aspects of Contemporary Greek Orthodox Thought* (London, 1923), pp. 384 ff.; Bishop Sylvester, *Orthodox Dogmatic Theology*, 4 vols. (Kiev, 1897), pp. 539 ff.

[2] N. Suvorov, *Kurs Tserkovnago Prava* (Manual of Canon Law), (Yaroslave, 1889), II, 331 ff.

Orthodox seem to invoke so often in order to solve all kinds of difficulties? I think that no answer can be given to any of these questions before an attempt is made to understand the complexity of the Orthodox teaching about marriage.

A western Christian may not realize that this teaching has never taken the form of a consistent and systematic doctrine in which the liturgical rites, the canonical requirements, the theological interpretations and finally the demands of reality would be expressed within a unified framework. Does it mean, however, that there is no Orthodox doctrine of marriage, doctrine which would in turn serve as a norm for practice? No! But it means that this doctrine has not been given a "juridical" formulation and remains, as much of Eastern Orthodox theology in general, in the state of affirmations rather than explanations, is expressed more often in liturgical rites rather than canonical texts, and finally, serves as a guiding principle rather than explicit legislation.

The starting point for any elucidation of this doctrine is, of necessity, in the Orthodox understanding of matrimony as *sacrament*. Here one must keep in mind that in the Orthodox Church, sacramental theology has never been formulated in clear and precise definitions as in the West. It is true that in postpatristic manuals of dogmatics much of the western approach to sacraments has been rather uncritically adopted. This "westernized" theology, however, so obviously contradicts the earlier and more normative Orthodox tradition, that of the Fathers and of the liturgy, that it cannot be accepted as an adequate expression of the Orthodox "*lex credendi.*" When speaking of the sacrament of matrimony, we must, therefore, see it within a wider perspective of the Orthodox meaning of sacraments in general.

It is sufficient for our present subject to stress that the sacrament or *mysterion* in the Orthodox tradition implies necessarily the idea of a *transformation*, of a "*passage*" from the old into the new and, therefore, an eschatological connotation.[3] The sacrament is always the passage from "this world" into the Kingdom of God as already inaugurated by Christ, and of which the Church herself is the "sacrament" in "this eon." Thus, in the baptismal death and resurrection, man is not simply absolved of his original sin but is truly "transferred" from the old creation into the new. In the sacrament of anointment, he is introduced into the Kingdom inaugurated on the day of Pentecost by the Holy Spirit. In the Eucharist the Church fulfills herself by ascending to the Kingdom of God, to "His table in His Kingdom." All sacraments are considered eschatological in the sense that they manifest and communicate in this world the reality of the world to come. Hence, and this is the second important observation, all sacraments are fulfilled in the Eucharist which, according to the patristic teaching, is the "sacrament of sacraments" because it is in a very concrete sense the sacrament of the Kingdom. Finally, all sacraments are truly sacraments of Christ, i.e., are ontologically connected with his death, resurrection and glorification.

---

[3] See my book *Sacraments and Orthodoxy* (New York, 1965).

How are these categories applicable to matrimony which, different in this from all other sacraments, does not seem to be directly and immediately connected with the "Christ event" and which exists as a universal and natural institution outside the Church? The answer to this question is given partially at least in the liturgical celebration of matrimony.

II.

The present liturgy of matrimony in the Orthodox Church consists of two services—the Betrothal and the Crowning—the first service taking place normally in the vestibule of the church and the second, having primarily the form of a procession which introduces the couple into the Church. We may leave out of this paper the description of the complex development of these services and the various strata of symbolism with which they were adorned on the liturgically fertile soil of Byzantium.[4] Let us rather concentrate on the fundamental significance of this peculiar "liturgical dualism" of matrimony.

There can be no doubt that the first service—the Betrothal—is nothing else than the Christianized form of the marriage as it existed always and everywhere, i.e., as a public contract sealed before God and men by those entering the state of marriage. It is, in other terms, the Christian "blessing" or "sanction" of the marriage, its acceptance by the Church. It appears rather late in the

[4] See A. Raes, S.J., *Le Mariage dans les Eglises d' Orient* (Chevotogne, 1958).

history of the Church and at a time when for all practical
reasons the civil society coincided with the Church and
when the Church was given an almost exclusive control
over family. In the early pre-Constantinian Church, the
only requirement for the members of the Church who
wanted to marry was the preliminary permission of the
bishop.[5] This means that the Church did not consider herself to be the performer of the marriage as such and early
documents stress the recognition by the Church of all
civil laws governing the marriage.[6] But if the Church did
not "institute" the marriage, she was given the power to
"transform it" and such is the real meaning of *matrimony
as sacrament*. "Lo, I make all things new": this from the
beginning was also applied to marriage. And, it is this
"transformation" of the marriage that constitutes the content of the second service mentioned above—the Crowning
—which begins precisely as all Christian sacraments with
a *procession*. The procession signifies that the "natural"
marriage is taken now into the dimensions of the Church
and, this means, into the dimensions of the Kingdom. The
earliest form of this service was the simple participation
of the newly married in the Eucharist and their partaking
as "one flesh" of the Body and Blood of Christ.[7] Even

[5] St. Ignatius, *Ad Polycarpum*, 5 v.

[6] See for example, *Epistola ad Diognetum*, v. 6; Athenagoras,
Lecatio Pro Christianis, chap. 33, Migne, *PG* 6, 965; Ambrose,
De Inst. Virg., 6, Migne, *PL*, 16, 316; John Chrysostom, *Hom 56
in Genes*, 29, *PG* 54, 488.

[7] See A. N. Smirensky, "The Evolution of the Present Rite of
Matrimony and Parallel Canonical Developments," *St. Vladimir's
Seminary Quarterly*, 8 (1960), 40, n. 1.

today, though it has severed its connection with the
Eucharist, the rite of matrimony keeps the indelible mark
of its Eucharistic origin and the common cup given to
the couple at the end of the service points back to the
Eucharistic chalice.[8]

In this sacramental transformation, the marriage ac-
quires new dimensions. Its content and goal now is not
mere "happiness" but the *martyria*, the witness, to the
Kingdom of God. It is given the power to be a service of
Christ in the world and a special vocation within the
Church. Above everything else it is a sacrament of the
Kingdom, for the family is one of the basic *antitypa* of the
Kingdom.[9]

The whole patristic tradition deals with matrimony almost exclusively in these categories in which the marriage
is connected with the great mystery of Christ and the
Church.[10] This tradition, in other terms, is interested in
the marriage as transformed and fulfilled in Christ and
the Church—this transformation being also the fulfillment
of the natural marriage. It deals, so to speak, with the
ideal marriage which has died to its natural limitations
and has risen to a new life in which it is totally transpar-
ent to Christ and to His Kingdom. This marriage, it is
obvious, is indissoluble and the very categories of dissolubility or indissolubility simply do not apply to it. It tran-

[8] See A. Raes, *op. cit.*, p. 49.

[9] See *Sacraments and Orthodoxy*, pp. 59 ff.

[10] See A. Raes, *op. cit.*, p. 8 and also S. Troitsky, *Christianskaia
Philosophia Braka* (Christian Philosophy of Marriage), (Paris,
1934).

scends them because by its very nature it is already a transformed and transfigured marriage. And, in a certain way, it is only such marriage that the Church teaches and reflects upon and, in a sense, only such marriage is recognized by her and it is only to such marriage that her positive evaluation of matrimony is referred. An example of this can be seen in the canonical regulations forbidding the ordination of all those whose marriage is not "perfect," i.e., first and unique on both sides. The marriage, thus, belongs to the *theologia gloriae* as in fact a part of ecclesiology and eschatology. The Church rejoices, so to speak, in this foretaste and anticipation of the Kingdom of God.

III.

There exists, however, another dimension of the marriage—this one rooted in the pastoral mission of the Church in the world. If the fundamental doctrine, or better to say, *theoria*, vision of the marriage, as still expressed in the liturgy, belongs to the early, maximalistic and eschatological period of the Church, this second dimension is the fruit and the result of the long and painful pilgrimage of the Church through history. It would be improper to describe it as a lowering of the standards and as compromise with all kinds of "real situations." For it belongs to the very essence of the Eastern Orthodox tradition to keep together, in a truly antinomical way, on the one hand the "impossible" demands on man—demands that entered the world when God became man so as to "make man God"; and on the other hand the infinite compassion toward man of the One who took upon Himself the sins of the world. Regarding marriage, it is as if, in one and the same breath, the Church were proclaiming its Divine nature and destiny, yet also, its existential ambiguity—the marriage as one of the major battlefields between the good and the evil, between God and the devil, between the New Adam and the old; marriage as inexorably rooted in the tragedy of the original sin. The Church keeps the glorious vision revealed to her by Christ; she gives the gift to all, but she also *knows* the "impossibility" for man fully to accept both the vision and the gift. Just as in the Eucharist the Church, while inviting her members to communicate says: "Holy things are for the holy," shows that only "One is Holy," the maximalism of the Church's revelation about marriage is precisely that which makes her condescending to the unfathomable tragedies of human existence.

The whole point therefore is that this is not a "compromise" but the very antinomy of the Church's life in this world. The marriage *is* indissoluble, yet it *is* being dissolved all the time by sin and ignorance, passion and selfishness, lack of faith and lack of love. Yes, the Church acknowledges the divorce, but she *does not divorce!* She only acknowledges that here, in this concrete situation, this marriage has been broken, has come to an end, and in her compassion she gives permission to the innocent party to marry again. It is sufficient, however, to study only once the text of the rite of the second marriage to realize immediately the radical difference of its whole "ethos." It is indeed a penitential service, it is intercession, it is love, but nothing of the glory and joy of that which has been broken remains.[11]

In practice, all this may be deeply misunderstood. During the long centuries of the Church's organic connection with Christian states, she had to accept many functions and duties, if not contrary, at least alien, to her nature.[12] This has been reflected in the liturgy and in ecclesiastical legislation and requires a detailed and patient study. If, however, one asks about the "essence" of the Orthodox teaching about marriage, one finds it in this apparently paradoxical tension—its belonging to Christ and His Kingdom and, therefore, its indissolubility on the one hand and the pastoral recognition of its human frailty and ambiguity on the other hand. Only within this tension a fruitful study of the Orthodox concept and practice of both marriage and divorce becomes possible.

[11] See Hapgood, *Orthodox Service Book*, pp. 302 ff.
[12] See A. N. Smirensky, *op. cit.*

COMMENT

AND

DISCUSSION

The ancient Christian traditions of the East converge with the belief of the Catholic West in a common affirmation of the sacramental holiness of marriage. In the plan of redemption the earthly reality of marriage has been transformed in Christ into an image, an icon, of the union of Christ with the Church. Man and wife are joined in a permanent relationship to each other that transcends the limitations of natural compatibility as a witness of the fidelity of the Lord to His people. In this perspective divorce and remarriage are more than a failure of personal commitment. They are a tragedy for the Church, the broken pieces of a holy ideal shattered by sin and human weakness.

The pastoral concern of the Church for the tragedy of broken marriage is to respond to human frailty with healing forgiveness. In the Christianity of the East, this forgiveness implies permission to marry again. The Church neither grants nor acknowledges divorce, but to the lonely and abandoned it sorrowfully grants the right to take another spouse. For the person and for the Church this is a penitential recognition of the harsh reality of sin and the deep need for God's grace. The liturgical form of the second marriage itself expresses the paradox of sin and grace in the words of an antinomy that encapsulates the very life of the Church itself. For the Church's role in the world is a constant reconciliation of opposites, the glory of ideals *in statu Patriae* and the reality of sin *in statu viae*.

The theology of marriage, its liturgical expression and canonical discipline belong to the area of antinomy. It is precisely in the acceptance of the consequences of this antinomy in the life of the Church that there is to be found the greatest difference between Orthodox and Latin belief. Between Oriental and Latin traditions the most fundamental discrepancy does not lie in the interpretation of the exceptions of Matthew's Gospel or even in the understanding of sacramentality in regard to marriage. Rather, it is to be found in diverse conceptions of the nature and role of the Church in the world.

In Byzantine ecclesiology the life of the Church moves constantly upon two different levels of reality. The dichotomy of the Kingdom of God revealed and present in a yet unredeemed and sinful world gives rise to a conflict of opposites that belongs to the very nature of the Church. Within this context there exists the parallel development of theological reflection upon the sacramental indissolubility of marriage and the canonical provisions designed to meet its failure. There is a theology of marriage as a reflection of the Kingdom and a juridical counterpart mirroring human weakness.

Three main stages mark the historical evolution of the Oriental Church's approach to marriage and divorce. In the primitive Church we find a basic acceptance of marriage as it existed in the world. The writings of St. Ignatius of Antioch portray a bishop living among his people and uniting them into one community in Christ. He knew the faithful and brought the blessings of the Church to them at every personal change in the status of their lives. It is not clear that St. Ignatius speaks of a sacramental action in the blessing of marriage, but his words fit into an ecclesiological concept in which all sacraments are involved in the one sacrament of the Church. The holiness of marriage lies within the holiness of the Church. It is the Church that transforms life and marriage. But first the Church had to accept and bless the life that existed. She had first to accept the worldly reality of marriage.

In the pre-Constantinian Church we find an acceptance of marriage as it existed in Roman society, including all the regulations and customs of marriage prevailing at that time. At the same time the great effort to proclaim the Kingdom of God effected a gradual transformation of society. Within the community of the Church all things are made new. Marriage came to have a new meaning for the baptized in relationship to the central and all-embracing reality of the Eucharist. Marriage received the acknowledgment of the bishop as the head of the community of the faithful. With this came the gradual integration of matrimony into the constitutional act of the Church, the holy Eucharist.

Then came the great and tragic confusion created by the reconciliation between the Church and the empire. On the one hand it was a glorious triumph for the Church. On the other it created enormous problems for both Church and state. An extremely complex semi-Christian society provided an environment for a disconcerting mixture of roles. At this time the Church had not yet developed its own specific system of canonical legislation. It made every effort, however, to influence the civil legislation by Christian principles. The state sanctioned the canons of the councils as state laws, but the Church did not sanction state law as canons. The Church's legislation was integrated into civil legislation, but civil legislation was never to become a part of the Church.

Between Church and state there was a hesitant and uneasy balance. The Church saw itself as the Body of Christ and the temple of the Holy Spirit. Yet to the state it was mainly a society, a corporation, a visibly structured organization. The conversion of Constantine, real as it was, was still completely within the pagan presuppositions of conversion. The Edict of Milan was not a Christian document. It was a typically syncretistic pragmatic gesture. The more Constantine became Christian the more intolerant he became. By the end of the century Theodosius said that everyone who was not a Christian was a mental case and should be burned. This is far from the freedom in which the Church rejoiced at the Edict of Milan.

The Church's teachings on marriage could not be imposed upon the state in their entirety, because the reality of greatest concern to the Church lies beyond the province of the state. What occurred was a gradual effort to transform society in general and, in so doing, bring to bear upon the law a strong moral influence. Divorce became more and more difficult to obtain. Women moved up the social ladder to a greater equality with men. Fundamentally, however, the tension continued to exist between the human reality and the Christian ideal. Marriage was one of many great sectors of society to be Christianized, transformed and introduced to new dimensions of meaning. But this was only possible within the Church and not within the logic of civil legislation.

The third stage occurred when the Church, in the person of bishop or priest, became the minister of marriage. In a vacuum of leadership, the Church received the total responsibility for the familial sector of social life. Born of this necessity were the purely temporal dimensions of the Church's dealings with civil and societal realities. It seems that the Church was almost forced to take on functions that do not naturally belong to it. Christianity assumed the role of the pagan state religions of the old empire. The Church was given a responsibility by the state to fulfill a civil role in society in regulating the temporal life of man. At this stage the sacramental view of marriage began to be translated into canonical prescriptions.

The notion of the indissolubility of marriage took on extensive juridical implications.

Looking back upon this era, Orthodox theology makes a distinction between the disciplinary tradition of the Church as a whole and the various canonical traditions of the particular churches. Reasons for divorce and remarriage changed, were expanded or restricted by the different national churches at various times in history. But the Church itself always looked upon divorce with the greatest reluctance. It always sought to distinguish a temporal responsibility on the level of social relationships from its essential role in integrating man into the Kingdom. The Church felt no basic need to exercise judicial authority in the temporal order. Its primary task was to refer temporal life to the order of revelation and sacramentality.

Today the Church no longer controls the destinies of civil society. It no longer exercises a purely social jurisdiction. But in the present stage of transition, it still acts as if it must cling to that power and responsibility. The Church still feels the weight of an ancient responsibility for all temporal arrangements. Within the ambiguities of this situation, Orthodox practice now wavers between the Byzantine or Russian imperial legislation on what constitutes grounds for divorce and the legal rules of the states and nations in which she lives.

The ambiguity of the Church's stance between a theology that stresses the indissolubility of marriage and the canonical practice that allows dissolubility is not to be understood as a compromise with the world. It is precisely the lot of the Church in the world. Sin is not a juridical crime. It is a rebellion against God. The Church confronts the reality of sin both *in statu Patriae*, from which stems her teachings and eschatological orientation, and *in statu viae*, from which comes her pastoral concern for man.

Within Orthodox tradition there is no such thing as divorce. The Church can no more remove the sacramentality of a marriage than she can remove the consecration from the Eucharistic Host. The Church simply grants the right to remarry in certain cases. What about the previous marriage? The ontological status of that first marriage is simply never made a matter of question. To ask the question supposes a static view of reality. Within the dynamic action attributed to the Holy Spirit by Orthodox theology, marriage can exist only while people actually live a marriage. If the marriage is not lived, it is dead. It is nothing. The real problem is not the abstract, Aristotelian essence that might remain, but what is to be done in pastoral terms with the existing situation. This is where the mechanics of canonical procedure in allowing remarriage are rooted.

The basic question today is not how to delineate various new juridical reasons to allow divorce and remarriage. It is rather the question of what constitutes the sacramentality of marriage and how close does this sacramentality constitute a reality that can be expressed in juridical terms. What is the relationship between what can be described as the maximum of the Church's teaching, which is not only an ideal, but the revelation of the true ontology of marriage and the real situation of man?

Is the dialectic between indissolubility and dissolubility just a matter of toleration or rather a category of tension which has to be kept if the Church is to fulfill her mission among men? Unless we ask the most basic questions about the nature of marriage and its relationship to the mission of the Church, the very sensitive question of divorce and remarriage will not be solved. The whole complicated development of the Church's teaching on marriage is one expression of her fundamental relationship to the world. It is only from a study of this relationship in which the problem is truly rooted that a solution can be found.

In Orthodox tradition sacrament or "mysterion" implies necessarily the idea of a transformation, a passage from the old into a new dimension of both meaning and reality. The Church's salvific mission to the world is fulfilled in a presence to the world in as far as the world can be transformed and has to be transformed by it. The world is not something wholly separated from the Church. It is the very matter of the Kingdom. In this sense, marriage is transformed by the Church and in the Church, while divorce remains a part of the morality of the world. It is a morality that the Church cannot be indifferent to or spurn. She must not only be interested in the morality of the world but must also transform it to a new reality.

Dr. Noonan's paper concluded quite convincingly that some Christians considered marriage dissoluble at a particular time in history. He did not go beyond this premise to generalize upon this practice of the Church as being decisive for a later period. "It has been done for two hundred years in the past. Therefore, it can be done today" was not his conclusion. This type of argumentation would run counter to the reality of growth inherent in the nature of man and religion. It would be a type of legal positivism foreign to Christianity.

Morality develops into a greater refinement of norms and a greater perceptiveness of judgment from reflection upon the existing situation of man in the light of primary principles. At one time slavery was accepted by Scripture, by tradition and by the Church. But today no one can consider slavery morally acceptable or even indifferent. The argument that it was accepted at one time does not prove that it can be accepted again. The Church moves with history and adjusts itself to developing human reality. As with the eventual rejection of slavery, so in the understanding of marriage there may be an evolution from an acceptance of dissolubility to belief in its absolute indissolubility. The ultimate criterion will not be the practice of the past, but the meaning of Christian marriage in the light of the real human situation today.

On the other hand, the argument from the *praxis ecclesiae* does have a negative value. Development cannot imply contradiction. The Church is based upon a revelation and an institution in which tradition is implied. The *quod traditur* is an essential element in a revealed religion. To be Christian means to be traditional because tradition belongs to the essence of a revealed religion. So there exists the antinomy of developing human nature that precludes a happening of one time from being normative for all time and the need to study history to find the negative limit beyond which contradiction excludes continuity. The problem of tradition is closely connected with the meaning of the theology of real development in doctrine.

We cannot say that at one time the Church believed one thing and at a later time she believed another in contradiction to it. The Church, in fact, in the early period was largely unconcerned with the institutional expressions of society. However, from the very beginning she had a notion of man, a notion of society and a notion of the destiny of man, which ultimately excluded the possibility of man's being enslaved. Again, the Church had from the beginning, in the New Testament and in the Fathers, an intuition, an understanding, a vision of marriage as indissoluble. Yet this vision could not be made an immediate practical possibility because of the extremely adverse social conditions of the time. The teaching had to develop gradually. It was only at the time of the Emperor Leo VI in the tenth century that matrimony as a liturgical service was made obligatory for all Christians of the empire.

This became the pastoral and missionary means of the Church to reach the people. Legislation prior to this time was mainly concerned with problems of regulating marriage and divorce. Now it became a question of how to impose upon the people the Christian view of marriage. The liturgical form developed as a teaching of what marriage should be. Christian history shows the explicitation, not the change, of a particular truth. There is a slow and patient evolution within society that brings about a real development.

When we study the past, we study it not only in the effort to see how many metamorphoses took place, but how certain basic ideas—God, man, history, world, nature—developed and were refined. It would be a catastrophe if today we suddenly proclaimed, as a kind of ecumenical achievement, that whereas in the past we had thought of marriage as indissoluble, today we all agree that it is dissoluble. On the other hand, to simply maintain the old tradition of absolute indissolubility would be equally intolerable. We are moving today, not in the direction of a liberation of marriage from medieval conceptualizations, but rather toward a deepening awareness of what has always been central in the belief of the Church, regardless of the inadequacy of the juridical or philosophical categories in which it has been expressed. For almost two thousand years, the Church has proclaimed that marriage is sacred and indissoluble. Yet all the while she has reluctantly accepted its dissolution to some extent as a tragic human failure.

There will always be a clash between the Kingdom and the world, the ideal and the exception, the eschatological hope and the reality. This dialectic between lofty goal and the reluctant acceptance of failure must maintain a proper balance in order that a real development may occur. Where the dialectic is ignored or overemphasis is given only one side, ultimately the impasse results in stagnation. Both sides of the dialectic have a role. St. Paul said that in the Kingdom "there is neither male nor female," yet he treated women in the same category as children and slaves. The role of women in the Church suffered in the imbalance of the latter perspective. It is only when we explore more fully the reasons why St. Paul enunciated the fundamental equality that a restoration of balance can be achieved. In similar fashion, between ideal and exception the imbalance resulting from an overemphasis upon the ideal will be corrected by exploring the implications of the human reality that makes exception possible.

In the theology of marriage of the Eastern traditions the primary point of departure is not the natural properties of marriage, but the supernatural union that it images. In the liturgy of matrimony the last act of the rite is the coronation: "Now receive these crowns in God's Kingdom." In its ultimate reality marriage is not measured by its current cultural acceptance. It is an icon of the Kingdom. Marriage transcends happiness. It transcends contract and even the family. But having defined marriage in these supernatural terms, Orthodoxy still remembers the natural dimension of marriage. The tension between the two exists and is inescapable. It is important, however, that the starting point of understanding begin, and not end, with revelation. The modern reduction of marriage to happiness and sexual fulfillment to which the Church may add a transcendent demand is not adequate. For Christians marriage is primarily a union witnessing the union of Christ and the Church.

At the time of the revival of the study of Roman Law which inspired the science of canon law in the Western Church, a juridical conceptualization overtook the personal and theological vision of marriage. The canonical conception came to center upon consent and copula, instead of divine mystery and human relationships. With this came a canonical refinement of the conditions for the validity of the marital contract. Rather than the *consortium totius vitae* of an earlier humanism or the "mysterion" of the Fathers, marriage came to be equated with contractual obligations and rights. A whole machinery was set up in the Latin Church to adjudicate the validity of marriages according to the canonical definition of a unique contract giving the right to bodily acts of reproduction. In an effort to achieve legal clarity, both the personal elements of this unique relationship and the supernatural context of mystery were pushed to the background. Consequently, where we in the Church should be speaking of the common life of two spouses who are children of God, we are probing in tribunal practice the conditions of a contract for bodily acts. The result is a sterility of vision that has reduced the great mystery of human and divine love to an unreal formulation of legal rules.

The Church's primary task in marriage today is to proclaim the full richness of both divine revelation and human understanding. It is not to inform the world that the Church now accepts new rules for allowing divorce and remarriage. We must become less interested in the judicial forum, and more concerned about a catechesis of marriage. In fact, all that we say about the indissolubility or dissolubility of marriage implies a grasp of the preliminary question, what is marriage. It is toward an understanding of this sacred mystery that we must now strive together from all the traditions of the Christian experience.

4

The Marriage of Christians— Valid Contract, Valid Sacrament?

WILLIAM W. BASSETT[*]

The subject of this paper evokes many problems to which the present matrimonial legislation of the Catholic Church has afforded only partial answers. The problems and the answers given them must be reexamined in the light of current theological and sociological consensus so that we may form a more effective pastoral ministry to the married. Accordingly, my purpose in this paper is to state as fairly as possible the canonical position regarding the juridic nature of marriage and its relationship to the Church. I shall then give a brief evaluation of this position.

The apparently overriding concern of the Catholic clergy for the validity or invalidity of marriages, the dispensations from the impediments to marriage, given when possible, and the formalities involved in the celebration

_[*]Assistant Professor of Canon Law, The Catholic University of America. He is the author of *The Determination of Rite* (1966). This paper was prepared with the generous collaboration of Robert H. Dailey, S.J., Professor of Moral and Pastoral Theology, Alma College, Los Gatos, California, and Professor in Area IV, Religion and Society, The Graduate Theological Union, Berkeley.

3117

of marriage are, quite frankly, a real puzzle for most people. The consternation is deepened on those rare occasions when after divorce and an ecclesiastical process some Catholics are allowed to marry again. Not uncommonly, formerly married non-Catholics are "permitted" to marry again after they have entered the Church. Questions are asked, answers are given or evaded and yet the perplexity remains. The legislation of the Church regarding the discipline of marriage is elaborate and of ancient vintage. The longest of all the sections of the Code of Canon Law covers the regulation of the Holy Eucharist and the sacraments of Penance, Holy Orders and Matrimony. By far the most complex of these is the law of marriage. It is for most laymen, and not a few priests, an arid stretch of recondite legal reasoning.

Related to this is a question being asked more and more frequently today: why and how did the Church ever become involved in adjudicating the validity or invalidity of marriages. Parallel to the law of marriage is an elaborately detailed treatise containing the procedural rules for trials of almost every sort. Criminal and civil actions are exceedingly rare, yet there are ample provisions for them. Ecclesiastical tribunals, however, including the Holy Roman Rota devote almost all their time and effort to the adjudication of the validity of marriages. There are historical and theological reasons why the Church has reserved the responsibility for making these judicial decisions. Today, however, many people seriously concerned with the mission of Christianity in the world are asking whether the Catholic Church can now withdraw from this responsibility. They are probing at the deepest level the rationale for a practice that may have arisen from the exigencies of historical circumstance and continues into the present so much at variance with other kinds of religious experience. A distinct note of urgency marks the questioning. How relevant or how important is the work of the marriage courts? Only an infinitesimal number of the thousands of marriage cases involving Catholics ever reach the Church courts. Of these only a small portion receive favorable decisions allowing remarriage. Yet the details of the adjudicative process literally consume the time and energy of countless numbers of priests.

Catholic belief has given marriage the significance of a holy relationship, transformed it from the merely human and seen in it a sacrament. It is a symbol and a cause of divine grace. While the sacral has always been primary in the perspective of faith, it must be admitted that a worthy theology of marriage is only gradually being developed and is still incomplete at this time. The law and jurisprudence of marriage, on the other hand, are quite clear and highly perfected. These latter govern the pastoral ministry and discipline of the Church in matters of matrimonial concern. Herein is the paradox that underlies the procedural impasse of the present day. The law has been elaborated from deductive principles derived from the legal meaning of consent to a contractual exchange of rights and duties. The sacred mystery of faith and the life relationship of human experience must contend with the strictures of an adjudicative process that binds decisions to an interpretation of marriage only within the narrow limitations of a secular contract. That which began as a discipline to protect the rights of persons and the holiness of marriage has become largely impersonal and almost wholly modelled upon the secular.

Canonists have defined as the object of marital consent a contract for the performance of those acts which are per se apt for the procreation of children. The consent of marriage is exclusive of all other persons and conveys a permanent right to such acts. A legal definition, however, exposes only a part of the reality of marriage. It offers grounds for the exploration of the legal properties of marriage, but it places major emphasis only upon a relationship to the physical. But marriage, like any lived relationship, clearly transcends the legal meaning of contract. Marriage, it is true, begins with a free and specific act of consent, but then unfolds into the mutual giving of oneself and the receiving of the other for the total sharing of life together. It is a bond of trust, a continuing covenant eliciting the most profound personal response to life. A marriage comes to be in the ineffable mystery of choice, choosing and being chosen by another as a spouse. It is initiated and lived in the acceptance of the personhood of another. The affection. and devotion of husband and wife in their deep commitment to each other cannot be encapsulated in the terminology of the present law. Yet this dynamic and continuing personal relationship lies at the very heart of marriage and bespeaks its meaning more clearly than the static categories of contractual law. Thus it must be contended that the definition or existence of marriage must be decided upon a broader basis than merely the legal grounds of the validating conditions of contract now in force.

The notions of contract and sacrament in regard to marriage have a long history. This history enshrines the work of theologians as well as canonists, but is largely directed by the exigencies of a juridical imperative. I shall try to state briefly the teachings of the canonists about the relationship of contract to sacrament in marriage and the positions that have emerged from them. As they arise, further questions will be articulated and evaluated within this context.

THE CANONICAL PREMISE

The basic canonical premise underlying the practice and procedure of the Catholic Church in its elaborate judicial system of matrimonial courts is the result of a closely argued syllogism concluding in the equation of matrimonial contract and sacrament.[1] In Catholic belief, Christ entrusted to the Church the sole responsibility for safeguarding the integrity of the sacraments. Marriage is one of the sacraments. Therefore, it is the sole responsibility of the Church to safeguard the integrity of the sacrament of marriage. Furthermore, marriage is a unique interpersonal relationship established upon free mutual consent granting certain rights and accepting certain re-

---

[1] The Code of Canon Law: Canon 1012; cf. also Pope Pius IX, "Syllabus errorum," props. 65 and 66—Denz. nn. 2965 and 2966.

sponsibilities. Thus marriage involves a consensual agreement as well as a sacrament. The valid consensual relationship between two baptized persons belongs to the
very integrity of the sacrament of marriage. Therefore,
the Church has the sole responsibility of safeguarding
marriage both as a sacrament and a consensual relationship.

Further, the authority of the Church over Christian
marriage includes everything that concerns the bond: the
exclusive power to establish prohibitive or diriment impediments,[2] the independent right to determine the legal
form essential to the validity of the bond of marriage[3]
and the inherent prerogative not only to pass judgment on
the validity of a particular marriage[4] but also to break
the bond in certain cases where the marriage has not
been realized between two baptized persons.

In the canonical practice of recent centuries the stance
of the Catholic Church before questions of divorce and
remarriage has been largely legal and contractual. Defective consent or personal incapacity for the contract of
marriage are grounds for decisions of nullity, allowing
the right to remarry. Juridical dispensations from the obligations of the marital contract are granted in cases where
one party, at least, has never been baptized. In these cases
the Church's power over the marriage contract is consid-

---

[2] Canon 1038/2; The Council of Trent, sess. xxiv, *de matrimonio,*
can. 4.

[3] Canons 1094 and 1099; the Decree *Tametsi* of the Council of
Trent, sess. xxiv, chap. 1—Denz. n. 1813.

[4] Canon 1960; the Council of Trent, sess. xxiv, can. 12; Pius IX,
"Syllabus errorum," prop. 74—Denz. n. 2974.

ered unlimited because the full unity of faith and baptism has not completed an absolutely indissoluble union verifying the notes of a sacrament of the New Law. Where a marriage has not yet been consummated, the Church dispenses from the obligations of an only partially fulfilled contract.

To adjudicate the conditions of both nullity and dispensation, Church courts follow an extremely tight and intricate system of procedure. A lapse of many months or even years between the initiation of the process and the final conclusion is common. The reasoning supporting this rigorously legal approach is derived from the obligation of the Church to preserve the sacred character of marriage and the use of a tight judicial process to prevent deception or error. The keystone of such an approach is firmly planted upon the equation of the sacrament of marriage and the socio-juridical conceptualization of the personal exchange of consent as a contract.[5]

The first title of the treatise on marriage in the Code of Canon Law affirms the identity of the contract and the sacrament of marriage.[6] This identity is the principal reason why Christian marriage has a relationship to and exists fully within the Church. Christian marriage is not a secular entity subject only to the regulation of civil au-

[5] Pope Leo XIII, Litt. encycl. "Arcanum," Feb. 10, 1880, n. 12— *Fontes C.I.C.*, n. 580.

[6] Canon 1012: 1. "Christus Dominus ad sacramenti dignitatem evexit ipsum contractum matrimonialem inter baptizatos. 2. Quare inter baptizatos nequit matrimonialis contractus validus consistere, quin sit eo ipso sacramentum"; *cf.* P. Leo XIII, "Arcanum," *op. cit.*, and P. Pius IX, "Syllabus errorum," props. 66 and 73—Denz. nn. 2963 and 2973.

thority. Over the marriages of Christians only the Church is competent.

Before the Council of Trent the canonical doctrine that mutual free consent constitutes both the sacrament and the bond of marriage was the commonly accepted opinion. Many, however, denied the logic of extending this equation to an understanding of marriage primarily as a contract and to an absolute inseparability of the sacrament and the bond of marriage. Many canonists were of the persuasion that a valid marriage could be entered clandestinely, that is, without the knowledge and blessing of the Church. The free and mutual consent of the two persons and their living together as husband and wife essentially constituted marriage. In such a case, a true marriage would exist, but it would not be a sacrament, even for the baptized. Similarly, if two baptized persons did not intend to receive the sacrament of marriage as instituted by Christ, they could be truly married. But in rejecting the sacramental character by their exclusive intention, they did not, of course, receive the sacrament. Proxy marriages, where one party was absent at the time of consent, were held to be valid, but not sacramental. The understanding of sacrament as a visible sign of grace would be absent from the celebration of consent where there was no true tangible union of the spouses.

The Council of Trent explicitly affirmed, however, that in each of these cases a true marriage exists which is also sacramental.[7]

---

[7] The Decree *Tametsi, op. cit.*; sess. xxiv, chap. 1—Denz. n. 1813.

After Trent most theologians and canonists (Suarez, Bellarmine, Sanchez, DeConinck, Pirhing, Laymann, Gutierrez, Castropalao, Catalani, Leandro) taught that the sacrament of marriage was identified with a natural contract of marriage and inseparable from it in a single entity. For Christians neither was possible without the other. Dissent from this opinion, however, continued well into the nineteenth century. Gabriel Vasquez, Ferdinandus Rebellus, Pontius, Hurtado, Dicastillus, Bonacina, Tamburini, Gobat and others,[8] distinguishing between the intention to contract marriage and the intention to receive a sacrament, taught that the sacrament of marriage is not the same thing as the contract, and thus separable from it.

Melchior Cano held that the matter of marriage is the consent of the parties and the form is the blessing of the priest. The Church, he said, is only responsible for the sacramental and liturgical aspects of marriage.[9] M. A. DeDominis asserted that the sacrament and the contract

---

[8] Cf. H. Conrad, "Das tridentinische Konzil und die Entwicklung des Kirchlichen und weltlichen Eherechts," in *Das Weltkonzil von Trient*, hrsg. von G. Schreiber (Freiburg, 1951), I, 297-324; A. Verhamme, "Sacramentum est ipse contractus matrimonialis," *Collationes Brugences*, 47 (1951), 359-364; *idem.*, "De ministro matrimonii," *ibid.*, 48 (1952), 83-89; F. Claeys-Bouuaert, "De inseparabili unione inter matrimonium sacramentum et matrimonium contractum," *ibid.*, 18 (1931), 81-85; J. De Baciocchi, "Structure sacramentaire du mariage," *Nouvelle Revue Theologique*, 74 (1952), 916-923.

[9] *De Locis Theologicis Libri Duodecim* (Salmanticae, 1563), L. 8, c. 5, n. 6.

can be separated as primary and accessory elements.[10] A similar opinion was held by the Jansenist author J. Launoy.[11]

In modern times the popes have repeatedly emphasized not only the exclusive competency of the Church over the marriage of the baptized, but also, as the reason for this competency, the inseparability of the sacrament of matrimony and the natural contract. The historical occasions warranting these affirmations have invariably involved the condemnation of opinions indicating a tendency to separate the contract from the sacrament in such a way as to justify the jurisdiction of civil authority over all marriages as purely civil contracts. Within the Church the post-tridentine regalists, and the followers of Jansenism, Gallicanism, Josephinism and Febronianism, as the principal supporters of the separation theory, were most frequently condemned. Except in the very limited area of civil effects bearing upon name, property and social status, the right of civil authority to any jurisdiction in the regulation of marriage and divorce for Christians has been strenuously opposed. The popes have simply affirmed against the efforts of modern civil jurisprudence that the marriage of Christians belongs solely to the responsibility of the Church. Marriage is a unique, ecclesial entity as a sacred, contractual exchange of consent.[12]

---

[10] *De Republica Ecclesiastica* (Londini, 1617), 1.5, c. 11, p. 2.

[11] *Regia in matrimonium potestas vel tractatus de iure saecularium principum christianorum in sanciendis impedimentis matrimonium dirimentibus* (Coloniae Allobogorum, 1731), t.1, p. 2.

[12] P. Pius IX, "Syllabus errorum," props. 66 and 73–Denz., nn. 2966 and 2973; *Allocutio*, Sept. 27, 1852–Denz., n. 2991; Ap. litt.

The common canonical teaching today affirms that a valid marriage of two baptized persons is always a sacrament, whether these persons are Catholics or not. The marriage between one person who is baptized and another who is not baptized, according to the more common opinion, is a valid contract, but not a sacrament.[13] Between two unbaptized persons there is no sacrament, but a true, legitimate marriage of the natural order. The terminology adopted by the Roman dicasteries for a marriage which is not a sacrament is a *vinculum naturale* or *legitimum*. This *vinculum naturale* automatically becomes a sacrament of marriage when both parties have been baptized. No further ceremony is required. In the absence of the sacramental characteristic, however, the natural bond of marriage may be dissolved, either according to the conditions of the Pauline Privilege (I Cor 7, 12-16), or by the vicarious power of the Holy Father.

Clearly, this brief sketch of canonical conclusions leaves many serious questions unanswered. The validity of this line of argumentation depends upon the meaning of the premises themselves and whether the illation de-

ad Regem Vittorio Emanuele, Aug. 9, 1852: "doctrina est ecclesiae sacramentum non esse qualitatem accidentalem contractui superadditam, at esse de ipsa matrimonii essentia"—*Fontes C.I.C.*, n. 869; P. Leo XIII, "Arcanum," n. 12—*Fontes C.I.C.*, n. 153 ff.; P. Pius XI, Litt. encycl., "Casti Connubii," Dec. 31, 1930—A.A.S., 22 (1930), 550. In a decision of the Holy Roman Rota, August 27, 1910, the inseparability of the contract and the sacrament of marriage was termed a doctrine "proxima fidei"; A.A.S., 2 (1910), 933.

[13] For a further development of the opinions in this matter, cf. J. C. Didier, "Le mariage entre baptisé et non-baptisé est-il sacrement?," *Ami du Clergé*, 72 (1962), 60-62.

rived from them merits the conclusion as a necessary consequence. Is marriage essentially a contract? If the sacrament of matrimony implies also a kind of contract, does it follow necessarily that the validly given consent to marry by two baptized persons must always be sacramental? Must the marriage of two baptized people be both sacrament and contract? Furthermore, must the relationship of the Church to the sacrament of matrimony find its disciplinary expression only within the logic of contractual law?

For the purposes of this study we must probe more deeply two specific areas of this position: the exclusive competency of the Church over the marriages of the baptized and the meaning of the contractual theory of marriage. We shall delineate the evolution of these concepts and then propose a canonical critique of the contract-sacrament theory. On the basis of current developments in sacramental theology and ecclesiology, we shall finally attempt to cast this problem in a new light.

THE COMPETENCY OF THE CHURCH OVER
THE MARRIAGE OF CHRISTIANS

A summary perspective of the historical background and development of the institute of competency in the canon law of the Church will be useful for the understanding of the meaning of the principle itself. To trace the full history and the entire jurisprudence on the subject in a thorough manner would be beyond the scope of this presentation.[14] A concise summary, however, will serve to indicate the trend of development.

In the early centuries of the Church bishops exercised very little, if any, direct jurisdiction over marriage. After the Edict of Milan (312), Constantine granted the bishops some judicial power, yet this did not extend directly to the regulation of marriage or settlement of cases of divorce. The later legislation of the Christian emperors, Theodosius, Justinian and Leo the Sage, undoubtedly ceded greater authority to the establishment of bishops' courts for marriage cases, but historical evidence is so sketchy that it is impossible to draw a clear picture. In the Western empire, however, clear traces of the Church's efforts to take decisive influence over marriage can certainly be detected in the canons of the provincial synods of the Frankish kingdom. A corpus of matrimonial law gradually developed in the Carolingian era that enlarged the disciplinary control of the bishops over the marriages of the faithful. It is difficult to assign a precise date to the translation of the authority of the state to the Church, particularly in matters of marriage and family rights.[15]

---

[14] Cf. J. W. Goldsmith, *The Competence of the Church and State Over Marriage* (Washington, 1944); L. Gerke, *Christian Marriage: A Permanent Sacrament* (Washington, 1965); G. Joyce, *Christian Marriage* (2nd ed., London, 1948). An abbreviated treatment may also be found in the *Dictionnaire de Theologie Catholique*, art. "Mariage," cols. 2123-2317.

[15] "We cannot assign a precise date at which the Church commenced to exercise jurisdiction over matrimonial causes in her own name. . . . The change took place gradually and was not effected by

The process was probably complete by the end of the tenth century. In rudimentary form there is clearly evident by this time a firmly established canonical system of matrimonial legislation.[16] Thus through the first ten centuries there occurred a gradual extension of the Church's authority over marriage, particularly in the West. What had begun as a pedagogic influence grew to become a full-blown legislative and judicial competency. Capping this progress came the development of a jurisprudence of the ecclesiastical decrees.

The *Decree* of Gratian (ca. 1140), which marked the beginning of the science of canon law in the application of scholastic methodology to the study of the Roman and patristic sources, contains a lengthy accumulation of laws on marriage drawn from the Fathers and the early councils.[17] The fourth book of the *Decretals* of Pope Gregory IX (ca. 1292) shows the extensive influence of the Church, not only in the law of matrimony itself but also in related matters, such as espousals, dowry, legitimacy, separation, etc. The *Decree* of Gratian and the *Decretals* of Pope Gregory IX form the core of the *Corpus Iuris Canonici*, which for many centuries was the official sourcebook for the positive law of the Church.

---

a formal grant. . . . It began as a matter of custom, and gradually was recognized as a matter of right." Joyce, *op. cit.*, p. 225.

[16] A. Esmein, *Le Mariage en Droit Canonique* (2nd ed., Paris, 1929), I, 27.

[17] Ten causes (nos. 27-36) in the second part of the *Decree* are devoted to the laws on marriage.

Elaborate matrimonial regulations and procedures for the judicial control over marriages indicate a clear presumption of the possession of jurisdiction. Through the Middle Ages and until modern times a steady refinement of canonical jurisprudence has strengthened and confirmed this canonical tradition. It can be said without exaggeration that since the time of the *Decretals* scarcely has a synod or council met, either for the whole Church or a particular part of it, that has not enacted legislation concerning marriage and marriage cases. Nearly every pope since the Middle Ages has become involved in marriage cases as a major concern of his office. For thousands of priests from the Holy Roman Rota through courts of appeal down to the diocesan tribunals, the tradition of an absorbing interest in the adjudication of marriage cases has been taken without quibble as a vital part of the apostolic mission of the Church.

In the *Corpus Iuris Canonici* there is no clear enunciation of the principle of the exclusive competency of the Church over the marriages of Christians.[18] There are many instances, however, of decisions made by churchmen over various aspects of marriage and family life. The accumulation of these decisions led the canonists who commented on the *Corpus* to deduce the principle of exclusive competency.[19] The full legislative and judicial

---

[18] Goldsmith, *op. cit.*, pp. 5-8.

[19] Hostiensis, *Lectura*, c. 3, X, *de ordine cognitionum*, II, 10, ad verba *Forum ecclesiasticum*: ". . . scriptum est., quod Deus coniunxit, homo non separet, et per consequens pronunciare non fuisse

power over marriage from the tenth to the fifteenth centuries confirmed a presumption of principle.

At the time of the Reformation the authority of the Church over marriage was severely contested. Many of the Reformers professed that marriage was a purely secular arrangement, subject only to the regulation of civil authority. Against this position the Council of Trent in its twenty-fourth session (1562) strongly emphasized the belief that the marriage of Christians is a sacrament, fundamentally related to the Church and exclusively under its control.[20]

The rise of the secular states after the French Revolution occasioned further reiteration of the sacramentality of marriage in contrast to a purely civil marriage and a purely civil divorce mentality.[21] Pope Leo XIII said, "Christ . . . having renewed marriage to such and so great excellence, commended and entrusted all the discipline bearing upon these matters to his Church."[22] The right

---

matrimonium inter coniunctos non sit hominis sed solius Dei vicarii; ipse solus vicarium, et cui hoc committit et non alius, talem quaestionem examinare et definire potest." Panormitanus, *Commentarium*, c. 3, X, *de ordine cognitionum*, ii, 10, n. 3. Note the use of the words "forum ecclesiasticum" in the decretal of P. Innocent III; C. 11, X, *de foro competenti*, ii, 2.

[20] Sess. xxiv, proem., can. 1. Cf. also, cans. 3, 5, 9—Denz. nn. 1797-1812.

[21] P. Pius VII, Const. "Auctorem fidei," Aug. 28, 1794, props. 59 and 60—Denz. nn. 2659 and 2660; P. Pius IX, "Syllabus errorum," props. 63-74—Denz. nn. 2969-2971, 2974.

[22] "Arcanum," *op. cit.*, n. 9—*Fontes C.I.C.*, n. 580.

of the Church over the marriage of the baptized, in the words of Pope Pius XI, stems from the belief that the only guardian and interpreter of the divine law is the Church of Christ.[23]

In summary, then, the Catholic Church has vindicated since the early Middle Ages the belief that the complete regulation of the marriage of baptized persons is the sole right and prerogative of the Church. This belief has been substantially confirmed by the Second Vatican Council[24] and the most recent decrees of the Church containing matrimonial regulations.[25]

THE THEORY OF CONTRACT

The doctrine of the classical canonists from the Council of Trent until the present is that marriage is a contract granting the mutual and exclusive right to the body for those acts which of their nature are ordered to the procreation of children.[26] Essentially constitutive of marriage is an exchange of rights and obligations that is effected in the manner of a consensual contract. This opin-

[23] "Casti Connubii," *op. cit.,* A.A.S., 22 (1930), 552.

[24] *The Constitution on the Church and the Modern World,* nn. 47-52 in W. M. Abbott, *The Documents of Vatican II* (New York, 1966), pp. 247-258.

[25] Cf. the Decree *Matrimonii Sacramentum* of the Congregation for the Doctrine of the Faith, March 18, 1966 in *The Jurist,* 26 (1966), 361-366.

[26] J. Bank, *Connubia Canonica* (Rome, 1959), p. 7; cf. canon 1081.

ion leaves aside the stress of the Roman Law upon the necessity of the common life[27] and the opinions of the earlier medieval theologians, who had located the essential characteristic of marriage in the mutual affection of the spouses.[28] It places primary emphasis upon the conditions of valid consent to a contract. Freely and legitimately given contractual consent basically constitutes the juridical reality of marriage.

The theory of contract was hammered out through a gradual process encompassing the efforts of hundreds of years. An explanation that would safeguard the freedom of persons entering marriage and at the same time supply a sure and clear legal criterion for deciding upon the existence of the marriage bond was the point at issue.

It is difficult to discover in the earlier canonical collections any attempt to analyze and closely define the nature of marriage. In response to questions sent him by missionaries in the Balkans, Pope Nicholas I in 866 spoke of the necessity of consent for marriage.[29] Hincmar of Rheims at the end of the ninth century taught that marriage consists primarily in the common conjugal life, of

[27] E. Volterra, *La conception du mariage d'apres les juristes romaines* (Padova, 1940).

[28] J. F. Noonan, "Marital Affection in the Canonists" in *Studia Gratiana XII, Collectanea Stephan Kuttner, II* (Bononiae, 1967), pp. 479-509.

[29] "Sufficit secundum leges solus eorum consensus, de quorum coniunctionibus agitur; qui consensus si solum in nuptiis forte defuerit, cetera omnia etiam cum ipso coitu celebrata, frustrantur."—Denz. n. 643.

which sexual intercourse was the most essential part.[30] The theory of copula, as it is called, or the location of the essence of marriage in the sexual relationship of husband and wife, was later taken up and defended by the canonists of the famous law faculties of the University of Bologna.

Peter Damian in the eleventh century finally denied the absolute necessity of intercourse for marriage, on the score that a real, though virginal, marriage would still be the sacrament of matrimony.[31] The canonists of the University of Paris followed Damian in adhering to a theory of consent, rather than sexual relations, as essential to marriage.

Between these two extremes a middle way can be found in the canonical collection of Yvo of Chartres, a very influential compiler living in the beginning of the twelfth century.[32] According to Yvo, consent was necessary to enter marriage, but sexual relations completed and made permanent the marital bond. Hugh of St. Victor, in the line of scholastic theologians, then defined the object of the mutual consent of marriage as the common life of husband and wife.[33] In his *Decree*, Gratian speaks of the

---

[30] ". . . inter ingenios et aequales legitima fiunt coniugia, cum a parentibus, quorum interest petita et legaliter desponsata et dotata et publicis nuptiis honestata femina coniugii copulae sociatur et ex duobus unum corpus unaque caro efficitur." Migne, *PL*, 126, 137.

[31] *De tempore celebrandi nuptias*, Migne, *PL*, 145, 662.

[32] *Ep.* 246—Migne, *PL*, 162, 253.

[33] Migne, *PL*, 176, 488.

necessity of consent, but takes a common ground between Hugh of St. Victor and the School of Bologna in specifying both sexual relations and the common life as the object of marital consent. Consent begins the marriage, he said, but sexual relations with true marital affection perfect and complete it.[34]

Peter Lombard defined marriage essentially as the union of man and wife realized in full common life.[35] For this union the mutual, free consent of each party was necessary. He said that the consent to live a married life, not the consent to have intercourse or merely cohabit, was necessary for marriage.[36] Finally, Pope Alexander III (+1181) settled the issue in decreeing that it is consent alone which is absolutely necessary for the existence of marriage;[37] the essential quality of this consent, however, should be one of true marital affection. Thus before the determination of the canonical formalities for the validity

---

[34] c. 3, C. 27, q. 2.

[35] *Sent. IV*, 28, 3—Migne, *PL*, 192, 915: ". . . consensus cohabitationis, vel carnalis copulae non facit coniugium, sed consensus coniugalis societatis." The bond of marriage, he said, consists of the love of husband and wife, not carnal union. Note St. Thomas, *IV Sent* d. 27, 9.1, ad, ad lum: "Matrimonium non est ipse consensus sed quaedam unio ordinatorum ad invicem."

[36] *Ibid.*

[37] "Si inter virum et mulierem legitimus consensus interveniat de praesenti, ita quidem, quod unus alterum in suo mutuo consensu verbis consuetis expresse recipiat utroque dicente: 'ego te accipio in meam' et 'ego te accipio in meum,' sive sit iuramentum interpositum sive non, non licet mulieri alii nubere. Etsi nupserit, etiamsi carnalis copula sit secuta, ab eo separari debet." c. 3, X, 4, 4.

of matrimony laid down by the Council of Trent, the free, mutual consent of a man and a woman to marital cohabitation was sufficient and necessary for marriage. The emphasis upon the meaning and conditions for valid consent has been retained to this day.

Today the Code of Canon Law enshrines the theory of consent in law, saying simply that consent makes marriage.[38] This consent in the theory of modern canonists results in a real contract between husband and wife. It is a bilateral agreement between two persons involving an exchange of rights and binding in commutative justice. Thus marriage is a sacred consensual contract.

The contract of marriage differs from other contracts in that its essential properties, that is, unity and permanence, are decreed by God, and not by the parties themselves. A man and a woman freely enter a predetermined type of contract in marrying. Such a contract is nonrescindable, and in this sense absolutely unique. It results in a sacred bond which is not completely dependent upon the will of the contracting parties. In order to enter this contract it is sufficient that both parties be free and capable of marriage and, at least, do not positively exclude one of its essential goods, i.e., offspring, fidelity and indissolubility.

It is the natural contract of marriage, the canonical position holds, that Christ raised to the dignity of a sacrament, without changing its basic nature as a contract itself. He transformed the contract of marriage into a sac-

[38] Canon 1081/1: "Matrimonium facit partium consensus."

ramental sign capable of conferring grace. Thus, for Christians, Jesus identified the natural contract of marriage with the sacrament.[39] For Christians, therefore, marriage is no longer a natural, but a sacramental contract.

The contract of marriage is a consensual contract, essentially constituted by mutual consent through words or signs bearing upon the present reality. Consummation is not required for the marriage bond to be established. From the contractual point of view, the requisites for validity are similar to those required for other consensual contracts. There must be genuine internal consent, without substantial simulation, and freedom from force or fear.

For the marriages of Catholics the legal formalities of the celebration of consent in the presence of an authorized priest and two witnesses are necessary for the validity of the contract. This law regarding the canonical form of marriage was given in the decree *Tametsi* of the Council of Trent and finally extended to the whole Catholic world in the decree *Ne temere* of Pope Pius X. Over the span of these years theologians disputed, but then finally conceded, the right of the Church to require these formali-

---

[39] P. Leo XIII, "Arcanum," *op. cit.* "Nec quempiam moveat illa tantopere a regalistis praedicata distinctio, vi cuius contractum nuptialem a sacramento disiungunt eo sane consilio, ut Ecclesiae reservatis sacramenti rationibus, contractum tradant in potestatem arbitriumque Principum civitatis. Etenim non potest huiusmodi distinctio seu verius distractio probari, cum exploratum sit in matrimonio Christiano contractum a sacramento non esse dissociabilem, atque ideo non posse contractum verum et legitimum consistere, quin sit eo ipso sacramentum . . . Christus Dominus dignitate sacramenti auxit matrimonium, matrimonium autem est ipse contractus, si modo sit factus iure." *Fontes C.I.C.*, no. 580.

ties over and above the mere exchange of consent for the valid administration and reception of the sacrament of marriage.

From the identity of the contract and the sacrament of marriage the following canonical consequences are drawn:[40]

1. The ministers of the sacrament of marriage are the contracting parties themselves. Thus, if two baptized persons legitimately exchange mutual matrimonial consent they receive the sacrament of matrimony. This will be true even though they do not intend the sacrament explicitly, for they cannot intend a true marriage without its being a sacrament. The blessing of the priest is merely accessory.

2. The existence of the sacrament of marriage depends on the existence of a true marital contract. If the contract is invalid, there is no sacrament.

3. The sacrament of matrimony, insofar as it is a contract, can be given and received by any external act manifesting true consent.

4. The sacrament of matrimony can also be received conditionally.

5. The sacrament of matrimony can be received by proxy, in the absence of one of the contracting parties.

6. Since the sacrament itself is the contract between baptized persons, it follows that marriage is regulated not only by divine law but also by canon law. This canon law can stipulate conditions, such as personal impediments and the legal formalities of contract, which if not dispensed or fulfilled, render the contract and the sacrament null and void.

7. Since between two baptized persons there cannot be

[40] Cf. Bank, *op. cit.*, pp. 16-18.

a marriage which is not a sacrament, if the marriage was legitimately contracted while one or both parties were not baptized, it automatically becomes a sacrament when both become baptized. No further formalities are required.

THE LIMITATIONS OF THE
CONTRACT-SACRAMENT THEORY

The theory of contract and the theory of the inseparability of the sacrament of marriage from the natural contract are quite obviously the result of reflections upon the necessities of a judicial practice. They are heavily conditioned by historical factors and suffer from all the difficulties inherent in this type of theologizing. Marriage is more than a consensual contract. It is a personally and socially institutionalized way of life. Both on a theoretical and a practical level the position that marriage consists essentially in a contract leaves in its wake enormous anomalies. These difficulties can be delineated from two different points of view: the jurisprudence of canon law and the problems of tribunal adjudication. The theology of the sacraments can then provide a basis for evaluating the absoluteness of the equation.

A. *The Jurisprudence of Canon Law*

Perhaps the principal anomaly to be found in the contractual theory in settling upon consent to a contract for the exchange of sexual rights as the essential constitutive of marriage is that simple error concerning the essential properties of that contract has no effect upon its validity.

Error regarding the unity and permanence of marriage has no effect on the validity of marriage,[41] provided that there has not been a positive exclusion of these properties in the will of one of the contracting parties.[42] This seems to be tantamount to saying that a person can validly enter and be bound by a contract, the very existence of which depends on his consent, while at the same time being ignorant of the nature of that contract. In the existence of such error, where is to be found the true exercise of free will necessary for consent?

For the validity of a human act it is necessary that a person know what is essential to that act. This is an accepted moral principle. Only that which is known can be truly willed. The substance of what marriage actually is must be known to be willed. The will of a person who is ignorant of what he is doing hardly differs from the will of one who excludes from intention what he is doing externally. Both simply do not intend the essential meaning of a particular action. To speak of the properties of marriage as substantial or accessory to it seems hardly relevant.[43] The fact remains that there is no real consent given to them. Yet in canon law a real marriage exists.

[41] Canon 1084.

[42] Canon 1086/2.

[43] A. Szentirmai, "Matrimonium non est contractus," *Revista Española de Derecho Canonico*, 1 (1965), 155-164. This article is a reply to one written by O. Robleda upholding the contract theory. Cf. O. Robleda, "Matrimonium est contractus," *Periodica*, 3 (1964), 374-408. For a survey of the discussion between those who hold the contract theory and those who hold a theory of institution, cf. G. Michiels, "Mariage—contrat ou mariage—institution," *Apollinaris*, 33 (1960), 103-117.

The law itself must acknowledge essentially more in marriage, therefore, than a mere consensual contract. Marriage must be an institution fundamentally oriented, not only to a contract between two persons but also to a broader dimension of humanity. Marriage cannot be essentially constituted only by consent to contract.

In total simulation, which is a lie, marriage is substantially not intended. In this case there is no real marriage. In partial simulation it is held by canonists, and by the law, that the substance of marriage is intended, but one or other of the properties essential to it is not. Therefore, the marriage is valid. But how can one and the same thing be distinguished from its essential properties, so that it can be intended without intending something essential to it? What is not known or desired is not willed. If the essential constitutive of marriage is only the consent of the will to a contract, marriage does not exist where there is no true act of the will. But a marriage is valid in law even in ignorance of its basic properties or partial simulation of them. More is clearly necessary for marriage than merely a consensual contract.

Secondly, the supporters of the contract theory generally light upon a clear physical criterion to define the object of consent. The object of consent, they say, is the *ius in corpus.*[44] The common life and the union of two persons, they say, are consequent to this, but not essential. The *ius in corpus* is principal, to which married life is accessory. But is it not more correct to say that two

[44] Canon 1081/2.

persons enter a total life relationship in which the *ius in corpus* is a part? The union of bodies supposes a union of mind and heart in marriage. Those acts which are per se apt for the procreation of children hardly constitute marriage where the common life and the union of mind and heart are absent. The intimate life and love of two persons lead to their natural expression in sexual union, not the converse.

The physical acts of marriage are not marriage itself. Marriage is more properly realized in the unity of life of husband and wife. This common life cannot prescind from full personal involvement or be separated from the physical acts of sexual union. In this sense, marriage implies, but is not merely a contract for bodily acts. It is a way of life more like a social institution. The intention of living a common life is far more than the consent to a contract for physical activity. If the object of consent is essentially the handing over of a permanent right to sexual acts, how does marriage differ from concubinage? Concubinage also supposes common consent and may not preclude permanence.

Consequent and incurable impotency would also seem to vitiate a contract essentially ordered to sexual activity. Yet in canon law only antecedent and perpetual impotency is an invalidating impediment.[45] The object of marital consent, therefore, must be essentially more than an unrealizable *ius in corpus*.

The *ius in corpus* is a necessity of the common life of

[45] Canon 1068.

husband and wife. But the common life of marriage is not
a necessity of the exchange of the right to sexual intercourse. Therefore, the common life of marriage is equally
the object of consent together with an exchange of sexual
rights. But the totality of married life is institutional. It is
not only contractual. Therefore, marital consent is ordered
of its nature toward an institutionalized way of life, not
just a contract.

A contract of its nature is an institute of private law.
Marriage, however, belongs to the order of public law as
a social institution. Thus, a private contract between two
persons is not sufficient to establish marriage, as it is not
sufficient to determine any public status in the social order. The intervention of public authority, either of the
Church or the state, must also accede to the institutionalization of married life. Consent is required for marriage,
but more than a consent to mere bodily acts and more
than consent to a mutual contract between only two persons. It is a consent given to a way of life with another
person which is integrated into the structure of society
and acknowledged by society as such. In the institute of
the canonical form and *sanatio in radice* the Church
clearly recognizes this. The perpetuity and exclusivity of
marriage do not come from the act of the private will
alone, but are a part of marriage by the will of God,[46] as

---

[46] "Consensus utriusque personae est causa proxima matrimonii,
sed simul cum institutione divina." St. Bonaventure, *In IV Sent.*
d. 24, 9.1, art. 2. Cf. *The Constitution on the Church and the Modern World, op. cit.,* art. 48.

a way of life responsive to both personal and societal exigencies.

The theory of marriage as a personal and social institution led in a common life with the mutual affection of husband and wife would seem better fitted to the reality than that which is explained by the theory of contract. A sacramentalized way of life rings a truer note than a sacramentalized contract for the meaning of Christian marriage.[47]

---

[47] It seems significant that the teaching of the Second Vatican Council on the nature of marriage carefully avoids reference to or the use of the word "contract." From a highly personalist perspective the meaning of marriage is unfolded in terms such as "community," "institution," "union," "covenant," "a whole manner and communion of life." The closest the Council came to the contract theory was in a single use of the word "compact" (foedus). Furthermore, the debate and decision not to include in the document a hierarchy of primary and secondary ends of marriage brings into question whether the sole essential object of marital consent is only "actus per se aptos ad prolis generationem." Surely it must be supposed that the nature and theory of the matrimonial contract as taught traditionally by the canonists were well known. It must also be supposed that the bishops were acquainted with current trends bringing this theory into question. Cf. *The Constitution on the Church and the Modern World, op. cit.,* arts. 47-52. In explaining the conciliar teaching on marriage, Bernard Häring says: "The Council sees marriage as a covenant patterned after the covenant between Christ and the Church. No Christian would dare to call that a contract. In the face of strong pressure from those who followed older thought patterns, the Council commission refused to use the word 'contract.'" "Marriage and the Family" in *Vatican II: An Interfaith Appraisal* (Notre Dame, Ind., 1966), p. 440. J. Dominian, "Vatican II and Marriage," *ClR* 3 (1967), 47-52.

B. *Problems of Tribunal Practice*

A purely contractual law is severely limited in providing for many of the problems with which tribunals must cope today. A truer, more humane and more expeditious approach must prescind from the narrowness of contract and must see marriage more broadly within the context of a total life relationship. There are many cases of marital failure in which it is impossible to prove the absence of a true contract. But it is quite easy to see that a viable heterosexual relationship constituting marriage never really existed. There are people who can truly consent to and fulfill a contract demanding the permanent and exclusive exchange of the rights to sexual activity. These same people, however, may be totally incapable or unwilling to sustain a true interpersonal marital relationship. To illustrate the difficulties of the contractual theory let us take, for example, the cases of sociopathology and homosexuality.

Both a sociopath and a homosexual can consent to a marriage strictly considered as a contract. They can know, desire and intend such a contract. To invalidate the marriage of these persons according to the jurisprudence of a strictly contractual theory, canonists offer two alternatives. Either a new impediment must be established to exclude these people from marriage or the notion of mental and emotional capacity for marital consent will have to be stretched to invalidate their consent. A new impediment would be extremely onerous in its implementation and bring in its wake enormous legal contradictions from the very lack of precision in which it must be cast. The transferral of the meaning of impotency from the realm of the physical to that of the mental and emotional would stretch the notion of capacity for consent far out of proportion. It would also be equally difficult to adjudicate. More impediments and more personal grounds for declarations of nullity on the basis of deficient consent are peripheral considerations, leaving the basic premise yet unexplored.

Can it not be said that in some cases a real contract may have been made, but there was never a real marriage because a true married life was never possible? In many cases marriage was not possible in its true institutional significance for life. It does not take a professional expert to make such a decision. Where the common consent of mankind agrees there is no marriage, however, and the lawmakers must struggle so hard to find a loophole in a legal theory to prove this, some suspicion may be cast on the adequacy of the theory itself. A courageous jurisprudence must be preeminently attuned to life and adjust itself according to that reality. We will now examine briefly some of the difficulties encountered by the contractual theory in the cases of marital failure as a result of sociopathic personality disorders and homosexuality.

1. The Sociopath

The Holy Roman Rota has never looked favorably upon petitions for a declaration of the nullity of marriage on the grounds that the respondent in a particular case is a sociopath. In fact, I have been unable to find a single case that has received an affirmative answer on this ground. Sociopathy, or psychopathy, according to the Rota, does not deprive its victim of the power of sufficient consent to the matrimonial contract.

"Although the principal characteristic of psychopathy is a defect of the will or affections, sufficient and often exceptional intelligence is present. . . . The marriages of psychopaths are often unhappy. But they cannot be declared invalid on grounds of defective consent from *amentia* (insanity) because the consent is not *per se* affected by pathological impulses."[48]

The Roman Rota has developed a jurisprudence which requires *due discretion* or a *critical power*, over and above the simple use of reason, in the contractants of marriage and has found this lacking at the time of marriage in persons afflicted with *amentia* or psychosis. The consent of these would be invalid. But in the case of sociopaths, the Rota has not found this power wanting at the moment of matrimonial consent. It has focused its attention on the moment of consent and has found the marriages of sociopaths valid.

An acute sensitivity to the overall significance of marriage would suggest that we shift our inquiry away from the capability of the sociopath to know and understand the contract of marriage to relevant questions about his

[48] Rotal Decision, coram Filipiak, Feb. 15, 1958 in *Monitor Ecclesiasticus*, 71 (1959), 612 ff.

ability to covenant with another for the sharing of a common life from a sufficiently profound sense of marital affection. But we do not have any legal guidelines by which to test this approach. Therefore, there is a growing tendency among canonists to look at the case of the sociopath outside traditional lines. Attention is being focused on his ability to fulfill the duties of marriage as a whole. If it can be proved that an individual sociopath is unable to fufill the duties of marriage because of sociopathic deficiency, they argue, the marriage is invalid. No one, they reason, can validly assume obligations which he cannot fulfill because of a defect in himself rendering him incapable of carrying out those obligations. This kind of person knows well the nature and obligations of marriage. He wants to assume them. But he cannot. If he cannot fulfill an obligation because of a permanent deficiency that cannot be overcome, how can he validly assume it?

This approach to the problem of the sociopath in marriage is a valid one. It emerges from a broader notion of marriage and it relies upon the essential requirements for marriage in general. One of these requirements is that the life of marriage be possible. This is the object of the consent. If the matter about which two persons consent is impossible, right reason, the natural law, must affirm that the consent is invalid.

The literature about sociopathy is abundant.[49] The incidence of sociopathy in the general population is be-

---

[49] F. Kobler, *Casebook in Psychopathology* (New York, 1964); Cavanagh and McGoldrick, *Fundamental Psychiatry* (Milwaukee, 1953); J. R. Keating, *The Bearing of Mental Impairment on the*

lieved to be very high. Experience teaches that sociopathy is very often the determining factor in the breakup of marriages. The following actual case is typical.

Mr. X was married at the age of twenty-five years. He is more intelligent than his siblings. He had learned a good profession and had his own profitable business before he was thirty. But he had to give it up within five years because of mismanagement, extravagance and irresponsible negligence in making collections and in paying his bills. Since the loss of his business, he has had a succession of ordinary, salaried jobs which he has not been able to keep because of his unreliability. At this time he is in the civil service with a modest salary, but he is unreliable there, too. He has a friendly and usually pleasant personality; he makes friends easily, but loses them rapidly.

Thirteen years of an unstable, stormy, unhappy married life ensued during which four children were born. Finally, his wife demanded and obtained a divorce. After his marriage broke up, Mr. X gradually descended on the

---

Validity of Marriage (Rome, 1964); H. Cleckley, *The Mask of Sanity* (St. Louis, 1964). The Diagnostic and Statistical Manual of the American Psychiatric Association says that the term sociopathy refers to chronically antisocial individuals who are always in trouble, profiting neither from experience nor punishment, and maintaining no real loyalties to any person, group or code. They are frequently callous and hedonistic, showing marked emotional immaturity, with lack of sense of responsibility, lack of judgment, and an ability to rationalize their behavior so that it appears warranted, reasonable, and justified. (*Mental Disorders, Diagnostic and Statistical Manual* [Washington, D.C., 1952] p. 38.)

social scale; he became shiftless, jobless and increasingly hostile toward his relatives, his wife and anyone who tried to help him. Finally, at the age of forty, he was almost on skid row. He submitted to a psychological study of himself and a brief period of psychotherapy which included self-commitment to a mental hospital for a few months. He was discharged from the hospital in excellent physical condition but emotionally he was about the same. The diagnosis based upon the psychological study was *sociopathic personality*. The therapists in the hospital agreed with this diagnosis.

There is a pattern of behavior which, the testimony of many witnesses reveals, extends back into his adolescent and premarital life. He seeks immediately realizable goals at the expense of possible, more remote and more satisfying goals. To achieve his immediate purposes, he lies easily in an effort to impress others and to escape from difficulties he himself has caused. But he never seems to learn from the experience of being constantly caught in his lies. He is unconcerned about not paying bills: utilities, car and house payments, insurance, taxes, entertainment bills and charge accounts. These are always in arrears and most have never been paid. He is notorious for self-display among his friends and acquaintances. He appears to be insensitive to the feelings of others closest to him. He was often cruel to his wife and his attitude toward his children varies from unconcern to anger and kindness. But he rarely fulfills his promises to them. Since the divorce he has never paid for the support of these children. He rarely sees them except to use them in some subtle way for his own purposes. Somehow the children sense this, because they return from visits with him with their spirits crushed. Sometimes his hostility toward others appears openly and irrationally. He disregards laws and obligations, but when he is caught he always has an explanation. He seems to be without insight into himself, but he is clever at manipulating others for his own advantage. There is no remorse for the disorder of his life. He is now remarried and is following the same pattern of behavior with his second wife.

This man has been diagnosed as a sociopath. But the kind of diagnosis a therapist makes depends very much upon the purpose of the diagnosis. Is he trying to make a statement with a view to future therapy or is he making it in order to inform a court of law about the quality of the acts of the person under diagnosis? Furthermore, does the diagnostician know that this man might be reacting to the situation in which he lives: to the personality of his wife and the pressures she brings to bear upon him; to her attitude toward the children which might be described as possessive and dominating; to an exaggerated desire of hers for a kind of neat, orderly fiscal solvency? These considerations raise the question as to whether he reacts only to her or also to almost all situations, both inside and outside the home, in a sociopathic manner.

Regardless of whether the pattern reveals a generalized condition of his personality or a constant, repetitious reaction to the personality of his wife, this man has *de facto* not fulfilled the duties of a spouse and a parent which he assumed in marrying. Is he capable of doing so? Is all of this deviant behavior merely a gravely sinful dereliction of duties which he could perform if he wanted to? Or is he afflicted by a psychic disability to perform long-term and ever-recurring obligations? He is able to understand what he is doing when he makes a promise; he is able to perform the marital act properly; he had not been sexually unfaithful to his wife; he is able to fulfill small obligations which require single acts and are not troublesome. But is he able to fulfill the long-term, constantly demanding duties which marital and parental life demand? If it can be proved that he cannot and that the disability existed at the time of the wedding, this marriage would be invalid because he tried to assume duties which are impossible for him to fulfill. The marriage would be invalid because married life was impossible for him or with him.

Not every sociopath is incapable of marriage. There are cases in which such persons fulfill their obligations with some success. In other cultures, too, it is possible that the external constraints of society would help to hold such a person to performance. But in our permissive society most of these restraints are absent. Left to themselves, many sociopaths simply cannot perform and we know that they cannot. The sociopath's problem is one of defective will power and confusion in the affective areas of his personality. But he also has a defect in his *critical faculty*. This faculty is described as: "A power of judging and of reasoning judgments together so that a new judgment can logically be deduced from the former ones."[50] The

[50] Rotal Decision, coram Sabattani, March 24, 1961—*Monitor Ecclesiasticus*, 73 (1961), p. 645, n. 4.

Rota has never applied this dictum to the sociopath. Psychiatric evidence, however, supports the belief that he is unable to make appropriate judgments about himself, his relations with others and proper modes of behavior. It further supports the belief that in cases of marital failure as a result of sociopathic deficiency there has rarely been any true interpersonal relationship between the spouses. Therefore, the failure of marriage is attributable to an incapacity for a particular marriage. This is more than just an incapacity to consent to a marital contract.

2. The Homosexual

Marriages which have failed because of the homosexuality or lesbianism of one of the spouses have, in some instances, been declared null by local ecclesiastical tribunals. But these affirmative decisions have been reversed when they were sent to the Roman Rota on appeal by the Defenders of the Bond.

The grounds alleged in support of the claim of nullity have been framed in different ways. For example,

1. It has been alleged that the respondent (the homosexual) gave a conditional consent to the marriage, the condition being against the *bonum fidei*, i.e., he would be permitted to continue his homosexual practices.[51]

2. It was claimed that the respondent (a lesbian) simulated consent by internally excluding the giving over of the *jus in corpus* to her husband and reserving "to herself

---

[51] Rotal Decision, coram Parillo, Aug. 12, 1929—*Decisiones ac Sententiae Sanctae Romanae Rotae*, 21 (1929), 434 ff., n. 1.

full freedom to continue her perverse relations with other women."[52]

3. In another case the petitioner asserted that the respondent (a homosexual) simulated consent by excluding the *bonum prolis* and the *bonum fidei* and also that he was unable to give consent because of his habit of homosexuality and, finally, he suffered from functional impotence.[53]

When it has been alleged that the homosexual simulated consent by excluding the *bonum fidei*, the Rota has held to the principle that there is a distinction between the exclusion of the right to the *bonum fidei* and the intention not to fulfill the obligation. A man might wish really to marry and at the same time intend to continue his extramarital liaisons; he might assume the obligation of fidelity and at the same time intend to violate it. Validity of the marital contract requires that one give his spouse the right to demand fidelity; it does not require that the husband actually give up his proposals of not honoring her claim. This distinction is subtle and hard to see, but it is constant in Rotal jurisprudence.

But even if one should grant that the homosexual has excluded the right of his spouse to demand that his fidelity include abstention from homosexual practices, there is another difficulty which removes homosexuality from being against the *bonum fidei*. For "the will or intention

[52] Rotal Decision, coram Doheny, Dec. 14, 1953—*ibid.*, 45 (1953), 765 ff.
[53] Rotal Decision, coram Lamas, March 15, 1956—*ibid.*, 47 (1956), 237 ff.

(concomitant with the matrimonial consent) to give one's body to other persons for the doing of acts which are against nature, such as homosexual acts, from which the generation of children cannot result, is not against the *bonum fidei* in the strict sense. Since sodomy is a sin against nature, it is worse than fornication and adultery. It is a grave injury to the innocent spouse and gives that spouse the right to ask for a separation from bed and board. But it is not that division of the body (*corporis divisio seu sectio*) which is opposed to the unity of marriage, because it does not bring about incertitude regarding the parentage of a child."[54]

The *bonum fidei* means, in other words, that the spouses have the exclusive right to ask of the other the performance of certain sexual acts. These acts are, taxatively and restrictively (the words are the Rota's), acts which are per se apt for the generation of offspring. Homosexuality, in practice, consists in sodomitic acts with persons of the same sex. The homosexual performs acts with others than his wife which are not per se apt for the procreation of offspring. Therefore, so the reasoning goes, the intention of continuing to practice homosexuality is not an intention against the *bonum fidei*.

The Roman Rota concedes that the practice of homosexuality can become an ingrained habit and that habit is a kind of second nature. Nevertheless, it strongly rejects a determinism which would thoroughly do away with

---

[54] C. Holbock, *Tractatus de Jurisprudentia Sacrae Romanae Rotae* (Graz, 1957), p. 133. Cf. also W. Tobin, *Homosexuality and Marriage* (Rome, 1964).

liberty. Therefore, it holds, even the habit of homosexuality does not preclude the possibility of a valid consent to a heterosexual union, such as marriage, by a homosexual. It rejects the idea that a habitual homosexual is able to give only a defective consent to marriage. In confirmation of this conclusion it points to the fact that many homosexuals choose to enter marriage, a relationship repugnant to them, precisely in order to overcome the habit and to become normal individuals. This motivation indicates that the consent to marriage of the homosexual is a clear and free act of consent because it is against a habit which had become per se a kind of second nature.

These decisions leave one wondering whether there is not something more to be said. Married persons who have discovered after the marriage that their spouses are homosexuals and lesbians find small comfort in the knowledge that they can obtain a separation from bed and board. They are convinced that the confirmed homosexual cannot really enter into a true marriage. They know theirs was never a real marriage. Pastors are not satisfied with these legal decisions and many canonists today strongly contest the interpretation of the facts and theory upon which the courts rely. More than one canonist holds that constitutional homosexuality renders the afflicted party unavoidably incapable of a true and lasting heterosexual relationship. The following is a recent case.

This man was twenty-seven when he married. The union lasted about five months. During this time there were approximately five attempts at sexual relations with his wife and none of these was successful. The first at-

tempt was on the fourth day after the wedding. The previous day she had asked him about consummating the
marriage and he replied by hitting her viciously in the
stomach. During the period of cohabitation, he went out
every night, Monday through Saturday, and stayed out
until early in the morning. This occurred every night except Sundays, with no exceptions. On the wedding night
he left her shortly after they had checked into their hotel
and returned about three in the morning. Later she discovered that he had spent that night with a homosexual
partner. After the marriage broke up, the bride's parents
had an investigation made and it was discovered that the
man had been a known homosexual for years and that he
had been with a homosexual friend the night before the
wedding. He has since remarried, the woman being a divorcee with four children. Apparently he is carrying on
the same kind of life now. Before his marriage he had
tried psychotherapy for some time. The prognosis of his
therapist is poor. This particular man will receive little
help from psychotherapy.

Cases such as this have been presented to the courts
under the rubric of defective consent to the marriage
contract. The courts have found that intelligence was not
impaired, that the homosexual knows what marriage is
and the rights it confers and the duties it imposes. Indeed, as we have said, it is not infrequent that a homosexual wishes to get married in order to overcome his
problem. Therefore the courts have found that contractual
consent was neither lacking nor defective. They have
ruled such unions true sacramental marriages! Is it not

possible, then, to look elsewhere for the grounds of invalidity?

Marriage implies more than the mere mutual giving and receiving of the rights to corporal acts which are per se apt for the procreation of offspring. The exchange of rights and duties applies to a true married life. The exchange gives each spouse a claim upon the other, a claim for the human performance of the duties of a spouse. These rights, duties, claims are exclusive and perpetual. The question is, therefore: is the homosexual able to honor the rights and claims of his spouse? Is he able to perform this duty in response to his spouse? The fact that a homosexual can respond or has responded *occasionally* to the desire of his spouse is not an affirmative answer to the question. For the right of one spouse implies an enduring obligation for the other. The wife has an enduring claim upon her husband's love. Yet he cannot love her normally and give her true marital affection. A union without human response and marked by rare and merely biological activity to fulfill a sick sense of duty is not marriage.

There are cases of homosexuals in which it is evident *after the fact* that they could not be expected to perform the duty of husbands in a human way over a long period of time. This inability arises from the psychic nature of homosexuality. If this disability existed at the time of the marriage and the present state of the individual is a kind of continuum of it, the homosexual could not have validly assumed the obligations of a husband. A person cannot validly assume an obligation if, at the time he attempts to assume it, there is a cause in existence which will prevent his fulfilling that duty.

The contract theory telescopes the reality of marriage into a clearly and closely defined legal entity. The question remains: is this marriage? Is a valid marriage only a valid marriage contract? Surely consent and agreement are necessary for marriage. Is this consent to a contract for bodily acts, however, or a total way of life? The basic response of marital consent is not to intercourse or procreation, but to the person of the spouse. Does it not seem that there can be consent to a contract, and yet in reality never be a marriage, because as marriage is lived and understood by people, such a relationship simply never existed? The basic juridical reality of marriage is not merely contractual. In most cases of homosexuality marriage would not exist *in fieri* nor *in facto esse*. To bind an innocent person to such a union is grotesquely unjust.

The theory of marriage not only as a contract, but also as an institution or total way of life, is receiving broad acceptance in the Church today, not only by theologians and psychologists but by a growing number of canonists as well. It has not yet been received into the jurisprudence of the Holy Roman Rota, however, because some of the proponents of this theory have stretched it too far in the other extreme of denying the causal significance of consent for marriage.

Garcia Barbarena, one of the first in recent times to contest the theory of contract, said that the free and mutual consent of the parties is not an efficacious cause of the marriage bond. The consent is only a necessary

condition for entering a marriage, which is totally determined in essence and existence by God and the social
authority of either Church or state.[55] The obligations of
marriage, he said, come not from a contract, but from the
will of higher authority. This theory of marriage as a
social institution was derived from a partial understanding of the meaning of convalidation without the
renewal of consent of one party to marriage, *sanatio in
radice*, and the implications of simple error in marriage.
In these cases, he said, the Church intervenes to constitute the marriage without the consent of the parties. By
this presentation he hoped to give marriage a permanence
beyond that possible by the normal understanding of
contracts and the autonomy of the individual will.

Such a theory, however, can hardly fit into the teaching
of the Church. It is too positivistic. The consent of both
parties to marriage is absolutely necessary. No human
agency can supply for this consent, if it is lacking. Moreover, this consent has a causal efficacy in bringing about
the existence of marriage.

I should submit, however, that though marriage is
surely a consensual contract, that is not all it is, even
essentially. It is more than this. In the context of the
common life, more than a contract constitutes marriage
as a personal and social reality. An institutional theory
of marriage would embrace and extend the theory of
consent to include not only the intention of the parties,

---

[55] G. Barbarena, "Sobre la idea contractual del matrimonio,"
Miscelanea Comillas, 16 (1951), 157-179.

but the possibility of a real married life following it and flowing from it. The acceptance of such an understanding would be a great pastoral advance in the theory and practice of the law.

Such a theory, of course, would less easily lend itself to a clear criterion for adjudication. It would considerably broaden the grounds of nullity to bring them into line with the best contemporary understanding of marriage. A broader human perspective would, however, render judgments less clear-cut and legally definable. Life itself is this way. But, then, we may ask: is the purpose of law to establish conditions for the ease of administration and adjudication by fitting life into clear-cut and definable niches, or rather, to meet and serve life in its fullest dimension?

C. The Contract-Sacrament Equation

The marriage of two validly baptized persons is termed a sacramental marriage (*matrimonium ratum*). If the conjugal act has been completed, marriage is not dissolved by the Church nor by any cause save death.[56] It makes no

[56] Canon 1118. Note that the canon says a ratified consummated marriage cannot be dissolved by any human power. Does the Church have power from Christ, a vicarious power, to dissolve such a marriage? This has long been disputed by canonists. (Cf. W. R. O'Connor, "The Indissolubility of a Ratified, Consummated Marriage," in *Ephemerides Theologicae Lovanienses*, 12 [1963], 692-722.) From the principles of the present law there is no intrinsic reason to prohibit dispensation from divine law as such. By vicarious power bishops now dispense vows (Canon 1313). Dispen-

difference whether the baptism was conferred in the Catholic Church, in any one of the Protestant communions, or even in any one of the smaller sects. All that is required is that the baptism be valid. The marriage is a sacrament and after consummation it remains permanent until death. Should separation and divorce occur, neither party can validly marry again until one is set free by the death of the other.

Whenever a case occurs in which both parties were baptized and there is question of the conversion and re-marriage of one of them in the Church, the practice is simply to reply that nothing can be done about it. Nevertheless the exigencies of the pastoral ministry and the *salus animarum* leave one dissatisfied with the way the doctrine claims to cover all cases without discernment of the differences which occur in life. We must ask ourselves whether such a broad and undiscerning doctrine is really all there is to say about the problem. The following case is typical.

Mr. X was born in a small rural community of culturally deprived parents. From time to time traveling minis-

---

sation from a vow is certainly not a dispensation from merely ecclesiastical law. This involves a relationship to God, a divine law. Pope Gregory XIII in the constitution *Populis* (cf. appendix to the Code) gave Ordinaries, pastors and Jesuit confessors the faculty to dispense marriages contracted in infidelity, so that one partner could remarry after baptism in the Church without the necessity of interpolating the former spouse. This delegation of authority certainly extends beyond the limits of the Pauline privilege. Thus there seems to be no intrinsic reason to deny the ability to dispense nor the delegability of such power to bishops.

ters of different sects would conduct revivals in the town. On one of these occasions, the parents of Mr. X had him baptized. He was an infant at the time. All evidence shows that the ceremony of baptism marked the beginning and the end of any connection with religion for him. His family did not practice any religion. There was never any talk about religion at home. He received no religious instruction, never entered a church and never prayed. In fact, he did not know about his own baptism. Mr. X married at the age of nineteen or twenty in a civil ceremony. The woman he married, though baptized in infancy, practiced no religious faith. The marriage lasted a couple of years and was terminated by divorce.

Mr. X now lives in California, has a good job in an industrial plant and is going to night school. At school he met an unmarried Catholic woman and came to know her family and some of her friends and their families. For the first time in his life he is learning what religion means. He has taken some instructions and wants to continue so that he can become a Catholic. His sincerity cannot be called into doubt. Love has grown between him and this young Catholic woman, and the possibility of a future Catholic marriage and family looms large in their thoughts. The case was sent in and petition made for a dissolution of his previous bond in favor of the faith. Then it was discovered that both he and his former spouse had been baptized as infants. On the basis of a contractual theory, the validity of the marriage appears unquestionable. Since he was baptized, it is also said that his first marriage was automatically a sacrament, whether he knew or intended it or not. In his early twenties on the threshold of entrance into the Church, with a religious faith for the first time and the desire for a Christian marriage, he stands barred from any possibility of marriage in the Church until his former wife dies.

Here we have a prior marriage of two baptized persons. In their personal histories there was a baptism in infancy, a baptism of which neither was aware. There was no religious life to follow, no incorporation into any kind of a religious community and no conscious understanding of the religious dimensions of matrimony. Yet in canon law this marriage has the same sacramental nature as the marriage of two intensely devoted religious persons, Protestant, Orthodox or Catholic.

To attribute Christian sacramentality to this kind of marriage is almost to attribute a kind of spiritual automaticism to the rite of Baptism and the matrimonial consent. It attributes a force to the unconscious reception of Baptism, followed by no other perceptible development of the religious life, and to the matrimonial consent, that need not be demanded by the Scriptures and the tradition of the Church.

In the Synoptics Jesus affirms the permanence of marriage. The "repudiation" of an erring wife which had allowed a Jewish husband to remarry, is not now allowed. St. Paul repeats this command which "is not from me but from the Lord" in the First Letter to the Corinthians.[57] Schillebeeckx comments: "It would appear that, according to the practice of the subapostolic and the ancient church, a straightforward breach between the partners

[57] I Cor 7, 10-11.

in marriage did not give the innocent party the right to remarry, even if the other party was guilty of grave misconduct."[58] Was marriage indissoluble? Yes. Was *every* marriage *absolutely* indissoluble? Not quite.

St. Paul makes an exception. When a marriage has been contracted in paganism and the husband becomes a "brother," i.e., baptized in faith and a member of the Christian community, while the wife remains an "unbeliever," the marriage is permanent if "she is content to live with him." The same thing is true if the woman becomes a Christian while the husband remains an unbeliever. "However, if the unbelieving partner does not consent, they may separate; in these circumstances, the 'brother' or 'sister' is not tied."[59]

The *absoluteness* of indissolubility depends upon the fact that husband and wife are Christians. The Christian is a "brother" or a "sister," persons who are identifiable as persons baptized in faith and members living in a Christian community. With the practice of infant baptism, this would be verified by the growing up within the community. The marriages of these persons are sacramental. They are the sign to men of faith of the union of Christ and the Church. How can we attribute such sacramentality to the marriages of persons who were baptized as infants, but who have never had faith nor life in the Christian community? To do so would be to attribute to the infantile reception of baptism alone, and unaccom-

[58] E. Schillebeeckx, *Marriage, Human Reality and Saving Mystery* (New York, 1965), p. 146.

[59] I Cor 7, 12-16.

panied by anything else that is Christian, a force which common sense ought to deny.

Because marriage is a lasting covenant of love proven in enduring fidelity, it is the sign of that relationship that exists between Christ and the Church. The *Constitution on the Church and the Modern World* of the Vatican Council speaks of the sanctification of married love, and thus its sacramental transformation, as the effect of the active and intentional presence of Christ in the lives of married people.

> Christ the Lord abundantly blessed this many-faceted love, welling up as it does from the fountain of divine love and structured as it is on the model of his union with the Church. For as God of old made himself present to his people through a covenant of love and fidelity, so now the Savior of men and the Spouse of the Church comes into the lives of married Christians through the sacrament of matrimony. He abides with them thereafter so that, just as He loved the Church and handed himself over on her behalf, the spouses may love each other with perpetual fidelity through mutual self-bestowal.[60]

The sacramentality of marriage cannot be seen in any magic way. It involves the acceptance of Christ and His constant salvific action in the lives and love of husband and wife. The love of Christian spouses transcends themselves as they consciously become cooperators with the Redeemer and witnesses to the community of the Church of His love. The sacramental reality deepens the experi-

[60] N. 48.

ence of love and gives it a prophetic function beyond the pale of words. Married love in Christ and only in Him is sanctified as a way of joy and sacrifice leading to God, the source of all love.

The Council did not see sacramentality as something alongside conjugal love, nor as something attached to a mere contract.[61] The covenant of marriage itself, referred in faith to Christ and the Church, is a way of salvation through the active presence of Christ. Mutual love, as Bernard Häring remarks, has a saving quality only if it is linked to the glory of God; it is holy only if lovers are also adorers of God.[62]

Acceptance of the nonsacramentality and thus, dissolubility of the marriage of those without faith or awareness of God would not involve a division of that unique, peculiar "one flesh" which belongs to Christian marriage, or rather to marriage between two Christians. For the "two in one flesh" means—over and above physical consummation of marriage—a single communion of life which acquires in Christian marriage a symbolic relationship to the mystery of Christ and his Church. The explicitness of this relationship emerges from baptism and visible incorporation into the Christian community.

CONCLUSION

Traditional canonical theory has attached sacramentality to the ratification of marriage and indissolubility to a

---

[61] Häring, *op. cit.*, p. 441.
[62] *Ibid.*

very narrow biological understanding of consummation. Thus has marriage been located within the septenary sacramental paradigm. Today, however, the understanding of sacramentality and its application to marriage are undergoing a profound reexamination from the positive bases of Scripture, the Fathers and the cultural expressions of marriage in history, to a systematic theological insight into its nature and meaning. To accept the simple equation of contract-sacrament is to accept only one way, and indeed, a very narrow way, of understanding sacramentality and marriage. Perhaps the real key to the great pastoral problems involved in the Church's solicitude for marriage today is to be found in the enriching developments of sacramental theology.

An examination of the canonical tradition and practice of the past few centuries on a practical and positive level gives ample reason to question the assumptions upon which they are based. The use of the exclusive category of contract in deciding cases of matrimonial nullity leads to conclusions and consequences in the lives of so many people that practically exclude a human and Christian answer to their suffering. The evident inadequacy of this approach lends credence to the real need for psychologists, theologians, biblicists and historians to reexamine the meaning of marriage itself. The very fact that such reexamination has begun and the theory has been called into question is a breakthrough that gives great hope for future development.

COMMENT

AND

DISCUSSION

The tradition of canonical legislation surrounding the institution of marriage is a development of centuries of solicitude for the attainment of the evangelical mandate. At the same time its pastoral orientation toward the good of persons reaches ideally to the greatest possible freedom within the range of humanly discernible truth. Thus the rigid norm of indissolubility is tempered in each particular case by careful investigation of all available evidence to determine the validity of marriage or the possibility of dispensation. The procedure of investigation has changed with history and further change can be expected. But the ultimate criterion for decision must firmly correspond to the reality of marriage itself. Is this union a real marriage or is it not? In the perspective of faith does the full sacramental reality of Christian marriage find its expression in this union or does it not? A negative finding yields freedom; a positive sentence bespeaks the permanency of a prior commitment to a perduring bond from which only death may grant release.

It is unrealistic to suppose that the Church can suddenly abandon the tradition of its past and forsake the responsibility for making such decisions. Progress and development within the continuity of tradition can come, however, from growth in the understanding of the nature of marriage itself and the nature of the judicial decision involved. The meaning of validity when applied to marriage is radically the meaning of marriage itself.

On what grounds should decisions of nullity be based to be most responsive to the truth of this greatly complex human and sacred relationship? Surely it can be said that marriage is more than consent, more than a moment of commitment, a happening that marks only the beginning, the "matrimonium in fieri." A valid marriage is more than a valid contract of marriage. Thus decisions must look beyond the moment and conditions of consent toward an appraisal of married life and love in continuity. Within the canonical tradition itself a more ancient precedent centered upon the significance of covenanted union and marital affection could be an aid toward the enrichment of contemporary theory.

Marriage in the teaching of St. Augustine is a union of mutual trust. St. Augustine carefully avoided an equation of marriage with either consent or contract, as this was understood in the Roman law of his day. "Pactum" or "foedus," used in reference to marriage as reflecting the union of Christ and His Church, is more closely akin to a perduring covenant than to a contract. Further, in St. Augustine the meaning of the sacramentality of marriage lies precisely in the indissolubility of the covenanted relationship. Two persons truly joined together as Christians cannot henceforth be separated. This is what indissolubility means. This, for Augustine, is the primary meaning of marriage as a sacrament, a holy and perduring covenant.

A biblical theology of marriage could more easily affirm the fuller theological concept of covenant than that of a limited synallagmatic contract. In Scripture, marriage reflects a covenant of life with life. This covenant of life and love has among its specifying characteristics the free gift of the body and the common identity of cohabitation. Marriage is a marital community binding two persons into a common destiny. If there is no authentic community of marital life, as in the extreme cases of sociopathy and homosexuality, there is simply no real marriage. In these cases a marked deficiency of marriageable personality renders a human, heterosexual community impossible. The rich biblical concept of covenant is an avenue of genuinely traditional theology to release decisions from the narrowness of a contractual stricture. The meaning of covenant emphasizes that which is truly human and unique about marriage. The unity of life toward which man- and womanhood, our sexuality, points is the covenant of life with life. What excludes this total covenanting excludes marriage. Within such a conceptualization development can be expected with fidelity to the underlying principles of tradition.

Furthermore, the meaning of marital affection has a long and good history in canonical literature. Marital affection in the pre-tridentine canonists is what characterized both the consent and the union of husband and wife. Consent to marriage is much more than consent to those acts which are suited to reproduction. This type of consent leads to fornication and concubinage, not marriage. Consent to marriage involves the deepest kind of commitment to the personhood of the other and the intention of joining life with him as spouse. Unfortunately, the exigencies of proof confined the use of marital affection in judicial procedure. How do you prove marital affection existed or did not exist? The legal tendency evolved to measure the presence of marital affection by the desire for the three goods of marriage, i.e., offspring, fidelity and indissolubility. If these were excluded, there was no marital affection. In reality, however, marital affection even in the teachings of the early canonists is wider than the mere expression of the three goods would indicate. In many cases marital affection was actually proved or disproved in marriage ratified after having been contracted with force or fear. The problems of proof are not insurmountable. The meaning of validity in marriage certainly involves the intention and the possibility of taking another as a spouse. This considerably broadens contemporary grounds for nullity. Is it not more true to reality? Furthermore, can we not project in this line a development that would ultimately lead to antecedent and continuing extreme incompatibility as a grounds for nullity? Such a concept of incompatibility in terms of extreme alienation would be both traditional and mark an advance without a contradiction of Trent.

What is meant by saying that marriage is a "sacrament"? As the history of theology suggests, consciousness of the sacramentality of marriage emerged only gradually. And marriage still remains one of the most difficult of sacramental realities to grasp. For unlike the other sacraments, marriage cannot be considered abstractly or in purely sacramental terms. As we are accustomed to think, a true and valid Baptism is a sacrament or it is not true and valid. But a true and valid marriage which is not considered a sacrament can still be acknowledged as a true and valid marriage. And thus an important question is raised.

Where is the sacramental reality in marriage located? When one speaks of the "sacrament" of marriage to what exactly is he referring? If it is a reality, in what does this reality consist? It cannot consist in either the canonical or ceremonial form of its celebration. Too narrow a focus on this aspect has led Karl Barth to suggest that Catholics do not have a theology of marriage so much as a theology of the marriage ceremony.

And, in fact, there do seem to be instances in which a marriage might easily be recognized by Catholics as sacramental even when these formalities could not be observed.

Is sacramentality located in the religious character of the marital "vows"? Apparently not, for a marriage can embody a genuine religious commitment to each other by the married partners without being technically considered a "sacrament." It cannot be located in the "consent" of marriage, either, because free consent is necessary for any marriage, whether "sacramental" or not. The mere intention to contract permanent union or to be absolutely faithful does not constitute the sacrament, for such an intention is common to many marriages outside the Christian community which are not considered in sacramental terms.

The sacrament cannot be effected simply by the intention of the partners to bring about a sacramental action when they marry, as this sort of interiorization of the sacrament would fail to fully account for its sign value. An intention is not an external sign, as a sacrament must be in order to be recognized as such.

The sacramentality of marriage cannot be located in the contractual institution of marriage since this, too, is present and effectual in all marriages. The very fact that Christian marriage has an ecclesiological or eschatological significance does not constitute it as a sacrament, since virginity is traditionally recognized to contain equally ecclesiological and eschatological significance and yet is not thought of technically as a sacrament.

If one suggests that the sacramentality of marriage consists in its having been so instituted by Christ, then further questions must be asked to avoid begging the issue. If Christ "instituted" marriage as a sacrament, what precisely did He effect in so doing? Long before and long after Christ, genuine marriages occur which Catholics do not normally consider as technically "sacramental." Is one then to presume that Christ did not "institute" these marriages? If so, what does this mean? Have some marriages been transformed by Christ in the Church and given a new reality so that they are really, even categorically, different? Does this not return us to the original question, in what does this new reality, the sacramental reality consist? It cannot be an absolute degree of indissolubility, because unconsummated "sacramental" marriages are dissolved.

What these plain but insistent questions strive to do is obviate an excessive formalism of response. Is there any static category that can be made a niche into which the sacramentality of marriage can be fitted? For trained ecclesiastics who too readily assume that the difference between sacramental and nonsacramental marriages is a clear one, it is worthwhile to ask if this difference is in any way experiential in the lives of married people. Unless one takes the position that sacraments have no term of reference in human experience, the hesitancy of response to such a question should itself be enlightening.

The effort to evade formalism must be made, for formalism in theology can lead to absolutism in law. The institution of marriage may flow from the sacrament, at least in part, or it may be infused with a new meaning because of the sacrament. But if the institution and sacrament are not truly related but merely confused, then a sacral absolutism can effect the legislation of the Church concerning even the institutional or contractual aspects of married life.

Pursuing the possibilities of a deeper development in the Christian consciousness of the sacramentality of marriage, one might advance a series of related suggestions. The teaching of "what God has joined together" may not refer to a contractual institution, but rather be intended to be evocative of Genesis and refer to the union in the flesh of man and woman. God is not somehow the "bond" of the marital contract. This would more readily account for the practice of the early Church of setting aside marital contracts for the sake of the Kingdom as well as the ongoing practice of the Church through history in annuling marriage contracts surrounding sacramental unions. It would also account for the hesitation of the Church to annul consummated marriages without escalating that hesitation into an absolute impossibility.

The sacramental character of marriage involves a relationship to the Church and to the reality of the world. It has a cosmic dimension. We have achieved in recent years a much more fully developed historical sense of the sacraments. This has provoked serious questions about the absoluteness of an essentialistic or abstract understanding of them. What an awareness of their cosmic dimensions will add is the clear consciousness that sacraments are not merely standardized ritual patterns of action applied to an unlimited succession of individual recipients in a basically repetitious manner, but are Christo-centric dynamisms which under symbolic form project and guide the further course of man. The symbolism of marriage, its sacramental sign and transcendant meaning bespeak an awareness of the sacred transformation of the human processes of life.

In this perspective, is not the legal category of "validity" quite confining and inadequate when one seeks to reflect on the full scope of sacramental action? Are not the Christian sacraments linked in a deep continuum with the religious projections of man as man rather than isolated in categoric difference and distinction from all other unifying events? Of the "established" sacraments, marriage is one which most forcefully suggests a "yes" to that question.

Accordingly, in regard to the nature of the decision made in response to questions bearing upon the existence of particular marriages, a correlative deepening of the understanding of marriage would mark more closely the limitations of human capability for judgment. Both as a sacrament and as an intricately complex interpersonal relationship marriage in its essential and dynamic reality may exceed the grasp of objective comprehension in a particular case. Can any third party be morally certain of the substantial absence of a true marital relationship? Furthermore, does not such a decision presume to enter with clarity an area of sacramental mystery? Perhaps judicial decisions should be more modestly drawn.

Both the oriental traditions and the ancient canonical practice of the West refrained from deciding absolute nullity. A decision, when called for, was not that there was no marriage, but rather that in certain circumstances remarriage would be allowed. When in reality spouses no longer lived together as husband and wife, there were conditions in which one or other of them was allowed to marry another. The significance of the former marriage was simply left unexplored. How can it be said that marriage continues to exist when there is no common life and no real union of either mind or person between those who were formerly husband and wife?

This occasions a further question: in order to reach moral certitude regarding the nullity of a particular marriage, does not a third party have to shrink its meaning to fit it into a manageable human construct? Is this not precisely what has happened when marriage is robbed of both the richness of personal interaction and its divine mystery in confinement to the prescriptions for validity of contractual consent? The judicial process, as a human means for arriving at truth, always falls short in its approximation of reality. This essential imperfection of human law and human judgment should be plainly acknowledged in canonical procedure to temper the meaning of moral certitude, and in many cases even to alter the object of decision itself.

Marriage as a human reality and a divine mystery cannot be completed in a single moment of time. Indeed, marriage is a state of life and a permanent sacrament. One of the underlying difficulties in current canonical practice, however, is the persistent determination to fix the fullness of sign and sacramentality upon a moment of consent. Fixation upon particular moments to discover when the sacrament comes into being is a juridical compulsion. The static and departmentalized, however, is but a single mode of comprehension of the dynamic processes of life.

The system of ecclesiastical courts of the Catholic Church for the adjudication of marriage cases is a unique religious phenomenon. It is a late development in the life of the Church. The present procedures followed in the courts stem largely from the legislation of Pope Benedict XIV (+1758) and the rules adopted in the nineteenth century by the Roman Rota. The procedural principles of the Italian Civil Code formed the basis of the treatise on processes of the 1917 Code of Canon Law. This discipline reflects but a single mentality in the Church and a legal philosophy notably at variance with the spirit of American jurisprudence. The role of the Church in directing the marriages of people who live in vastly diverse cultural and social circumstances need not be narrowed to a single procedural discipline. The very confidence that the faithful should have in the law of the Church demands that that law reflect the best legal tradition known to them. Thus both a departure from strictly contractual law and a great flexibility for adaptation in procedural law should be expected in the reform of canon law.

The responsibility of the Church for the marriages of Christians can be expressed in many different ways. The traditional role exercised by the Church in deciding marriage cases could be met by summary administrative processes, similar to counselling sessions. Within the ecclesiology of Vatican II should not a fuller responsibility for these cases be placed once again upon the shoulders of the local bishops? The regional and national conferences of bishops can well decide procedures that fit the Christian and cultural standards of their people. The system of accusatorial court practice need not prevail. Finally, the good of persons individually and the Church as a whole would seem to call for the fullest measure of confidence in the just and expeditious solution of all marriage cases at the local level.

5

The Indissolubility of Christian Marriage and the Common Good

LOUIS AND CONSTANCE DUPRÉ[*]

The Church's present position on the indissolubility of marriage is based upon a certain interpretation of the Scripture, more than upon the natural law. All philosophical arguments must therefore be viewed as additional evidence corroborating this reading of the Scripture, not as the only or even the main support of its position. We insist on this point in the beginning in order to place the present study in proper perspective.

Yet if the main argument is scriptural, the authority of the Church's traditional reading of the Scripture far surpasses that of any exegetic support. It is therefore necessary to determine what has been defined authoritatively by the Church. As late as the sixteenth century

[*] Professor of Philosophy, Georgetown University. Mrs. Dupré is an attorney with the Office of Economic Opportunity in Washington. Prof. Dupré is the author of *Kierkegaard as Theologian* (1953), *Contraception and Catholics* (1964), *The Philosophical Foundations of Marxism* (1966). He is co-editor of *Approaches to Morality* (1966) and editor of *Revelation and Reflection* (1968).

some theologians denied that there was a fully authoritative definition on this issue. Cardinal Cajetan, after having interpreted Mt 19,9 as clearly permitting divorce and remarriage, concludes: "I understand from this law of Our Lord Jesus Christ that a Christian is allowed to dismiss his wife because of adultery on her part and is allowed to marry another woman. But my interpretation is subject to a definition of the Pope, which so far however is not extant."[1] Somewhat in the same vein is the position of Catharinus, one of the most important Fathers of the Council of Trent, who in his *Annotationes contra Cajetanum* (1542) concurs in Cajetan's conclusion and considers the existing legislation simply a legitimate means to prevent the increase of adultery.[2]

With Trent the picture changes altogether and we have two canons on the indissolubility of marriage. "If anyone says that the marriage bond can be dissolved by reason of heresy, domestic incompatibility, or willful desertion by one of the parties: let him be anathema."[3] "If anyone says that the Church is in error when it has taught and does teach according to the doctrine of the Gospels and apostles that the marriage bond cannot be dissolved because of adultery on the part of either the

---

[1] *Comment. in Evang. S. Matt.*, xix, 9.

[2] See G. H. Joyce, *Christian Marriage* (2nd ed., London, 1948), p. 393. See on all this also F. von Gunten, O.P., "La doctrine de Cajetan sur l'indissolubilité du mariage," *Angelicum*, XLIII (1966), 62-72.

[3] Denz, n. 1805.

husband or the wife; and that neither party, not even the innocent one who gave no cause for the adultery, can contract another marriage while the other party is still living and that adultery is committed both by the husband who dismisses his adulterous wife and marries again and by the wife who dismisses her adulterous husband and marries again: let him be anathema."[4] For adultery only the charge of error on the part of the Roman Church is condemned. Divorce after adultery was not *directly* condemned in order to avoid displeasing the Republic of Venice by proscribing the existing practice of its many Greek subjects. However, divorce and remarriage because of desertion and incompatibility are condemned outright. Some theologians claim that the canon on adultery also affirms dogmatically that marriage remains indissoluble after adultery.[5] But this theory is not generally accepted.

To make our argument more stringent, we will not go into the problem of the "theological qualifications" of the Trent canons. According to a well-known thesis, they were not intended as dogmatic definitions but rather as disciplinary rules.[6] Yet that does not necessarily make them less *binding* in faith. We also leave out of consideration the question of whether Trent decided that a mar-

---

[4] Denz. n. 1807.

[5] C. Palmieri, *De Matrimonio* (Rome, 1880), p. 142.

[6] Peter Fransen, S.J., "Réflexions sur l'anthème au Concile de Trente," *Ephemerides Theologicae Lovanienses*, 29 (1953), 657-672.

riage *could* not be dissolved by the Church or simply that it *should* not be dissolved by the Church.[7] We will simply assume that a direct condemnation forecloses any further discussion.

The arguments behind the Church's negative attitude toward divorce are based partly upon the sacramental nature of matrimony, partly upon divine positive law and partly upon the natural law. First let us consider the sacramental character. Among many other documents, the Council of Florence (1438-1445) declares matrimony indissoluble "because it signifies the indivisible union of Christ with the Church."[8] *Casti Connubii* strongly emphasizes the relation between the sacramental symbolism and the indissolubility of marriage: "Never, for any reason whatsoever can this sort of possibility [dissolution of a marriage as in the Pauline privilege] occur for a sacramental, consummated Christian marriage. For such a marriage, as it realizes the fullness of the marriage bond, has, by the will of God, supreme stability and indissolubility, and may never be undone by man's power."[9]

A comparison between these and other texts on indissolubility as resulting from the sacramental character of marriage seems to lead to two conclusions. One, the sacramentality makes marriage *absolutely* indissoluble, while a nonsacramental marital contract still allows for

[7] William Van der Marck, "De recente ontwikkelingen in de theologie van het huweljk," *Tijdschrift voor Theologie*, 7 (1967), 127-140.

[8] Denz. n. 1327.

[9] Denz. n. 3712.

certain exceptions. Two, the sacramental nature "strengthens the indissoluble unity" of the nonsacramental marriage.[10] Apart from the Pauline privilege, the sacramental character merely confirms an indissolubility which exists independently of the sacrament. Even the possibility of dissolving a *matrimonium ratum non consummatum* seems to result from an incompleteness in the marriage contract rather than from an incompleteness in the sacrament. Otherwise we would have to assume that the sacrament is fully constituted only in the physical consummation of marriage, rather than in the act of consent as theology has traditionally thought. Such an assumption would imply that those who for religious reasons abstain from the consummation of marriage are never able to share the fullness of the sacrament. But even if we consider sexual intercourse an integral part of the sacramental union, it still remains obscure why only this final stage of the sacrament should make the marriage absolutely indissoluble. On all these grounds one may well conclude that the sacrament alone does not constitute the indissolubility, nor does it exclude dissolutions which would be possible in nonsacramental marriages (save for the Pauline privilege). The sacrament gives a symbolic dimension to the marriage contract, but it does not make it more of a marriage, nor does it change the contract from being generally indissoluble to being absolutely indissoluble. The indissolubility is "strengthened" by the sacramental character because the natural obligation now also becomes a sacred

[10] Denz. n. 1797.

commitment. We feel therefore justified to repeat what we wrote at an earlier occasion: "The marital obligations of the Christian are essentially the same as those of the non-Christian, although the former has stronger motives to fulfill them."[11]

This conclusion obviously does not take away from the Church's legislative authority in these matters. Aside from the fact that for almost a millennium the Church was the only true society beyond the family, marriage for the Christian is even today a sacrament and therefore subject to the Church's regulation.[12] But since the sacrament only sanctions and deepens a natural contract and a natural institution, the Church's legislation must basically follow the nature of this institution and this contract. We therefore should analyze its indissolubility from the point of view of natural law.

Most medieval authors held that the indissolubility of marriage is a point of natural law as well as of divine positive law. Yet the arguments which they present for the natural law conclude at most to a relative indissolu-

[11] "How Indissoluble Is a Catholic Marriage?", *The National Catholic Reporter* (March 8, 1967).

[12] The Church's right to regulate in sacramental matters does not necessarily entail the need for a detailed legislation of a natural institution, particularly today when the state itself takes care of such legislation. In fact, there was little or no canonical legislation of marriage before Trent. (See P. J. M. Huizing: *De Trentse Huwelijksvorm* [Bussum, 1966].) But the purpose of the present paper is to show that even if one grants the appropriateness of the Church's legislative presence in the institutional aspects of marriage, some of this legislation should be reexamined.

bility (perhaps better termed "stability"). G. H. Joyce describes the problem as the medieval theologian saw it: "It was manifest that the law of nature demands that the union of husband and wife should, in general, be permanent: were it otherwise it would fail of its essential purpose. For the chief end of marriage is not the advantage of the married pair, but the procreation and due training, physical, intellectual and moral, of the offspring: this would be impossible were the marriage liable to be hastily dissolved. Was it, however, possible to go further, and say that it must be altogether indissoluble?"[13] In his Commentary on the *Sententiae*, St. Thomas considers the problem exclusively from the point of view of the offspring.[14] To justify indissolubility after the children have grown up, he falls back upon a feudal concept of marriage as a property channel and concludes that the parents must provide for the children during their entire lives by ensuring them the best possible inheritance after their death. Apparently this argument was satisfying, for it was repeated much later in the *Supplement to the Summa Theologiae*.[15] Even the objection of a childless marriage in which one of the partners would be able to have offspring with another spouse does not disturb him too much. He simply answers: "Matrimony is directed toward the common good principally by its primary end, the good of the offspring. Yet by its secondary end, it is also directed toward the good of the person who contracts it, namely,

---

[13] *Op. cit.*, p. 384.
[14] *Sent.* IV, d., qu. 2a,2.
[15] Qu. 67, a.1. *Suppl.*

as a remedy against concupiscence. Therefore the laws of marriage are made more in view of what is good for all than of what may be beneficial to one. Even though the inseparability may prevent the good of the offspring for one man, it still is convenient for the good of offspring in general."[16]

This, of course, is a very poor argument.[17] For although Thomas is right in presuming that the institution poses certain requirements that are not inherent to the individual contract, it does not follow that a general dispensation for sterile marriages would affect the indissolubility of fertile marriages. Thomas himself seems to realize that his argument does not carry too far, for he adds in the next article that although indissolubility is required by the law of nature, it falls under the secondary precepts of this law, which allow for exceptions.

Because of the dearth of good arguments and perhaps also because of the permission accorded to the Jews to divorce their wives, many medieval theologians did not consider the absolute indissolubility of marriage a precept of natural law but of divine positive law. However, since the words of Christ on the indissolubility of marriage were addressed to unbaptized Jews, they were assumed to apply

[16] *Ibid.*, ad 4um.

[17] But not so poor as one advanced by a contemporary commentary on Canon Law in favor of marital indissolubility: "the irreparable consequence which the consummation of marriage entails for the bride." Bouscaren and Ellis, *Canon Law: A Text and Commentary*, p. 447 (1957).

universally and not only to Christians.[18] This assumption is reflected in the decretal of Innocent III ordering converts who before their baptism had divorced their first legal wife, to return to her. Even here, then, we see that the sacramental character is not the determining element for indissolubility: it merely confirms the universal, divine positive law.

The argument for indissolubility based upon revelation still retains its force as long as one does not interpret it in a legalistic way, as if God by a special decree imposed indissolubility upon the institution independently of the intentions of those who enter into it. As the Dutch canonist P. J. M. Huizing writes: "Indissolubility does not mean that the two spouses enter upon a state which is indissoluble by God's will whether they want it or not. Indissolubility means that the spouses themselves in a Christian marriage *want* to conclude an unbreakable bond."[19]

Returning now to the natural law, it would seem to us that three essential values are at stake: the interpersonal relationship between the spouses, the well-being of the children and the good of society as a whole. Many of our contemporaries decide the issue exclusively on the basis of the first factor. They conclude that marriage is "indissoluble" only as long as it psychologically enriches both partners, which for all practical purposes means, as long as

---

[18] Joyce, *op. cit.*, pp. 381-386.
[19] "Katholieke Kerk en Huwelijksorde" in *Bijdragen*, 27 (1966), 384.

they do not want to dissolve it. Aside from the fact that the relations between the spouses alone is too narrow a basis for a decision in which society as a whole has a stake, this attitude may jeopardize the very ideal which inspires it. Indeed, to many escapists the very possibility of "getting out" could weaken their efforts to overcome inevitable difficulties.

The second factor is the well-being of the children. An harmonious education definitely requires a stable home. Yet, it does not necessarily require absolute indissolubility. Indeed, the choice is often not between a stable and an unstable home, but between a stable misery and a less miserable change. It has been questioned whether the child profits from keeping the relationship together for his sake once the personal community of the parents has been destroyed.[20] By eliminating divorce, one does not eliminate broken homes.[21] The alternative is often not even a miserable home, but parental desertion or Church-approved separation. By permitting separation while excluding the possibility of a new marriage, one may well deprive the child of sufficient material support as well as of what he needs most under the circumstances—a second parent.

But however weak the argument based on the *bonum prolis* may be, particularly in the case of a sterile marriage, it has at least the merit of pointing out that a marriage

[20] See Rosemary Ruether, "Divorce: No Longer Unthinkable," *The Commonweal*, (April 14, 1967), 118.

[21] See Max Rheinstein, "The Law of Divorce and the Problem of Marriage Stability," *Vanderbilt Law Review*, 9 (1956), 633, 645-648.

contract always involves more than a private agreement between two individuals. Marriage is also a social institution in which the common good is at stake. The notion of "common good" (*bonum commune*) is the good of society as a whole, that is, the good of the relations between the individuals, but always considered with respect to the individual well-being of the members who compose this totality.[22] The inevitable tension between the totality and its individual parts gives the common good a dynamic character. Jacques Maritain describes this tension in the following terms:

> The end of society is the good of the community, the good of the social body. But if this good of the social body is not understood to be a common good of *human persons*, just as the social body itself is a whole of human persons, this conception would lead in its turn to other errors of a totalitarian type. The common good of the body politic is neither the mere collection of private goods, nor the good of a whole which, like the species with respect to its individuals or the hive with respect to its bees, draws the parts to itself alone and sacrifices them to itself. It is the good *human* life of the multitude, of a multitude of persons; it is their communion in good living. It is therefore common *to the whole and to the parts*.[23]

Since the common good consists of an ordered heirarchy of values, the balance between the good of society as a

[22] See, e.g., Morris Ginsberg, *On Justice in Society* (Baltimore, 1965), p. 81.

[23] *The Person and the Common Good*, trans. by John J. Fitzgerald (London, 1941), p. 39.

whole and the good of individuals constantly varies. As the individuals develop themselves culturally and economically, the interests of society change, and so does the relation between the two. In past centuries the social order was viewed as something to be preserved through a maximum of stability and a minimum of change. In our present civilization, the ideas of progress and evolution have made the social order much more dynamic. Concentrating on the relation between society and individuals, we notice that in a stage of society where a social institution needs all possible protection, legislation is directed almost entirely toward that end. But where the basic institution is already solidly established, legislation more and more recognizes the rights of the individual as expressed in contractual and other relationships. The difference between an institution and a mere contractual agreement is that the conditions of an institution affect not only the particular relationships of its members, but society as a whole.

Marriage is obviously an institution in which the community has a legitimate interest. At the same time, it is an inter-individual agreement based upon the most sacred rights of the person. We may say that it is a contract resulting in an institution. A decision of the United States Supreme Court in 1888 defines the relation between the two as follows: "The consent of the parties is of course essential to its existence, but when the contract to marry is executed by the marriage, a relation between the parties is created which they cannot change. Other contracts may be modified, restricted, or enlarged, or entirely released upon the consent of the parties. Not so with marriage. The relation once formed, the law steps in and holds the parties to various obligations and liabilities. It is an institution, in the maintenance of which in its purity the public is deeply interested."[24]

The question now is: What sort of marital stability does the balance of the common good between society as a whole and the rights of its individuals require today? The older legal concept of marriage, which almost exclusively considered its institutional aspect, required all but absolute indissolubility. This alone, it was believed, could elevate marriage entirely above the contractual freedom of the individual parties and ensure a stable society, well equipped to provide for its new members. In 1790 Sir William Scott gave a classical expression to this institutional view of marriage and its need for indissolubility.

Though in particular cases the repugnance of the law to dissolve the obligations of matrimonial cohabitation may operate with great severity upon individuals; yet it must be carefully remembered that the general happiness of the married life is secured by its indissolubility. When people understand that they must live together, except for a very few reasons known to the law, they learn to soften by mutual accommodation that yoke which they know they cannot shake off; they become good husbands and good wives from the necessity of remaining husbands and wives; for necessity is a powerful master in teaching the duties which it imposes. If it were once understood that upon mutual disgust married persons might be legally separated, many couples

[24] Maynard v. Hill, 125 U.S. 190.

who now pass through the world with mutual comfort, with attention to their common offspring and to the moral order of civil society, might have been at this moment living in a state of mutual unkindness, in a state of estrangement from their common offspring and the moral order of civil society, and in a state of the most licentious and unreserved immorality. In this case, as in many others, the happiness of some individuals must be sacrificed to the greater and more general good.[25]

In this text the stability of marriage is raised almost to absolute indissolubility. Nothing short of a direct threat to a spouse's life is a sufficient ground for separation on the basis of cruelty.

Such views were justified by the vital importance of the family for the fulfillment of most society needs. In most cases, education, recreation, protection all used to be provided exclusively by the family. From an economic point of view the family was the most important unit of production as well as *the* means of channeling the disposition of property. Over the last century enormous social-economic changes have transferred most of these functions, either partly or in their entirety, to other institutions. On the other hand, the importance of the family for companionship and a fulfillment of psychological needs has increased.[26] The civil law reflects these changes by de-emphasizing the institutional aspect of marriage in favor of the contractual (the juridical sanction of the bond be-

[25] Evans v. Evans, 1 Hagg. Con. 35, 161 Eng. Rep. 466.

[26] On this, one may consult Burgess and Locke, *The Family from Institution to Companionship* (New York, 1953), pp. 483 ff.

tween the two partners). We perceive this development in an extension of the definition of extreme cruelty to cover any unjustifiable, prolonged course of action by which one spouse deprives the other from attaining the ends of marriage.[27] It is evident also in the acceptance as grounds for divorce of any conduct by one spouse which compels the other to leave.

Simultaneously with the emphasis on the interpersonal aspect of marriage and partly as a result of it, a reevaluation of indissolubility as the optimum means of protecting the institution has taken place. Continuing a relation in which the legitimate ends of marriage have been destroyed long ago has a harmful rather than a beneficial effect upon the institution. As Justice Traynor writes in a 1952 California case: "The disruptive effect of divorce upon children is to be deplored, but in a given case it may be preferable to violence, hatred, or immorality when these are present in the home. The community as a whole also has an interest. Adultery, desertion, or cruelty, for example, *can only discredit marriage; their perpetuation is not lightly to be decreed.*"[28] It is now recognized that civil law should steer a realistic middle course between laxity and rigidity. The former encourages a sexual license that may lead to a total disintegration of the institution, as was amply illustrated in the Soviet Union after its introduction of new marriage laws subsequent to the Revolution. The latter becomes just as destructive of the institution when

[27] *E.g.*, Brown v. Brown, 171 Kan. 249, 232 P.2d 603 (1951).
[28] De Burgh v. De Burgh, 39 Cal. 2d 858, 250 P.2d 598 (emphasis added).

it no longer reflects the accepted standards of behavior and results "in meretricious relations, which would also be an impairment of the institution."[29]

In other areas of family law there has been a similar trend toward recognition of individual rights and duties and away from the unconditional protection of the family status (the institutional aspect). Rather than unconditionally granting the estranged wife a certain amount of material support, the law now takes into account each individual situation during separation or after divorce. Also, children born out of wedlock are no longer the victims of the bypassing of the marriage institution by their parents, and are gradually being granted many of the rights of legitimate offspring (including legitimacy itself).

A law always reflects the social and cultural conditions of the period which made it. As Cardozo pointed out, the conceptions at the basis of the law, rather than resulting from a purely logical, intrinsic process of thought, are accepted standards of a particular period.[30] A system of law, then, must be evaluated in terms of the factors which produced it. However, once the body of law is constituted, it acquires some degree of autonomy and consistency of its own. This independence of legal conceptions which originated in a different cultural and moral past makes necessary periodic adjustments to current social-economic and cultural needs.

[29] William McCurdy, "Divorce—A Suggested Approach," *Vanderbilt Law Review*, 9 (1956), 685, 706.

[30] Benjamin Cardozo, *The Nature of the Judicial Process* (New Haven, 1965), pp. 55, 112.

Does the Church's legislation on divorce sufficiently reflect the change in balance between the institutional and the individual aspects of marriage that has taken place in modern life? Is absolute indissolubility still the best way to protect the institution of marriage and to promote the common good? These are the two basic questions to ask. Yet before they can be answered we must be sufficiently sure that the Church itself has recognized the shift in balance between the institutional and the personal aspects of marriage. Otherwise, one might still argue that the civil law in liberalizing its restrictions on divorce is merely ceding to the moral decadence of modern times, as conservative Catholics often say at every single change in law concerning religion or morality. Reading the recent documents on marriage from Leo XIII on, we cannot but notice the unprecedented emphasis on the rights of the individual. In *Rerum Novarum* Leo XIII wrote: "In the choice of a state of life there can be no doubt that everyone has the power and the freedom to choose one of two courses: Either to follow the counsel of Jesus Christ about virginity, or to bind himself with the marriage bond. No man-made law can take away the natural and fundamental right of man to marry, nor can it in any way delimit the principal purpose of marriage, originally established by God's authority: 'Increase and multiply.' "[31] This freedom was never affirmed more strongly than in the recent constitution on *The Church and the Modern World*.

[31] AAS, 23 (1890/91) p. 645. This text was quoted by Pius XI in *Casti Connubii*.

Yet when it comes to the actual recognition of these individual rights, Canon Law remains exactly where it was hundreds of years ago. In cases where an annulment is sought, the presumption is still entirely on the side of the institution, that is, of the existing contract. May we not consider the institution as sufficiently established to allow the presumption to be shifted to the side of individual rights? One could ask the even more basic question of whether maintaining social stability should still be the concern of the Church today or whether the Church should rather, as Father Huizing suggests, take pastoral care of its members according to each one's individual situation.[32] However, as we indicated earlier, the problem of the appropriateness of ecclesiastical legislation in matters of civil concern lies beyond the scope of this paper.

In the Pauline privilege, for centuries the Church has recognized the right of the individual over against the institution with respect to the full exercise of his supernatural gifts. Could not the Church extend the application of this principle and consider any behavior so disruptive of the marital relation and society itself as consistent infidelity a sufficient ground for the dissolution of marriage? Must the rights of the individual still be held secondary to the maintenance of the institution? What does the inalienable right to marital fulfillment mean when the marital relation is invariably subordinated to the existing contract, however weak the grounds are

[32] See "Katholieke Kerk en Huwelijksorde," 386.

which support the contract? Father Schillebeeckx in his book on marriage justifies the Pauline privilege by declaring the communion in faith an essential element of Christian marriage. According to him, the Pauline privilege is merely the acceptance of the self-dissolution of marriage in the interest of the baptized partner's life of faith.[33] But as we have pointed out elsewhere,[34] however important the elements of faith may be to a Christian marriage, other elements are even more essential to marriage itself. Prolonged adultery strikes at the heart of the marital relationship. May we not apply to fidelity what Schillebeeckx says about faith, namely, that it forms such an indispensable element in the marital relationship that without it this relationship practically ceases to exist.

[33] *Marriage, Human Reality and Saving Mystery* (New York, 1965), p. 158.
[34] "How Indissoluble Is a Catholic Marriage?", *loc. cit.*

COMMENT

AND

DISCUSSION

The best modern legal and social thought places singular emphasis upon the dignity of persons and their rights in the face of institutional demands. This personalist perspective is clearly discernible in the jurisprudential principles that safeguard the processes of justice in the free democratic societies of the world. It is also predominant in the teachings of the recent popes and the documents of the Vatican Council. The implications of a shift of emphasis from the institution to the person in the reform of the canon law of marriage can be seen in the two basic propositions offered in the paper. In all annulment and dissolution cases the presumption of law should favor the freedom of the individual over the exigencies of the institution of marriage. And, since persistent adultery strikes at the very heart of marriage, this should be considered an equitable ground for divorce with the right to remarry. Though some may wish to go further, these moderate recommendations should be carefully investigated as real possibilities consonant with traditional Catholic thought.

Two important sources of the present discipline of the Church, the Council of Florence and the Council of Trent, would not inhibit the Church's ability to adjust her discipline of marriage to the exigencies of a highly personalist approach. It is only in the *Decretum pro Armenis* that divorce and remarriage are forbidden by the Council of Florence. Theologians generally deny the infallible or conciliar character of this decree. At most this was a disciplinary decree coming after the closing of the Council sessions. Cardinal van Rossum, among many other theologians, has already raised serious questions about the theology of the sacrament of Holy Orders enunciated in the decree. Since the decisions of Pope Pius XII we know that, contrary to what the decree states, the conferral of the sacrament does not consist essentially in the handing over of the instruments of the priesthood. It consists in the form with the imposition of hands. The general acknowledgment of a change in the teaching regarding Holy Orders indicates that the *Decretum pro Armenis* is not doctrinally normative. We know also that Pope Eugene IV did not intend to condemn the practice of the Greeks in granting divorce with the right to remarry in the case of adultery. Joseph Gill, in his probing study of the Council of Florence, concludes that a doctrinal rapprochement with the Orthodox was agreed upon by the Latin Church. This was done with the knowledge and acceptance of the oriental traditions of divorce and remarriage because of adultery.

At the Council of Trent the objection of the ambassador of Venice was not directed to the fifth canon of the twenty-fourth session, in which adultery was not mentioned. It was to an earlier version of the canon, which was later modified at his insistence. The first version had been a straightforward condemnation of all divorce and remarriage. This was the opinion of many theologians at the time. But, as a matter of fact, the Council did not wish to accept so strong a statement. Thus the Council said merely that the Church had not erred in forbidding remarriage after divorce because of adultery. Trent did not intend to condemn the practice of the Orthodox. Thus we cannot conclude that the Council demanded absolute indissolubility as a point of doctrinal belief. This was largely a matter of disciplinary concern. The main issue was the holiness and sacramentality of marriage.

Trent affirmed for marriage the fullness of sacramentality. This means that the Council affirmed that Christ has sanctified the natural elements of the human reality and associated them with God's salvation and redemption. Whether the natural reality of marriage essentially depends on consent or marital affection, it is consecrated and given a new order of intentionality in the faith. But even this consecration does not so radically alter the basic human reality of marriage that it is intrinsically changed. Sacramentality does not, in fact, confer upon marriage an absolute indissolubility. This is evident from the fact that a ratified, i.e. sacramental, but not consummated, marriage can be dissolved. Thus the fact of sacramentality is not a cogent argument for absolute indissolubility.

Two categories of approach may be taken in the natural law arguments to support indissolubility. One is an approach from the outside in, an attempt to argue indissolubility as something necessary to marriage as a support. This is the nature of the argument found in St. Thomas and most of the scholastic tradition. This argument fails, however, in isolating the various elements of marriage from the whole and in absolutizing the social milieu of marriage. When this changes, as it has, the argument fails. Another category would be to look at marriage from the inside out. This would start, not by asking what is necessary for marriage, but what is marriage itself. It is essential to this latter argument to consider fully the human reality of marriage, precisely as it is lived in the present condition of mankind.

Historically, great importance has been placed upon the legal safeguards of the institution of marriage because of the investment individuals have in it, namely its value and functioning for them. Today many of the functions formerly handled by marriage are supplied by other institutions of society. This is particularly true in most areas of education and economic life. Yet marriage remains a precious institution to fulfill personal needs and establish values that are otherwise lost in contemporary society. Thus the institution and the person are still closely bound together. Marriage, as it serves individuals, serves the common good. But today is not the service of marriage so essentially personalist that without this dimension in actuality marriage has failed and ceased to exist? Without companionship and common life today there is simply no marriage. In a period of transition and development the influence of the Church must be brought to the task of shaping those forms of life for the future that will genuinely contribute to human fulfillment. This demands a continuing sensitivity to the human situation of the present and a willingness to put aside outmoded traditions in favor of more positive alternatives.

The basic question is not a choice between individual rights and the institution of marriage. When these two have become exclusive of each other there is something very wrong. The real issue is one of emphasis. Today emphasis upon the interpersonal elements of marriage is long overdue for the good of the institution itself.

A general trend from institutional to individual rights does not necessarily indicate growth and maturation. In some areas of society this may be seen more correctly as a deterioration than an evolution. In some social institutions progress enables people to move from status to contract. But there is also evidence that some things mature in a movement from contract to status. For example, labor legislation in the United States has developed since the nineteenth century away from individualized contracts to a protected institutional status. The Roman legislation on marriage between the second and sixth centuries fluctuated from individual freedom to a great emphasis upon the institution. These developments responded to the real needs of society. But directions can be reversed, making the plotting of a unilinear process of development difficult. Thus today generalizations on both sides of individual social facts are precarious. Though the divorce rate would indicate that some doubt can be cast upon the relative safety of the institution of marriage, this sociological observation does not alter the judgment that a growth in respect for personal freedom and responsibility is a valid indication of social progress.

Finally, it may be observed from a civil point of view, that to speak of fault in the breakdown of marriage today is a legal anachronism. The divorce system may favor fault as a legal fiction. The actual reasons for divorce, however, tend simply to acknowledge the fact that, for one reason or another, the marriage has practically ceased to exist and cannot be restored. We could be a century out of date in arguing for adultery as the only exception to the absolute indissolubility of marriage. From the traditional point of view, adultery as an exception can be reconciled with the teachings of the Council of Trent. The substantial reasoning for this exception, however, would also obtain in other cases of complete marital failure, such as desertion or insanity. Thus there are valid theological and psychological reasons for arguing for the enlargement of the grounds for divorce in view of the practical cessation of married life in individual cases.

6

Psychological Influences on the Matrimonial Bond

JOHN W. HIGGINS, M.D. [*]

The context for the application of knowledge from the psychological sciences to considerations of matrimony is the relevance of health to establishing and maintaining the marital relationship. The major source of the most applicable and probably valid information comes from the clinical enterprise—that is, from experiences of the treatment of human problems and illness. For the most part, this origin of the information from—strictly speaking —*pathology* has not been fundamentally troublesome, since most of the familiar questions have related not to health, but to sickness. In fact, the ostensible readiness with which psychiatric expertness has been sought and used has tended both to bypass some real uncertainties and to ignore potential contributions to deeper questions relating to marriage.

This essay will review briefly some aspects and problems of the more familiar application of psychologic-psychiatric knowledge and then proceed to some slightly less

[*] Associate Professor of Clinical Psychiatry, Saint Louis University School of Medicine.

familiar aspects, particularly in regard to "neurosis" and
to the "normal."

SERIOUS PATHOLOGY AND THE
VALIDITY OF MARRIAGE

When psychiatry is defined as that medical specialty
devoted to the diagnosis, treatment and prevention of
mental disorder, its right to comment on the relation of
behavioral pathology to particular issues is generally re-
spected. The most common matrimonial problem of law
for which psychiatric opinion is sought has been and is
for some time likely to be the question of impediments to
validity. The principle is that demonstrable serious mental illness of different varieties may be adjudged to block
the individual's capacity to contract a marriage. This es-
timably humane position deserves protection and support. While psychiatry can clearly do this, at the same
time its ability to do so faces limitations.

First, as befits any scientific enterprise, there are unsettled issues within psychiatry about many features of
mental illnesses, most notably about their etiology. Yet,
while these vexing uncertainties remain, they do not con-
note absolute ignorance. For instance, in regard to the
generally agreed-upon "most serious" illness, schizophrenia, research into etiology continues, but at the same
time there is massive evidence that disturbances in family
constellation are highly important. Even in connection
with this illness, with all its puzzles, there are facts which,
for one reason or other, are insufficiently applied to ques-

tions about the marital contract. For example, the well-known possibility of insidious onset is not reflected in the requirement of "hard" evidence, such as a history of hospitalization or strenuous treatment to support the presence of illness. Nonexpert testimony may be all that is available to "prove" the previous existence of grave illness, particularly among the lower classes who may be very late in undertaking medical care. Therefore, ways must be sought to use and to evaluate such testimony more fully.

The predictable duration, the variability of course, the response or nonresponse to treatment are significant features in weighing the influence of illness on forming and maintaining a marital union. Such matters are just as weighty as the clinical diagnosis itself. In regard to grave psychiatric illness, the most painful problems are those "chronic" disorders from which recovery is improbable and when a perhaps young spouse has, in effect, no longer a meaningful marital partner, albeit a living one.[1]

Further—but properly—to complicate the matter, it is widely held in expert circles that clinical diagnosis alone is not a crucial index of aptness for marriage. For example, today the diagnosis of schizophrenia is fairly freely applied by some and thus includes patients who fall far short of the stereotyped psychotic on the disturbed ward of the mental hospital. A "borderline schizophrenic" (and even more definably "sick" people) may form as osten-

---

[1] J. Higgins, "Schizophrenia as a Consideration in the Annulment of Marriage," *Bulletin of the Guild of Catholic Psychiatrists,* 7 (1960), 87.

sibly "good" marriage. With some exceptions, we have no clear basis for universal predictions that such and such an illness per se precludes a lasting marriage, although the marriage may not be a "good" one. Only one author[2] tentatively proposes that there is high predictability of failure on the basis of the clinical diagnosis alone; this is in the instance of the marriage of a woman diagnosed as hysterical personality to a man diagnosed as paranoid. However concretely this opinion is to be taken is moot, but it touches on an issue which is less controversial. This is that the actually expected interaction of the marital partners is more important than what the clinical diagnosis may be for either of the spouses. Needless to say, this is difficult to predict.

Still another point can be raised about clinical diagnosis. Simply stated, the clinical diagnosis is ordinarily no more than an agreed upon name for constellations of behavioral signs and symptoms. The consensus concerning proper criteria for diagnoses is the principal safeguard against the ever-present danger of the influence of personal bias. The danger is that a clinical diagnosis has the potential for being a pejorative judgment—for becoming a name given to what is not liked or agreed with. This becomes a specially hazardous matter in the diagnosis of character disorders (as distinguished from symptomatic disorders) when the diagnosis comes close to being a judgment that the behavior in question is not acceptable by conventional social or moral codes.

[2] N. Reider, "Problems in the Prediction of Marital Adjustment," in *Neurotic Interaction in Marriage*, ed. V. Eisenstein (New York, 1956), chap. XVII.

In this connection, three points seem worth emphasizing. One is a warning about too easy reliance on anecdotal accounts in support of a diagnosis. Such accounts always need to be carefully scrutinized and considered from the viewpoint of differential diagnosis. The second is a strong recommendation that those who utilize psychiatric knowledge in judging marriages should continually seek up-to-date authoritative psychiatric sources.[3] Third, when at all possible, psychiatric opinion ought to be removed from the role of legal adversary and be considered in an advisory capacity to the court.

NEUROSIS AND MARRIAGE

In regard to questions of the validity of the marriage contract, the psychoneuroses and, in most instances, the "neurotic character disorders" are not frequently adduced as impediments. This is not because such diagnoses include nothing which could destroy a marriage.

There are several reasons for considering the relevance of *neurotic* disorders (psychoneuroses, neuroses, neurotic character disorders, etc.). One—not too important—reason has to do with the widespread use of the term, sometimes based on a supposition of clarity of definition which nowhere exists. Operationally, all clinicians know what a

[3] The following textbooks constitute excellent entries into current American psychiatric sources: (a) S. Arieti, ed., *American Handbook of Psychiatry* (New York, I & II, 1959, III, 1966); (b) A. M. Freedman and H. Kaplan, *Comprehensive Textbook of Psychiatry* (Baltimore, 1967); (c) R. Redlich and D. Freedman, *The Theory and Practice of Psychiatry* (New York, 1966).

neurosis is: a recognizable group of symptoms (of anxiety and depression and defenses against them), frequently precipitated by special experiences and, in the firm opinion of many, predisposed to by developmental circumstances. Beyond this, clear definition is in dispute. While casually referred to as "minor disorders" (in comparison with the psychoses) they are usually not "minor" to the afflicted individual and those close to him. A second reason is that by whatever definition, they are widespread enough so that on statistical grounds alone they may be expected to appear in the midst of marriage, which they do. In addition, on psychoanalytic theoretical grounds, they are capable of playing a crucially deleterious role in the maintenance of the marital union. Without here spelling out all the details, it seems reasonable that any exploration into the current state and problems of the bond of matrimony has to include awareness of the influence of neurosis.[4] The fundamental general thesis is that the same psychological forces and conflicts which eventuate in neurotic behavior can adversely influence the choice of mate in the first place and adversely influence the expectations of and participation in marriage in the second place.

Possibly the loudest spokesman for the role of neurosis in the causation of unhappy marriage was Edmund Bergler. The title of one of his books adequately conveys his view that "divorce won't help."[5] His point was that mari-

[4] An ample review of particularly the psychoanalytic literature about "neurosis and marriage" will be found in Eisenstein, *op. cit.*

[5] *Divorce Won't Help* (New York, 1966).

tal discord usually arises from neurotic conflict and that this conflict will last beyond divorce or separation and invest any new marriage. The problem left by him and others who emphasize neurosis is that they imply a distinction between those labelled "neurotic" and those not so-labelled which is often hard to find.

UNCONSCIOUS NEED AND MARRIAGE

It is not so much that the presence of an illness interferes with a marriage, but rather what that illness connotes, that is, the influence of neurotic needs, or—more generally and correctly—anxiety-provoking impulsions. Whether or not these impulsions eventuate in frank and recognizable illness, they play a role, and sometimes a discordant one, in human relations. The central ideas in regard to these needs are: first—however they are conceptualized—they exist; they seek satisfaction and inevitably are more or less frustrated; they require interaction with others; they develop, and the history of their mode of satisfaction is crucial in determining the structure of character. The psychoanalytic viewpoint emphasizes the meaningful relatedness of these needs to the body and, most importantly, maintains that "old" forms of needs may either persist into adult life or be revived in stressful conditions. However elaborated, the thesis is that human behavior is to be understood as a continuous process of seeking satisfaction which, psychologically speaking, is further understood as the reconciliation of inner needs and the demands of external reality. It is the mutual influence of the developing inner needs and the perception of external reality which instills the proper complexity into the meaning of "satisfaction", lest the term convey a wholly self-centered hedonism. For instance, in development, the individual incorporates the rules of his world which on becoming structured as personal standards become, too, needs or motives. The organized and organizing part of the personality—the ego— is, in health, in continuous development. One does not one day reach health and cling to it in the abstract thereafter. At any specific time, the inner needs of the individual, interacting with the reality as perceived, require a highly personal solution which may be more or less successful. Given the influence of developmental experience, very similar appearing circumstances of stress may be differently tolerated and responded to by different individuals.

In this context, marriage can be viewed as a state in which two people share and mutually satisfy their needs and in the process continue to grow. (If we had adequate measures for the last—growth—we could have a criterion for a "good" marriage.) The multitudinous variations among these needs, their interaction, the reality in which they exist and their modes of satisfaction are such that it is less a mystery why marriages are conflict-ridden than why they are not more so. Of the psychological forces favoring resolving the conflicts by maintaining monogamous union, a highly important one has to do with the ubiquitous human need to master the anxiety of separation from the primary object—the mother. Leo Stone refers to the institution of marriage as "the most general and comprehensive adult solution to the problem of separation." He adds that the usual eventuality of the birth of children closes the circle in unconscious fantasy through the parents' identification with the children.[6]

Other studies have attempted to examine more precisely the nature of the emotional aspects of marital interaction. Stein[7] has adduced evidence that in some marriages disturbances arise from the husband's apperceiving the wife dominantly as an extension of his own body, particularly the penis, so that his love (and hate and fear) of her is like that of his own body. Giovacchini[8] especially has been concerned with the symbiotic object relationship which he holds to be constructed in marriage. One form this may take requires similarity in underlying psychic conflicts, levels of psychosexual development and character structure for the maintenance of equilibrium in the marriage. It deserves emphasis that these similarities may not be manifestly apparent and may show up only when some change occurs. The total emotional involvement implied here involves large scale projections—a seeing of the self in the other, and ordinarily leads to lasting marriage. The extent to which the recipient of the projection fits the assigned role determines the stability of the relationship. How much of the self is projected will depend on the level of object relatedness which the indi-

[6] "The Psychoanalytic Situation and Transference," *The Journal of the American Psychoanalytic Assoc.*, 15 (1967), 238.

[7] M. Stein, "The Marriage Bond," *Psychoanalytic Quarterly*, 25 (1956), 238.

[8] P. Giovacchini, "Characterological Aspects of Marital Interaction," *Psychoanalytic Fon.*, 2 (1967), 7.

vidual has achieved. The more primitive the level, the more vulnerable is the marital adjustment. A much less stable situation occurs when the requirement of one partner for the other is less total, when the spouse represents mainly a personification of a particular defensive trait or need. The evanescence of such personality parts results in evanescence of union.

Aside from providing some insight into the nature of marital union, these latter notions particularly also comment on the fact that lasting marriages are not necessarily "good" marriages. They also allow reasonable speculation that one "bad" marriage does not necessarily lead to another bad one.

A matter open to psychiatric comment, but of sufficient importance and complexity to require separate discussion, is the question of the influence of children on the long-lastingness of marriage and the influence on children of discordant or broken marriages. In regard to the latter question, suffice to say that current evidence tends to support the idea that growing up in a seriously discordant marital atmosphere can be as deleterious to optimal development as growing up with one divorced parent. However, there are enough qualifications of this premise to warrant reserving any general judgment.

HUMAN NEED AND THE MARRIAGE BOND

When psychiatry's data are brought to bear on the normal, there is often concern about the validity of so doing. Yet, if carefully dealt with, the rich fund of information gleaned in the treatment situation can be drawn on and generalized from. In actuality, this problem of extrapolation from the clinic is the object of considerable thought, especially within psychoanalysis.[9] Touching more directly on the subject of the relation of law and marriage, there are two tomes which exemplify the seriousness with which this issue is taken.[10] In the end, this problem of the bias produced by a psychiatric viewpoint does not seem different from other determined efforts whose percepts are shaped by defined viewpoints.

The observations drawn from the clinical situation of psychotherapy of adults (particularly the closely intimate view obtained of human feeling and interaction as well as the reconstruction of life history), the longitudinal studies of development, plus common observation allow some general statements relating to the nature of the marriage bond. Most generally, marriage is a specially important instance of the individual's coming to terms with his world through meaningful relations with other people. In this sense, the preparation for marriage begins at birth: the expectations of marriage and of the spouse are rooted in the earliest relations with others and, of course, shaped by subsequent experiences.

Marriage itself becomes special through the intensity of the mutual investment—an intensity which is particu-

[9] Cf. H. Hartmann, *Psychoanalysis and Moral Issues* (New York, 1960) and R. Holt, ed., *Motives and Thought: Psychoanalytic Essays in Honor of David Papaport* (New York, 1967).

[10] Cf. J. Goldstein and J. Katz, *The Family and the Law* (New York, 1965) and J. Katz, S. Goldstein and A. Dershowitz, *Psychoanalysis, Psychiatry and Law* (New York, 1967).

larly signified in the multimeaningful sexual act.[11] Clinical observations say in a technical way what is commonly observable. First of all, the union of the partners must be seen, too, as a *process*, as a part of human development. The union begins, obviously, before any formal acknowledgment of it and will be influenced by a congeries of motivations, many of which are out of awareness and not subject to rational consideration. While the mutual commitment is reinforced by the social sanctions surrounding the one nuptial ceremony and contract, the fundamental task of cementing the bonds extends far over time and probably basically never ends. The multitudinous experiences of mutual pleasure, sadness, conflict and reconciliation, and support (spoken of more precisely in the "symbiosis" arising from projection and introjection of needs) lead toward the "two-in-one-fleshness" of the bond. In psychological terms, identifying with or being like the other is a central event. When these psychological ties achieve that integration we regard as optimal, the dissolubility of marriage is roughly as relevant as the dissolubility of the attachment to life. It is hypothetically possible, but in actuality is out of the question. The power of the forces to union—rooted, as proposed, in the whole of development—is great. and ordinarily transcends the power of externally imposed sanctions or threats.

However, when marriage is viewed in this way as a continuous process, other considerations apply, too. All of

[11] J. Higgins, "A Psychiatrist Looks at Human Sexuality," *Jubilee*, 12 (Feb., 1965), 36.

life, including marriage, presents problems. While sur-
mounting them enhances growth, not everyone is capable of good solutions in all circumstances. There may be
times in any average expectable marriage when the bond
is assaulted enough to become very flimsy. Much will depend on how potent are the psychological strengths each
partner brings to the specific situation. This is one of the
reasons why demonstrable serious mental illness at the
time of marriage becomes important in that it denotes
limited potential. But there are times when one can know
only in retrospect that the partners (or one of them) were
not sufficiently capable of fostering the process of marriage. In such instances, the previously existent bond
may, in fact, be broken, sometimes, unfortunately, ir-
reparably.

CONCLUSION

Having been concerned mainly with *problems*, it is fair
to conclude—if only in outline—with what must be considered as solutions. They lie in the areas of:

1. education for marriage, whose major fault is in its
   ease of prescription and difficulty in execution;
2. the requirement for more widely available and varie-
   gated *expert* marriage-counselling, particularly by
   the clergy;
3. the appreciation of the role of neurotic involvement
   in marriage and the concomitant appreciation of the
   need for available and adequate treatment;
4. the probable necessity to face the fact that the only
   outcome for some marriages is their dissolution.

Thus, in summarizing we may enumerate four pivotal points.

1. Serious mental illness has been long accepted as a possible impediment to the validity of marriage. Further to support this practice, various considerations have been adduced in regard to the establishing of a clinical diagnosis, and what it signifies.
2. Psychoneurotic (or "less serious") illness is fully capable of destroying a marriage.
3. Neurotic needs may always be expected to play a role in marital interaction and to cause conflict. There are powerful psychological forces favoring the maintenance of monogamous union.
4. Marriage is viewed psychologically as a continuous process with vicissitudes, aiming toward a state of mutual integration.

COMMENT

AND

DISCUSSION

Expert medical and psychiatric counsel quite frequently plays a decisive role in marriage cases submitted to ecclesiastical courts. As in parallel civil procedure, forensic medicine serves to establish evidence either of physical capacity or of due discretion in contracting marriage. A medical diagnosis of physical deficiency, for example, may underlie the judicial sentence of the nullity of marriage on the grounds of impotency. In this case the existence of a true marriage is ruled out because of the relative or absolute incapacity of one or other individual to fulfill the physical obligations of marriage. Depending on the diagnosis, impotency antecedent to and continuing in a marriage may render an individual incapable of marriage altogether or simply incapable of marriage to a particular person.

Psychiatric diagnosis, on the other hand, is considered decisive in canonical procedure only when it proves an absolute mental or emotional incapacity to give true matrimonial consent. A marriage may be declared invalid only when one or the other party is proven completely incapable of knowing or willing a true marriage. In contemporary canonical practice such a judgment must entail the decision that a particular person is totally incapable of marriage with anyone, not only with the particular person in the case. The sentence of nullity implies that the respondent in a marriage case is incapable of any true marital relationship.

Yet it is strongly questioned whether a finding of total incapacity is either necessary or real. Except in very extreme cases, can a psychiatrist so clearly and so absolutely diagnose general mental or emotional inability to marry? Instead of using psychiatric diagnosis to make such a radical decision, would it not be preferable to limit the decision only to the relationship of the individuals in question? The human limitations for such a serious decision should be more cautiously drawn. Is it not sufficient to say simply that in a specific case a particular couple is unable to sustain a true marital relationship? To cast a judgment beyond the particular to an absolute incapacity would seem unnecessary. Such a decision would also run counter to much of the findings of contemporary psychiatric research. There are major behavioral manifestations of mental illness generally agreed upon by psychiatrists. In many cases these criteria can supply a fairly stable opinion. Yet this opinion, when reduced to an absolute judgment, can almost always be disputed.

The inability of two persons to enter or sustain marriage is often due to deficiencies in one party which cannot be positively compensated by the other. In belaboring the illness or deficiencies of one party, judges often fail to consider the other party or the entire context of the interpersonal relationship of marriage. In many cases the deficiencies of one party may be due to the failings of the other. The very fact that a marriage fails because one party proves incapable does not mean that this same person cannot successfully marry someone else.

It bears substantial consideration that there are some schizophrenics, manic depressives, psychopaths, homosexuals, persons with character disorders or other mental or emotional disturbances, who are in satisfying marriages. Some persons seem to be able to live reasonably well with a sociopath. Others cannot. In some way these deficiencies are offset by other factors in a particular marriage. Can we say, therefore, because a particular person was beset by one of these disorders at a particular time and could not successfully contract marriage with one person, that he is not capable of contracting marriage later with another person? In too many cases the clinical diagnosis of one party fails to comprehend the broader context of the interaction of both parties in a marriage. It is this interaction which is of ultimate significance, not the psychological state of only one of the spouses.

Each marriage is a unique relationship between two unique persons. A realistic judgment will not look beyond these two. Were this man and this woman capable of entering a true Christian marriage with each other? We should not ask whether marriage in the abstract was possible at all for either of them. It is the presence or the absence of a true marital relationship between two specific individuals that is to be decided. Absolute judgments about generic incapacity are neither sound nor are they fair.

In this regard, the current acceptance in canonical literature of the term "mental or psychic impotency" is unfortunate. The term rests upon an analogy with physical impotency that simply does not obtain in most instances. Physical impotency is not a clear-cut phenomenon. There are many kinds of impotency and varying degrees of curability. The term "psychic impotency" offers only a spurious clarity and should be avoided.

It is becoming increasingly clear that the procedures of the ecclesiastical courts in handling cases of emotional or mental sickness are in need of radical revamping. The courts are simply crippled by difficulties that severely curtail any positive pastoral ministry. In most cases the burden of evidence is contained in briefs and written transcriptions of testimony. Very little personal contact between the judges and the persons involved is possible. Consequently it is extremely difficult to make decisions based upon a thorough understanding of the particular situation. Prolonged personal contact necessary to correctly evaluate personality disorders is absolutely indispensable. This is rarely possible for the courts.

Secondly, it is extremely rare that ecclesiastical authorities have any hope of restoring a happy or even reasonably successful marriage. Mental illness or sociopathic disorder has long since taken its toll and destroyed the marriage by the time the case is introduced. Divorce generally has already taken place—perhaps even a second or a third marriage. The petitioner comes to the tribunal in hope of release through a declaration of nullity, to contract another marriage or to obtain the Church's blessing for an existing union. In very few cases are positive decisions given that will be of any help at all.

There should be more attractive and easily available modes of coping with marital difficulties. It is to be desired that these disturbances cease to become the occasion for the use of psychiatric entities only for the adjudication of nullity. Instead, greater concentration should be put upon understanding and assisting persons afflicted with personal problems and deficiencies.

To be of real service to those beset by grave difficulties in marriage, informal counseling procedures or boards of equity would generally be of greater help than legal tribunals. Men or women qualified in theology, law and psychology should work with the people themselves to counsel and aid them. If such a board decides that in a particular case marriage is impossible or seems never to have really existed, the Church should simply accept that judgment. A closer cooperation of priests, lawyers and doctors would contribute to more effective pastoral care. It would bypass the complications of judicial procedure and lift the aid of medical and psychiatric experts out of the strictures of a narrow legal context.

7

The Family in the 1960's: Facts, Fictions, Problems, Prospects and Institutional Linkages

MARVIN B. SUSSMAN[*]

Social change is a paradoxical process—at once both cataclysmic and turtle-like. How one views the phenomenon of change involves multiple factors, including social, psychological, biological and economic elements which converge within each individual to form a unique perspective. Each of us perceives society from his own respective spatio-temporal position, experiencing change differentially.

[*] Professor and Chairman of the Department of Sociology at Case Western Reserve University. He is editor of the *Sourcebook in Marriage and the Family* (1955; 3rd ed. 1968), *Sociology and Rehabilitation* (1965) and *Community Structure and Analysis* (1959); co-author of *The Walking Patient: A Study in Outpatient Care* (1967), *Hough: A Study of Social Life and Change* (1959) and *Social Class and Maternal Health* (1957). Dr. Sussman is currently editor of the *Journal of Marriage and the Family*.

Special thanks are due Mrs. Donna Siegel, research assistant in the Department of Sociology, CWRU, for her painstaking work in the preparation of this paper.

An examination of the current status of the American family is thus a particularly difficult task, since the variables are so numerous and complex. At one level the family in the 1960's is functioning similarly to its ancestral counterpart in 1900 in providing adequate socialization, emotional sustenance and family continuity for its members. The institution of marriage persists, recurrently legitimated by the community. But from other stances, new patterns and trends are visible. Both intra- and interinstitutional relationships must be explored, and analytical attention focused on popularized myths of marriage and family. The urban kinship network is not, as some hold, primarily functioning on a level subordinate to other social organizations upon which it depends for survival, but rather the family is as much involved in producing changes in other societal systems as it is required to adjust to social changes produced by nonfamily systems. In this paper, we use a sociological perspective to examine the family today and the impact of social change. To begin, we shall look at some of the basic statistics of marriage in the 1960's and then discuss the broader implications for family functioning and solidarity.

Today the United States surpasses all other Western nations in the proportion of married citizens. Almost 90 percent of Americans are married at least once during their lifetimes; as few as four percent of men and three percent of women in their late twenties enter middle age without having married.

To a greater extent than in the past, persons are marrying at similar ages as marriages are compressed into a narrower age range. In 1960 husbands over 55 years of age were 3.6 years older than their wives on an average, and husbands under 35, only 1.9 years older. Furthermore, 42 percent of older husbands (over 55) were at least five years older than their wives, as compared with only 17 percent of younger (under 35) husbands.[1]

These factors can potentially influence the middle and late stages of the life cycle; they can determine, in part, the length of time of the child-rearing and child-launching periods and the wife's capability to obtain outside employment. Finally, the lessening of the difference between the ages of the husband and wife at marriage causes a significant improvement in the joint survival of the couple. Under mortality conditions in 1960, a woman married at the age of 20 to a man four years her senior ran a 42-percent chance of being widowed by age 65. If she married a man two years older, there was a 37-percent chance; and if they were the same age, a 33-percent chance.

Viewed from still another perspective, the chances a half century ago were about one in six that a man aged 25 and a woman 19 would both survive the next fifty years; currently the chances are one in three. These figures all represent the potential duration of marriage rather than the expected, since they do not allow for divorce or annulment. For the average couple who married

[1] Robert Parke, Jr., and Paul Glick, "Prospective Changes in Marriage and the Family," *Journal of Marriage and the Family,* 29:2 (May, 1967), 249-256.

in recent years, the expected duration has been about eight years less than the potential.

The relationship between expected and potential duration of marriage is affected by socioeconomic differences in divorce and separation. The general conclusion of Parke and Glick from assessing the findings of divorce and separation studies is that continuity of marriage is a condition shared less by the lower classes in society. In the 1960 census, special attention, they report, was given

> to social and economic analysis of the patterns of marriage and dissolution of marriage among men 45 to 54 years old, a group that has reached its peak earning capacity and among whom few additional first marriages will occur. There were one and a half million ever-married white men in the age group with incomes of less than $3,000 and more than two million with incomes of $10,000 or more. Fully 29 percent of the poor men, but only 16 percent of the affluent men, were no longer living with their first wives at the time of the census. . . . Barring a rise in the divorce rate or major changes in the pattern of divorce and separation by socioeconomic status, the reduction of poverty should result in a substantial long-term improvement in the average stability of marriages.[2]

Some caution and reservations are required here, since there are overall increases in the past ten years of the percentage of the population who are divorced. However, the major fact remains that the potentiality for joint survivorship of couples for longer periods of time is greater in the 1960's than at any previous time.

[2] *Ibid.*, 254.

With the beginning, in about 1860, of the urban period in this society and two subsequent world wars, marriage and divorce practices are characterized by two trends, secularization and liberalization. The family today largely functions under a value-free mandate that marriage is a civil rather than a sacramental contract and that, being an earthly transaction, it is amenable to dissolution under certain conditions. The consequence is a rather widespread acceptance of divorce, a fact often inflated by the mass media and thus resulting in a pronounced alarm for the survival of the family.

According to estimates and statistics available, the 1960 divorce rate was almost eight times that of 1860.[3] Yet, despite these data, within the past twenty years the divorce rate has not drastically increased, except for a brief rise caused by the war followed by a decline. In 1946, when many war marriages ended, the rate was 4.3 per 1,000 of the population, an all-time high. In that year more than 600,000 couples were divorced. For the next five years the rate fell, reaching 2.5 in 1951. In 1960 the rate was 2.2 per 1,000 of the population, identical with the 1941 rate. Provisional figures point to no abrupt change in the rate through 1970.

It is interesting that the wealthy and the highly educated, contrary to a popularly held notion, do not have

---

[3] Paul C. Glick, *American Families* (New York, 1957), pp. 120-145; Paul H. Jacobson, *American Marriage and Divorce* (New York, 1959), pp. 60-83; "Population: Marriages, Divorces, and Rates with Percent Changes from Preceding Years: United States, 1920-1959," *Vital Statistics of the United States*, 1959, Part 2, pp. 2-17.

higher divorce rates than the poor and those of limited education. Although comprehensive national statistics are not available on this point, a number of research publications[4] indicate that the higher professional and business groups have the lowest divorce rates, while the highest divorce rate is found among working-class families. The great publicity attending divorce actions of wealthy and prominent persons may account for the popular myth that these groups have the highest divorce rate.

Further, Bernard found that the probabilities for white and nonwhite men to achieve stable marriages vary, increasing with income, occupation and years of schooling. The probabilities for white men are greater than for nonwhite, but the differences between them decline as income, schooling and job level rise.[5] Such factors are intimately linked with the specific problems of the Negro family. High divorce and illegitimacy rates and weakened family solidarity are related to racial discrimination and poverty. It has been suggested that the most effective barriers to family deterioration in the long run are good jobs for Negro men—jobs with status, stability and potential.[6]

Other factors frequently held to be related to divorce are "mixed" marriages—both interracial and interreligious. As for Negro and white intermarriage, data are in-

[4] *Ibid.*

[5] Jessie Bernard, "Marital Stability and Patterns of Status Variables," *Journal of Marriage and the Family*, 28:4 (1966), 421-439.

[6] Elizabeth Herzog, "Is There a 'Breakdown' of the Negro Family?" reprinted from *Social Work*, January, 1966, by the American Jewish Committee, New York: Institute of Human Relations.

complete. There are now 31 states where such marriage is legal, but only three publish records. However, from information that is available, it has been tentatively concluded that racial intermarriage does appear to be increasing, although not at a rapid pace.[7] Scant research addresses this phenomenon, and no conclusive data have been presented concerning the effects of interracial marriage on family solidarity.

Regarding interreligious marriage, again, comprehensive data are unavailable, since there are only two states which require a statement of religious affiliation on marriage registration forms. There is, however, a recently published study on interfaith versus intrafaith marriage in one of these states—Indiana. One-ninth of all marriages in Indiana occur between couples of divergent faiths.[8] The interfaith marriages were found to be more by civil ceremony and to involve individuals who are members of religious minority groups, who have been previously married, who are older, who are in high-status occupations and who reside in urban areas; these marriages were also high in premarital pregnancy and divorce, although the difference in divorce rates between inter- and intrafaith marriages was quite slight.[9] With respect to premarital pregnancy among intrafaith marriages,

[7] David M. Heer, "Negro-White Marriage in the United States," *Journal of Marriage and the Family*, 28:3 (1966), 266.

[8] Harold T. Christensen and Kenneth E. Barber, "Interfaith Versus Intrafaith Marriage in Indiana," *Journal of Marriage and the Family*, 29:3 (1967), 468.

[9] *Ibid.*, 461.

Protestants were highest, Catholics in the middle position and Jews lowest in incidence.[10] The authors concluded that distinctions between inter- and intrafaith marriages were still doubtful; generally, investigators need more data and more control over other variables such as husband-wife combinations, i.e., Catholic husband-Protestant wife versus Protestant husband-Catholic wife, and degree of devoutness or rigidity of belief. The authors suggested that certain *intrafaith* religious differences may be more disruptive of a relationship than interfaith disparities taken alone[11] and also referred to Burchinal and Chancellor's suggestion that the age of bride and social status of the groom influence survival rates more than religious combinations.[12]

Overall, the increase in divorce rates does not appear to be as dramatic as commonly supposed; we may wonder why there is such alarmism. It may be the anxiety stemming from the view of society as increasingly impersonal and the debatable notion that the family is becoming obsolete. None of the evidence justifies this picture of a disintegrating family without functions in our future society, and we shall consider this aspect later in our analysis.

Another factor is that popularization of psychological and social science theory and findings and rapid communication of these through the mass media have undoubtedly served to heighten awareness and anxiety about marital maladjustment. Contributing to an explanation of

[10] *Ibid.*, 467.
[11] *Ibid.*, 469.
[12] *Ibid.*, 462.

the widespread alarmism about the stability of the family is, paradoxically, the increasing acceptance of, and even preference for, divorce as an alternative to marital unhappiness. Acceptance has served to increase the visibility of divorced persons, who are more likely to admit their status as the threat of social ostracism fades.

Increasing acceptance of divorce is in the continuing tradition of secularization and liberalization. It is supported by social science findings, such as that children of divorced parents seem to adjust better than children of unhappy parents who stay together. Acceptance and alarmism, seemingly paradoxical, can act as allies in efforts toward ameliorating marital problems. Acceptance of divorce may be a healthy trend which takes cognizance of some of the realities of interpersonal relationships and which assists understanding of malfunctioning. On the other hand, alarmism also may act as a spur toward rooting out the causes of marital dissolution.

Also part of the prevalent pattern of marriage and divorce is the earlier age of marriage and the freewheeling method of courtship and first marriage. For some individuals, the first marriage which ends in divorce is similar to the extended engagement characteristic of mate selection a generation ago and still found among selected class and regional populations of the United States. The first marriage in this sense is a "trial" marriage, with remarriage occurring quickly after divorce.[13]

Another value change is reflected in the fact that the presence of children does not necessarily shield a mar-

[13] Bernard Farber, *Family: Organization and Interaction* (San Francisco, 1964), pp. 157-175.

riage from dissolution. Latest published statistics show that more than one-half of divorcing couples have children.[14] It is considered better to generate a divorce if the married individuals do not prove to be successful parents and if the presence of one of them in the home is damaging to the character and personality development of the child. An intact family for intactness' sake should be ruled out. Support for this notion comes from the observation that, in divorce cases involving children, damage results not from the legal divorce proceedings or the separation thereafter but from the emotional divorce which precedes it. Further, children living in a home marked by marital conflict often are touched by family instability far more deeply and painfully than children living with only one parent. And, when the conflict is accompanied by strong attempts to deny the rift and present a solid front to "protect" the child, even more damage may result if the child, as so many are capable of doing, senses the deceit, sees himself as the center of responsibility for binding together two antithetical elements, and incurs guilt. Also, the child's conception of "what marriage is" is likely to be sadly lopsided.

The present patterns of divorce and remarriage are sustained, in part, by wider opportunities for women in the work world—available in large measure due to prosperous economic conditions, improved education, and increase in the number of welfare and social service agencies which often employ women and provide services for women who are gainfully employed.

[14] Jacobson, *op. cit.*, p. 131.

The phenomenon of the wife working outside the home for remuneration is likely to continue in the future. By the end of the decade, it is estimated that 33 million, twice the number in 1950, will be employed in the labor force. Currently, for the first time in history, more married than single women are in the employment brigade. In 1940, 36 percent of the women of the work force were married, compared to 60 percent in 1961.[15] Other reasons for the upswing are recruitment during the two world wars, survival during Depression days, family-life-cycle changes and the quest for independence, intellectual expression, gratification and satisfaction of material needs and desires. The working mother is no longer a deviant pattern.

The implications of this phenomenon are not clearly visible especially in relation to role reallocations and socialization functions in women's families and work systems. Who does what and to whom, who has major responsibility for socialization and who is chiefly responsible for handling affective expression and instrumental tasks are unsettled questions for parents of today's families.

Our current concern over the impact of women in gainful employment upon role relationships within the family, especially those related to child rearing, has colored our vision of the more obvious and potentially drastic changes for relationships within work systems. Suppose, for example, in our society that medical work became women's

[15] U.S. Bureau of the Census, *Statistical Abstract of the United States, 1962* (Washington, D.C., 1962), p. 225.

work as in Russia where 80 percent of the physicians are women compared to less than five percent in the United States. Such a shift in work roles, and even a less dramatic one, would require basic changes in value orientations within both society and the medical system. Consider only one facet of the patient-physician relationship, the fiducial, confidential and intimate aspects of the exchange. How can women deal with the physical examination of the male, and what are the required changes in orientations and values required of males in order to feel secure in such an examination? I do not want to get involved in arguments concerning the loss of femininity and maintenance of objectivity or appear to be "old hat" by indicating too many obstacles in the path of occupational emancipation. Rather, my point is that we blithely accept changes in sex-work roles without understanding their significance and implications.

Another aspect of social change involves orientations toward marriage and the family. Studies such as those by Cuber and Haroff[16] indicate that many marriages which are maintained over long periods of time are utilitarian in character. These marriages are maintained for purposes other than to express an intimate, highly important personal relationship between a man and a woman; the partners, if they receive satisfaction for sexual and emotional needs, do so largely outside the marriage bond. Such marriages are found increasingly among middle-aged

[16] John F. Cuber and Peggy E. Haroff, *The Significant Americans* (New York, 1965).

couples who have lost, or perhaps never developed, a close, personal and intrinsic relationship.

Related to this phenomenon is the increasing competence and capacity of both men and women to find satisfactory interpersonal relationships across sex lines and outside the marital bond. The posture that the two partners fulfill all their basic and derived needs within a marriage and upon marriage give up all or most relationships with individuals of the opposite sex is no longer a dominant one. The prevalent and accepted mode is that married men and women can have a variety of heterosexual relationships ranging from colleagueship to the most intimate and emotionally charged love affair. In general, while extramarital affairs are not condoned, neither are they strongly condemned. The reasons for this value change are quite complex; they must be associated with the integration of women into the work world and other institutional areas, the specialization of functions which even occur on a personality-emotional level, and the greater opportunities for both men and women to develop liaisons on a continuum of mild to serious involvement.

The implication of this phenomenon is that, once the pattern of heterosexual activity becomes institutionalized, one can anticipate no arresting of this behavior in the later years of life; it is probable that older people will seek to establish a variety of liaisons as they did in former years and arrange marriages on utilitarian or intrinsic bases. For example, there is clinical evidence of utilitarian arrangements among older people who develop common-law marriages for economic reasons and companionship.

Both marital and extramarital activities have been greatly affected by the development of oral contraceptives and the distribution of information about contraceptive methods in general. For example, one survey of college girls on a midwestern campus revealed that 22 percent had indulged in sexual intercourse. Over half of both the virgin and nonvirgin girls were judged "adequately informed" of contraceptives; a third were "well informed," and the remainder uninformed.[17] Undoubtedly, figures vary from campus to campus, and region to region, but various surveys confirm that numerous students possess, and moreover utilize, the vast array of available information.

It would be useless to generalize the psychosocial attitudes accompanying these practices, but a brief scanning is in order. Fundamentally, secularization and liberalization in society are the overriding factors. Another aspect is the power of groups—the fact that many young persons adopt what are the real or perceived norms of the reference or membership groups to which they aspire to belong. Also, some may sense a more general aura of "everyone's doing it" and thus join in; here the mass media contribute significantly. In their quest for personal happiness, young people are exposed to the intense physical expressions of life which enforce the inability or unwillingness to postpone sexual gratification until after marriage. Rebellion against authority, rejection of tradi-

[17] Robert E. Grinder and Sue S. Schmitt, "Coeds and Contraceptive Information," *Journal of Marriage and the Family*, 28:4 (1966), 473.

tion and quest for personal identity also pertain. A final aspect that must not be ignored is that some young people are *not* totally numbed by a desire for group acceptance, are not exploding with hate for and rebellion against society, but are, in nonmarital sexual relations, expressing something genuine and representative of newly emerging values. Against the backdrop of long established institutions, these persons may appear starkly outlined, out of context and incomprehensible. Indeed, they may be "different," but we cannot with any justification define them in toto as completely lacking in values and principles. At the root of much too easily labeled "anarchism" is the quest for a stable community life. For example, witness the recent hippie cults. Besides their dramatic boldness, these enterprises also exhibit strivings toward flexibly integrated and peacefully functioning communities. In one sense this represents a turning away from an electrified civilization and its complexities and malfunctions to a more primitive unit, a "tribe" in which members are not merely—to employ Schutz' terms[18]— "contemporaries" with one another, sharing space and time, but "consociates" who have more essential "face-to-face" relationships, almost forming a substitute kinship system.

There are, of course, many ways to interpret the trends of our age; any pursuit of real understanding, however, must recognize the impact of social change. Values and

---

[18] Alfred Schutz, *Collected Papers I, The Problem of Social Reality*, ed. by Maurice Natason (The Hague, Netherlands, 1962).

norms evolve through history; a few endure with scant modification, but most eventually undergo a metamorphosis and are transformed through time. Today many of our dominant values are under scrutiny at various levels. Some persons have already scrutinized and rejected certain values, and are now in the process of expressing what they deem most essential. Thus, there is much conflict and incongruency in our culture today.

Perhaps one of the most important implications of the development of the oral contraceptive popularly known as "the pill" is that individuals may have sex without fear. Particularly for women, intimate relationships have long been clouded by the possibility of unintentional conception, and for unwed females, resultant societal wrath. Now, with effective birth control measures, sex may be had in a purer, more meaningful form. The overwhelming fear of pregnancy, which colored relationships of persons not desiring children at the immediate time, was diminished, allowing intimacy to become an essential expression of love and concern.

The pill, however, is not the sole catalyst opening the gates of freer expression of love. Its development was based on quite solid practical necessities. The population explosion and starvation conditions of numerous populations have been well documented and here need no further elaboration. But even before the pill the demand for fuller sexual expression was voiced with deepening conviction. Literature and films portrayed the beauty of total love, aesthetically presenting not only the symbolic but also the realistic aspects of romantic love, while the sciences, such as psychology, discussed the naturalness of behavior and the harms of unwarranted repression. As knowledge and theory broadened, society could analyze itself objectively, seek out the seeds and evolution of its norms and examine scientifically their contemporary relevance.

Promiscuity, implying irresponsibility and immorality, is a less-often-used word. Influenced in part by such movements as existentialism, individuals have begun to take note of their personal responsibility for their own actions. Beyond the formula "I think, therefore I am" emerges the belief "my actions define my being." Sex, then, as a fundamental human action, has meaning beyond reproduction. It is a process of creation not only of new life but of identity. Sex on the campus is less closely linked to rebellion than to self-expression, i.e., activating one's particular human potentialities for love and commitment.

These developments have begun to filter out to various formal societal organizations. Last year's Notre Dame conference on human sexuality and fertility is a case in point. In the Cleveland area this fall, the Health Museum sponsored an educational television series on "Sex in American Culture," including such topics as "Human Reproduction," "Embryological Development," "Birth of a Baby," "Population Expansion," "Venereal Disease," "Education for Family Life" and "Adolescence and Sexual Identity." These are but two instances of the dominant trend toward open and enlightened discussions of sex in contexts beyond the bedroom or the back seat.

These are, however, only beginnings; much remains to be accomplished in the areas of enlightenment and education. Social change, we recall, does have a turtlish side. In the realm of education, the family stands out as a strong resource with many potentialities. Thus, it is well at this point to consider further some theoretical and empirical aspects of the current structure and status of the American kinship system.[19]

A current popular position is that as a consequence of industrialization there emerges a "mass" society with spe-

[19] For further reference see the following by Marvin B. Sussman: "Theoretical Bases for an Urban Kinship Network System," paper given at the annual meeting of the National Council on Family Relations, October 29, 1966, Minneapolis, Minnesota; "The Isolated Nuclear Family: Fact or Fiction?" *Social Problems* (1959), 333-340; "Kinship Family Network: Unheralded in Current Conceptualizations of Family Functioning," with Lee G. Burchinal, *Marriage and Family Living* (1962), 231-240; "The Urban Kin Network in the Formulation of Family Theory," The Ninth International Seminar on Family Research, Tokyo, Japan, forthcoming in *Yearbook of International Sociological Association*, ed. by Rene Konig; "The Help Pattern in the Middle Class Family," *American Sociological Review* (1953), 22-28; "Family Continuity: Selective Factors Which Affect Relationships Between Families at Generational Levels," *Marriage and Family Living* (1954); "Activity Patterns of Post-Parental Couples and Their Relationship to Family Continuity," *Marriage and Family Living* (1955), 338-341; "Intergenerational Family Relationships and Social Role Change in Middle Age," *Journal of Gerontology* (1960), 71-75; "Parental Aid to Married Children: Implications for Family Functioning," with Lee G. Burchinal, *Marriage and Family Living* (1962), 320-322; "Relationship of Adult Children with Their Parents in the United States," in *Family, Intergenerational Relationships and Social Structure*, ed. by Ethel Shanas and Gordon Streib (Englewood Cliffs, N.J., 1965), pp. 62-92.

cialized institutions providing educational, health, welfare, recreational, economic, political and social services. The modern urban family is thought to be dependent upon these other societal institutions and must adjust to their normative demands or be destroyed. However, this view is only a partial representation of the family's position. In addition to an adaptive stance, the modern urban family further demonstrates directive and integrative behaviors. The kinship network, composed of nuclear units related by blood or marriage, *both* influences *and* is influenced by other social systems. In some instances the family acts directly to produce specific changes in the policy, structure and activities of other institutions. In other circumstances, influence is less directional but more reciprocal and blends the normative requirements of the family-kinship structure with those of other social bodies. In still other situations the family has minimal influence and is in fact dependent upon other societal agencies for its existence.

The varied stances of the family are largely explained by the existence of a viable and functioning kinship network. Today the majority of American nuclear families are active with other units within a kin-related network which is capable of providing for its members' economic, emotional, educational, welfare and other kinds of support complementary or competitive to those furnished by other societal institutions. This condition affects intrafamily relationships and the individual's or his family's relationships with other kin-related, nuclear families and social organizations. Further, the kin network is a voluntary body and as such competes for the interest and participation of its members. Thus, the American nuclear family is neither isolated nor completely autonomous.

One of the key concepts for explaining the bases of the kinship network is reciprocity, a give-and-take exchange based upon activity for which one is rewarded. As George Homans[20] has suggested, the more an individual is rewarded as a consequence of his action in any situation, the more likely he is to engage in the same or similar activities later on. One common misunderstanding about reciprocity is the implied assumption that exchanges between two individuals must be equal or approach equality. To the contrary, the majority of reciprocal relationships which exist among individuals are based upon exchanges which are unequal and often involve unspecified, perceived obligations for which the individual giver can never be certain of the appropriate returns.

Related to reciprocity is the process of bargaining, which has as its objective getting some advantage in a transaction with another individual. Each party to the interaction directs his behavior in relation to his perception and expectations of what the other individual will accept in order to reach an agreement. Bargaining is actually an effort to determine what are acceptable expectations and to give the other person a minimum concession in order to obtain a greater advantage.

Social exchange or reciprocity is a basic element in integrating member nuclear family units within the urban

[20] *Social Behavior: Its Elementary Forms* (New York, 1961), pp. 53-59.

kin-family system. In the relationships between member units on intergenerational or bilateral kin lines, reciprocal relationships emerge partially out of tradition and feelings of familial responsibility and partially out of opportunity and the rewards that ensue from effective bargaining. Exchanges between member family units are not equal, nor do they occur, nor are they expected to occur, about the same time. For example, parents do a variety of things for their young married children and grandchildren with the expectation that when they themselves become less independent in their declining years the children, by then middle-aged and established, will take care of the parents' needs. Other subtle and less visible bargaining forms are exchanges which involve aid in time of need, maintaining communication and visitation patterns, sponsoring the job or career of the child of one's siblings and so forth.

One cannot, however, continue indefinitely in a reciprocal relationship without receiving some reward in return. The family network is one of several alternative social structures and becomes preferred when it provides real or perceived payoffs for participating individuals superior to those offered by other societal institutions. Individuals possess both service and self-interest motives, and the service orientation can be followed only so far, after which it loses its ability to sustain the individual in the relationship. Since the kinship network is a voluntary organization, persons can withdraw. Usually, however, the more involved one becomes, the more one builds credits and debits and becomes cemented to the viable and functioning network. It is likely that participants who find the family institution a preferred alternative cannot so freely withdraw from the tradition-laden relationships of the nuclear family and related kin. Thus, while reciprocity is fundamental to the kinship network, voluntary exchange is tempered by increasing commitments to the system.

This theoretical posture of family organization and behavior stresses the independent nature of family behavior as an antidote to the prevalent use of the family as solely a dependent variable. For example, observe the interinstitutional relationship between the family and the school. Educational activities are performed primarily by the school. When education is considered not only learning a body of accumulated knowledge but also learning new roles, the family, too, is an educational enterprise, since it performs vital socialization activities. In many societies the family-kinship network decides which of its children will be educated, how much financial support is to be given to the educational system and what type of education system is preferred. If the family finds the curriculum of the school not to its liking or the values espoused in the school in conflict with its own, there follow complaints, lack of support and cooperation, strikes and even violence—expressions of power and direct influence upon the educational system.

Influence of the family upon the school is expressed further in a more diffuse manner. Teaching methods, curricula, objectives and hardware are related to the social class of the family, its patterns of socialization and home-environmental conditions. Schools must cater to the demands, needs, faults and expectations of their clients. Of course, unequal reciprocities develop between the two structures at various stages of their respective development in relation to their specific needs. Consequently, one cannot generalize about the adjusting or dominating posture of the family or other societal institutions with which it is interacting. But one can identify problems involving interaction, the positions assumed and the mechanisms employed to achieve accommodation between the two.

In conclusion we note that family-school interaction is but one example of the capability of the family to exert influence upon other social organizations. Such influence is easily lost sight of in the fact of the more dramatic aspects of social change. Secularization and liberalization are pervasive trends, evident throughout this discussion of marriage and the family. Today with greater economic opportunities, more women are joining the labor force, a fact which affects marital role relationships and childrearing practices. The divorce rates, we have seen, are not severely accelerating; rather, divorce is more widely accepted, talked about more openly and thus more visibly practiced. Psychology and social science theories are reaching a broader audience; more are taking note of the effects of marital conflicts upon children, while both the acceptance of and alarmism about divorce have furthered investigations into the causes of marital dissolution.

Values and norms are being scrutinized and revised. Transformations wrought by social change are occurring at varying paces throughout different sectors of society, but they are occurring and they are inevitable. In the realm of sexual morality, certain changes are already observable. Men and women are sharing intimate relationships more freely, both within and without the marital bond, due partly to the improvement of contraceptive methods and partly to revised attitudes toward personal and sexual expression. Concurrently, the broader ramifications of sex, including the education of children, family planning, and medical, social and psychological aspects are being examined in greater depth.

Some persons too quickly assume that the various value and organizational transformations in our society forecast the inevitable disintegration of the family and kinship network. This assumption, however, is not supported by the facts. The family is a voluntary social institution offering services complementary and competitive to those offered by other organizations. The increased incidence of working wives, changing orientations toward marriage and the development of the pill are unavoidable facts of our time. All of them have significant impact upon the structure and function of the family and other societal systems—an impact by no means exclusively deleterious. These phenomena have brought alterations, and if we are responsive to the dynamic temper of this age, we must anticipate even more. Through these transformations the family has acted and been acted upon. It remains a preferred alternative, and we predict it will continue to function as a viable and influential social system in the future.

COMMENT

AND

DISCUSSION

The pastoral concern of the Church for the good of mankind has been expressed traditionally in many different ways. In fostering the stability and holiness of family life, a highly systematized legal structure of contractual conditions and judicial process has been developed over the centuries. If a radical change in legal discipline were to be contemplated at this time, not only would it be necessary to demonstrate a clear need for departing from the past; it would also be important to offer a positive prediction that change would lead to a more favorable implementation of the Church's saving mission. There is a fear that the law cannot be altered without seeming to compromise basic principles to the mores of the present age.

Would a much greater leniency and flexibility in matrimonial canon law lead to more divorces? Would this further weaken family ties and undermine an ideal for which ecclesiastical authority has always striven? The answer to these important questions will involve a careful evaluation of relevant sociological research. An equitable solution extending the pastoral care of the Church to the pressing needs of persons caught up in the agonizing trauma of a broken marriage cannot simply be deduced from abstract principles. Empirical investigation is crucial. Indeed, such empirical findings brought to bear upon this issue may substantiate authentically Christian reasons making fundamental change imperative.

Although our contemporary measures of what constitutes marital compatibility or stability are far from perfect, enough work has been done in psychology, psychiatry and sociology to give us some indices, scales and observational techniques to determine whether a marriage is thriving or deteriorating. If we probe the inner workings of a family, we may come close to estimating the psychological convergence of sacramentality with marital compatibility. On the other hand, we may be opening a Pandora's box. We may find in a particular marriage a high order of alienation and such disaffection that we may well wonder whether sacramentality is even possible in such a life situation.

We cannot be content with merely an external and legally imposed permanence in marriage. In situations involving profound conflict and repulsion, keeping a couple together by legal sanction may be more destructive of themselves and their children than permitting separation. The Church has too easily avoided these tragic consequences of marital discord by pointing to the strictures of her law.

Looking at the society in which we live today and the courtship system that brings people together for marriage, are we not expecting too much for the full sacramental reality to be in existence in all cases from the very beginning of marriage? Children mature to complete independence of their parents, so that there is very little parental control over mate selection. Property distribution occurs after death and is generally made in liquid assets, not in land. The obvious consequence is that some people are bound to have more freedom than they can psychologically handle. They often make terrible mistakes with their first marriage. Is there then no hope that the Church can give for the broken-hearted who have failed in marriage and now must contemplate a long life of loneliness?

Most in this situation simply leave the Church and remarry civilly.

Most individuals can fulfill the ritual obligations of the sacrament in getting married. Very few can do so with complete spiritual commitment. Two people have to grow together into a truly spiritual marriage. Is it too much to suggest that a sacramental marriage may be a state to be achieved only after years of successful striving? We may be expecting entirely too much in bringing to bear upon the young and the immature the full implications of sacramental indissolubility.

It would seem that a ritualistic concept of sacramentality dominates in a good deal of the discussion about marriage. Because of the close association between the sacred and the profane, both in law and in ceremony, there is the suggestion of marriage as a type of initiation rite where people enter into a new way of life. Perhaps historically it was the legal involvement in marriage that led to an association of the fullness of sacramentality with the initiation ceremony. The absoluteness of an ultimate ideal into which people should grow has been associated with the absoluteness of stepping from the profane into the sacred. Maybe sacramentality is better realized where the ritual ceases to be merely an event but actually becomes incorporated into life.

Divorces do not cause broken marriages. The breaking up of a marriage is a fact long before it is juridically recognized. In this regard, it is illusory to point to a steadily mounting divorce rate and call for more rigid divorce laws. The causes of broken marriages are profoundly personal, as well as societal. Though we do not have statistics on every broken marriage that does not result in divorce, there is a great deal of evidence to indicate that the proportionate number of broken marriages is not significantly higher now than in the nineteenth century, or than the present number in countries that do not permit divorce. There are other common ways of getting out of marriage, such as desertion, the use of mistresses or just informal separation. The fact that there are more women who are now economically and politically free means that there are more women now who will make the external break than would have made it before. Liberalizing divorce laws is not really a significant threat to the internal stability of the family.

Considering the legal grounds for divorce as constituted in the fifty states, one would have to suppose a liberal use of legal fiction in divorce processes. The actual reasons for divorce more frequently than not bear little resemblance to the alleged reasons. A change in legal grounds will probably not affect the divorce rate appreciably. Such a change has recently been made by the state of New York. A study is now being conducted there by the American Sociological Association to test the validity of this conclusion.

Regardless of all other experiments in group living, the family is the basic unit of society. The great majority of people strive instinctively for a stable marriage. They place a great investment in marriage and derive from its security the satisfaction of basic human needs that can be met in no other way. But there will always be some who fail. Because of imperfect socialization, either environmental or familial, some will be unable to sustain a permanent marital commitment. They become prone to make a shifting career of marriage. Some of these can be rehabilitated. Most cannot. For those who can, a second marriage may often constitute a permanent life involvement.

The reasons for the breakdown of married life are many and not all of them are of the same priority. It is not necessarily true, for example, that a higher incidence of divorce occurs in interfaith marriages. Iowa and Indiana are the only two states that require the posting of religious affiliation on marriage certificates. Harold Christensen's recent study based on data available in Indiana bears out that of Burchinal and Bachelor in Iowa. They both indicate that there were more family break-downs because of intrafaith differences, such as differences in social status, differences in educational levels or differences in consensus on the goals of marriage, than because of interfaith differences.

The findings of social research also bring into question the validity of an appeal to the good of children as a deterrent to divorce. The studies of Ivan Nye in this regard are worthy of a high degree of confidence. It seems well substantiated that the children of divorced parents adjust better to life than the children of unhappy parents who stay together merely for the sake of the children.

In view of these considerations, an alternative must be suggested to the Church's traditional canonical response to the failure of marriage. As an instrumentality to promote the stability and sanctity of marriage a system of legal impedi-ments and courts of trial is no longer adequate. It may not even be necessary.

There are valid criteria for the dissolution of marriages and the granting of annulments. In America today the civil courts could be entrusted with this task. Civil society does have a legitimate interest in preserving the family. The positive role of the Church may be shifted to pastoral counselling and a more intensified catechesis to sustain the ideal of indissolu-bility. The personal responsibility of the individuals themselves to institute civil proceedings would require that they seek counsel about the legitimacy of their reasons for seeking di-vorce. The Church may then accept the decision of the courts and honor the conscience of the persons involved. Though a departure from the practice of the past, this would not ap-parently involve a contradiction of the Church's fundamental doctrinal position regarding the sanctity and permanence of marriage. In freeing the Church of an absorbing entanglement in marriage courts, a more positive pastoral ministry to the married could be emphasized and implemented.

A STATEMENT OF CONSENSUS

Inspired by the Second Vatican Council, we have assembled as concerned Christian scholars to discuss the bond of marriage and its indissolubility, especially in the modern world.

The Second Vatican Council, after expounding "the dignity of the human person and the work which men have been destined to undertake throughout the world" (*The Constitution on the Church and the Modern World*, art. 46), goes on to consider "a number of particularly urgent needs" of the present time "in the light of the Gospel and of human experience" (*ibid.*).

The Council introduces the topics of marriage and family among these needs and considers specifically the indissolubility of marriage and divorce. It says that "the intimate partnership of marriage life and love [is] . . . by divine will and in the eyes of society, too . . . a lasting one" (*ibid.* art. 48). It also mentions "the plague of divorce" (*ibid.* art. 47).

These statements of the Council are not without their problems, precisely because of the "human experience" to which they appeal. For, first, the Council says that "although the Church has contributed much to the development of culture, experience shows that because of circumstances it is sometimes difficult to harmonize culture with Christian teaching" (*ibid.* art. 62) and, secondly, the Church, aware of rapid changes and of the plurality of thought, is convinced that she "must rely on those who live in the world" in order to "grasp their innermost significance in the eyes of both believers and unbelievers" (*ibid.* art. 44). Therefore, "in pastoral care appropriate use must be made, not only of theological principles, but also of the findings of the secular sciences, especially of psychology and sociology" (*ibid.* art. 62).

Thus we have proceeded to the study of this very important and delicate subject.

In the course of the Symposium we have concluded that the following questions need further consideration:

1. In what sense is Scripture conclusive about the indissolubility of marriage?
2. In the study of this indissolubility, what is the meaning and weight of tradition as reflected in these sources: the writings of the Fathers? the practice of the early Church? the norms of Roman Law enacted under Christian emperors? the doctrine and practice of the Eastern Churches ? the Council of Trent?
3. While the ideal of indissolubility applies to all marriages, its actual fulfillment is not urged in each concrete instance. Is it possible that the area of exceptions be extended to marriages of even baptized persons?
4. What can the theology, practice and experience of other Christian Churches contribute to the study of indissolubility?
5. What should be the juridical responsibility of the Church for marriage and what should be the province of the state?
6. In what precisely does the sacramentality of marriage consist? Is the place of the sacramentality of marriage sufficiently clear in the discussion of indissolubility?
7. What is the precise reason for the solubility of a nonconsummated sacramental marriage?

8. In individual cases how does the breakdown of the marital relationship affect the indissolubility of the bond?
9. What contribution do the findings and judgments of psychology and sociology make to the understanding of the indissolubility of the marriage bond?
10. What is the relation between the right of the individual person and the stability of the institution of marriage?
11. Within the context of the present discipline on indissolubility, what can be done to develop a jurisprudence adapted to the solution of presently insoluble problems?
12. Is there evidence that the dissolution of individual marriages would weaken the institution and detract from the ability of persons to persevere in marriage?

In order to implement the serious and prolonged study required, certain considerations deserve immediate attention. Effort should be made on the part of all Christian communities and their leaders to initiate and foster research into the problem areas. For this purpose the cooperation of scholars and universities could be obtained and even financially supported by appropriate grants.

Special effort should be given: (a) to the construction and setting forth of a new and effective catechesis on marriage and family life on all levels, one that is based on relevant theology, the findings of related sciences and the witness of Christian married couples; and (b) to the creation of counselling programs that will render all possible help to couples in marital difficulties.

Furthermore, it is the considered judgment of the Symposium participants that the present processes relating to the annulment and dissolution of marriages are clearly inadequate to the needs of the faithful. Therefore, the following principles should be enacted:

1. The existence of the marriage bond should be decided in law on the basis of the preponderance of evidence.
2. In the resolution of marriage cases far greater emphasis should be laid upon safeguarding the dignity and rights of persons.
3. All marriage cases should be solved on the local level, saving the right of appeal.

SYMPOSIUM PARTICIPANTS

Dr. Donald Barrett, Department of Sociology, University of Notre Dame

Rev. Anthony Bevilacqua, Diocesan Chancery Office, Brooklyn, New York

Rev. Paul Boyle, C.P., Executive Coordinator: The Canon Law Society of America

Rev. David Burrell, C.S.C., Department of Philosophy, University of Notre Dame

Rev. Raymond Carey, Archdiocesan Tribunal, Chicago, Illinois

Rev. Dr. Frederick Carney, Perkins School of Theology, Southern Methodist University

Dr. Ewert Cousins, Department of Theology, Fordham University

Rev. Robert H. Dailey, S. J., Alma College, Los Gatos, California

Rev. Dr. Robert Dodds, Department of Ecumenical Relationships, The National Council of Churches

Dr. J. Massingberd Ford, Department of Theology, University of Notre Dame

Dr. Piero Frattin, Department of Theology, University of Notre Dame

Rev. John F. Hotchkin, Catholic Bishops' Commission for Ecumenical Affairs

Rev. Peter Huizing, S.J., Department of Theology, Catholic University of Nijmegen, Holland

Rev. Walter Imbiorski, Director: The Cana Conference of Chicago

Rt. Rev. Msgr. Stephen Kelleher, Archdiocesan Tribunal, New York

Rev. Thomas Lynch, President: The Canon Law Society of America

Rev. Richard McCormick, S.J., Bellarmine School of Theology, North Aurora, Illinois

Rev. Alan McCoy, O.F.M., Provincial of the California Province of Franciscans

Rev. Sebastian MacDonald, C.P., The Passionist Theological College, University of Chicago

Dr. O. Hobart Mowrer, Department of Psychology, University of Illinois

257

Rev. Lawrence Mullins, Diocesan Tribunal, Davenport, Iowa

Rev. Ladislaus Örsy, S.J., Department of Theology, Fordham University

Very Rev. Msgr. Victor Pospishil, Department of Theology, Manhatten College

Rt. Rev. Msgr. John Quinn, Archdiocesan Tribunal, Chicago, Illinois

Rev. Dr. Paul Ramsey, Department of Religion, Princeton University

Sister Jeanne Reidy, C.H.M., Marycrest College, Davenport, Iowa

Dr. Paul Reiss, Department of Sociology, Fordham University

Rt. Rev. Msgr. John Schmidt, School of Canon Law, Catholic University of America

Rev. E. S. S. Sunderland, Marriage Court of the Episcopal Diocese of Massachusetts

Rev. William van der Marck, O.P., Department of Theology, University of Notre Dame

Rev. William Walsh, S.J., Department of Theology, Georgetown University

Rev. Lawrence Wrenn, Archdiocesan Tribunal, Hartford, Connecticut

Index